End

"... But the greatest (

That's what you will experience on every page of *"Just Add Sugar"* .... Love! A Mother's Love, a Father's Love, Family Love, God's Love!

This insightful, heart-felt, and yet, hard hitting book will bring you to hilarious laughter and tender tears. The story holds you spellbound while you consciously and unconsciously learn powerful eternal truths rooted in the fertile soil of Gods Kingdom.

Deby Scott writes with humility, unique wisdom, and powerful anointing. As you read, you will sense your problems seeming smaller and bitter experiences and memories losing control. That's because Deby is ***Just adding sugar.***"

Dr. Mike Brown
Strength & Wisdom Ministries

"In Just Add Sugar, Deby's transparent and heartfelt journals are inspirational and encouraging. Deby captures the difficult road she traveled during the process of adoption and how she was able to endure by adding sugar, God's sweet presence, to her journey. We recommend this book to all who are walking through the adoption process. You will be truly blessed."

Dr. Ronald and Pastor Judy Burgio
Lead and Co-Pastor, Love Joy Church
President, Elim Fellowship (Ron)

"Hilariously organic in childrearing and family, *Just Add Sugar* steals the heart! Encores to the mother of seven speaking in true "Erma Bombeck" tradition while sounding the high calling of birth mothers and mothers alike. Filled with antidotes both practical and spiritual, Deby teaches practicing the sweetness of God's presence throughout. And let us not forget to ask for a sequel on Nick alone!"

Rev. Nancy Clark
WILLOW Director, Elim Fellowship Women's Ministry

"Just Add Sugar – The Sweetness of His Presence" is a delightful book full of rich wisdom and encouragement for moms. Deby's stories touched my heart and resonated with me as a mother of three adopted children. Her devotional style makes reading easy for busy moms. I highly recommend this book to all mothers."

Lisa Osteen Comes
Associate Pastor, Lakewood Church

"Deby Scott's book, "Just Add Sugar," reflects on her life's journey. Her short stories grab your heart from the start causing you to stand in awe of our great God and His faithfulness. The passion and love she has for being a mom and all that goes with the demands of having a house full of children are evident throughout. Every parent can relate to her stories.

Deby is a very gifted and creative writer. Her stories grab your attention. I found myself laughing out loud one minute and grabbing a tissue to wipe my tears the next. She has an amazing gift to bring you into her story, find the lessons in the events of life, and make you feel like you were actually there when it happened."

Donna Fiorini
Donna Fiorini Ministries

"We have a very dramatic God, and the Scriptures are full of His epic interventions in the lives of people and His transforming truths. Just as in the Scriptures, where some people's hearts opened up to the divine, and others hardened themselves to His voice, in this life we also encounter people who notice the hand of God throughout the day to day, and others who are determined NOT to notice.

As longtime friends of Deby Scott and her family, I've watched them master the art of capturing those "aha moments" wherever and however they happen, and weave them into their ministry for the strengthening of others. In "Just Add Sugar," Deby displays on paper that gift of discerning where "Emanuel – God With Us" has revealed His Presence on life's journey. This devotional will take readers into the Lord's Presence each day with faith, love, and just the right amount of humor, while at the same time cultivating the grace in all of us to notice His handiwork in the lives of our own loved ones. Through their lives and this "Just Add Sugar," our days have been made sweeter."

Rev. Jack Hempfling
Senior Pastor, Living Waters Church

"One out of three people today have major insecurity problems. Deby's new book builds confidence – confidence in God, confidence in yourself, confidence in your future. This book will empower you to go from "I wish I could" to "I think I can" to "Yes, I will!"

Dr. Keith Johnson
America's #1 Confidence Coach
www.KeithJohnson.TV

"Just Add Sugar!" I loved it! This book is filled with Life and Hope, Truth and Laughter! Deby's heart stories make the mundane leap to life. Her faith in Christ shines through on every page! As Deby acknowledges the sweetness of His presence in her daily life, that same sweetness of His presence refreshes mine! Thanks Deby, for sharing your heart with all of us. I treasure your friendship!

Rev. Joan Wood
Friend!

Just Add Sugar

~ The Sweetness of His Presence ~

Dear Beth,
Never give up!
Your best days are ahead!
(Ps. 16:11)
Love,
Deby

DEBY SCOTT

WESTBOW
PRESS
A DIVISION OF THOMAS NELSON

WestBow Press books may be ordered through booksellers or by contacting:

WestBow Press
A Division of Thomas Nelson
1663 Liberty Drive
Bloomington, IN 47403
www.westbowpress.com
1-(866) 928-1240

All Scripture quotations are from the New King James Version of the Bible.
Copyright © 1979, 1980 1982, Thomas Nelson, Inc., Publisher.

ISBN: 978-1-4497-5314-6 (sc)
ISBN: 978-1-4497-5315-3 (hc)
ISBN: 978-1-4497-5313-9 (e)

Library of Congress Control Number: 2012909246

Printed in the United States of America

WestBow Press rev. date: 05/30/2012

This book is lovingly dedicated to my Heavenly Father Who prompted the idea of writing it so others with the desire of adoption would be encouraged. To You be the glory! May it accomplish all that You have intended for it to! Thank You for using me in this way, and for seeing me through every little event penned within these pages. I love You!

It is also dedicated to the "husband of my youth," Eric, who is not only a wonderful husband, but a devoted and fun-loving father as well. Without you our family would not be what it is today. Thank you for your strong leadership and guiding hand, and for not thinking I was out of my mind when I shared with you "my idea" of sharing our lives with the world! By your own example you have encouraged me to "lay hold of THAT for which the Lord has laid hold of me" (Philippians 3:12)! I love you with all that is within me!

I also dedicate this work to all six of my children ~ Erin, Sarah, Josiah, Hannah, Nicholas, and Deborah – who without you, I would not have occasion or reason to write about adoption, as well as Paul, my special surprise whom I have claimed as my son from the moment we first learned about you in 1987! All of your lives have forever shaped mine in a way that only God could have done through you! I thank Jesus for you every day for you are truly unique and special gifts from Him, hand-picked and perfect! I love you!

I also thank my Celebrate! Family Church congregation in Leicester, New York as you have been an integral part of my life since 1992. Some of you have cried with me, many have prayed with me, and most have laughed with me as I have shared each wild experience with you. You're great; and I love being your pastor's wife!

"For I know the thoughts that I think toward you, says the Lord, thoughts of peace and not of evil, to give you a future and a hope" (Jeremiah 29:11).

Contents

Foreword

A "foreword" is an opening word or statement. A foreword is intended to introduce the author or the topic, or in this case, "Just Add Sugar." In considering an introductory statement, my mind continually reverted to a different type of foreword. Rather than a verbal description, my thoughts go immediately to a declaration of movement – forward.

Forward! The dictionary says it is a description of placement (the forward part of a ship). Forward is also a direction (as opposed to rearward or to the side). One definition states that forward is progressive – when progress is stopped, forward is no longer occurring.

People stop looking and moving forward for many reasons. Sometimes they get stuck. Sometimes they are afraid or they get tired. Sometimes the process of moving forward becomes mentally or physically too demanding and they begin to doubt that forward is attainable or even desirable.

This book is intended to move you forward. The lives depicted are real. Sometimes the names have been changed, sometimes not. But the reality is there – the people in these stories could be anybody. They could be you.

The old spiritual says, "Through many dangers, toils and snares, I have already come; it's grace that brought me safe thus far, and grace will lead me home."

This book could have been called, "Grace to Go the Distance." The reader will find hope, encouragement, fresh fire, and new desire – that whatever you have come through, whatever is out there waiting – "Forward" is not only possible and available – "Forward" is fully attainable.

"Just Add Sugar" will delight you, challenge you – even provoke you. The foreword for this gripping little journal is – just keep moving forward!

Rev. Eric Scott
Deby's husband,
Their kids' father,
and
Senior Pastor, Celebrate! Family Church

Introduction

I never considered myself a big dreamer except when it came to motherhood. From the time I was a little girl I dreamed of the day that I would grow up, get married, and have babies . . . and lots of them. It never occurred to me that I might have some struggles along the way. I knew what I wanted and that was that. No career. No fame or fortune. Just a family, and hopefully one much like the one I grew up in.

I had a father who adopted me when I was seven years old after he had been married to my mom for five years. He had wanted to adopt me before this but my mom, having been through one failed marriage, wanted to make sure this marriage was going to work. My dad worked long and hard to provide for us. He loved the outdoors and made it a point to take the family on weekend getaways whenever possible. He had a funny sense of humor and seemed to be able to make a joke out of virtually anything.

My mother was a stay-at-home mom who I was sure had eyes in the back of her head! She was the lawgiver and disciplinarian of the family but also the one on whom I knew I could always count, regardless of my antics! I knew she loved me; and the fact that she held firm to her set rules no matter how hard I tried to wear her down, proved just how much. She was there when I got home from school. She was the chief cheerleader at my sports events. She was a good cook and seamstress and taught me to be the same. Best of all, she didn't rub a hole in the floor on her side of the car when I was learning to drive . . . well, maybe just a small one!

I had five brothers and sisters who came after me who I loved and doted on. I was proud to be their big sister. We did things most siblings did. We fought one minute over things that now seem unimportant, and stuck up for each another in the next breath. We laughed a lot too. It was a great life and a great family.

My days of playing with dolls came very early in life as it does with most little girls. I loved walking my babies up and down the sidewalks near my home in the pink stroller I was given one Christmas. It wasn't long after that I decided my goal in life was to be a mother. I just knew I'd be a good one!

As a teen I held the dream of a family in my heart even though I became rebellious for several years. I knew the things I was doing weren't right or good for me, but for the sake of popularity I participated in the party lifestyle – drinking alcohol I didn't like, taking drugs I was afraid of, and hanging around with people who were one step from jail.

I met my wonderful husband, Eric, while we were both stationed at Fairchild Air Force Base in Spokane, Washington. We married fifteen months later at age twenty-two. While I remained faithful to my husband, I couldn't get out from under the drug and alcohol cloud which followed me through those first eight rocky years. Finally, in 1985, I came to the sobering realization that I was a mess and needed help. I gave my heart and life to Jesus with the assurance that, regardless of what the future held, all would be okay. An exchange was made that afternoon that would forever change the course of my life: His beauty for my ashes; His oil of joy for my mourning; His garment of praise for my spirit of heaviness (Isaiah 61:3). My sinful, guilt-ridden life was surrendered. "He had redeemed my life in peace from the battle that was against me" (Psalm 55:18). And for the first time in many years I had rest from the torment of a disappointing and God-less life. The Lord and I together had won.

Eric and I were pretty sure what we wanted out of life. His plans never included a growing family per se, but he wasn't opposed to the idea either. He always felt that if it happened, great, if not, that was fine too. He always told me that he married me for me and not the children I would give him. While those words were reassuring, the anguish in my soul grew to unbearable levels with each passing month. We had to face the unspeakable and unimaginable truth – we were infertile.

It was true that we hadn't necessarily been trying to get pregnant . . . (let's just say he wasn't, BUT I WAS!) . . . neither were we trying to prevent it. As months came and went and still no baby, we sought the help of a doctor who I believed would have some reasonable explanation for our infertility as well as a quick-fix solution. I wasn't ready for the truth of his words. But tests, tests, and more tests, plus one surgical procedure after another, proved that pregnancy would not be an option for us. This devastating reality hit me right between the eyes – and deep down in my heart. I cried off and on for what seemed like months. I could barely stand to look at pregnant women or moms pushing their babies in strollers. It was a very dark time in my life. I felt like I was in a hole with no way of getting out. I didn't know Jesus at this time so I didn't know of His peace that passes understanding. I didn't know He had a plan for my life in spite of the sorrow in my heart. And I didn't know that He was already working and had, in fact, by now orchestrated events that would forever change my life.

We had been married five years when the call came in the middle of the night. John, a man my husband knew from work, knew a woman who was looking for an adoptive family for the child she couldn't care for. The baby was barely hanging onto life due to malnutrition, and it was at this time that she found her way to her friend for counsel and help. John shared his knowledge of such a couple and she agreed to meet us the next morning.

The phone's ring jolted us out of a restful night's sleep. The only word I heard as Eric spoke to the person on the other end was "baby." I was in shock. As Eric hung up the phone and explained the situation to me as best as he understood it, my mind raced. We agreed to get a few more hours sleep before going to John's house the next day, but my sheer and utter delirium prevented my immediate slumber. "How," I pondered, "could Eric sleep after this phone call?" Eventually I did too, but not for long. We had an 8:00 a.m. appointment and I planned to be on time!

The normal twenty minute drive to John's seemed to take forever! The wind storm the night before brought down many power lines and tree limbs, but Eric managed to get us there safely and on time in spite of the detours. I barely said a word as he drove; I was numb. The very thing my heart had desired for so long was finally coming to be. I can't tell you how I walked up the steps to John's front door because I don't remember doing so. Jesus must have carried me.

The door opened and my heart sank as I spied across the room the woman who held my future in her arms. She looked peaceful yet questioning. And as I suspected, she had many things to say as we began our conversation. What surprised me the most was how easy it seemed for her to place her baby in my arms, which she did almost immediately. It was at this time that the reality of what was happening flooded my awareness. The baby I longed for was finally coming into my life, yet MY joy was a direct result of HER sorrow. The very same baby I was privileged to receive was the same one she had to let go of. It was a bittersweet time, yet somehow I managed to choke back the tears until we were home with our new little addition. It wasn't until years later that I fully understood how wonderfully God's grace had adorned both of us "mothers," each for different tasks in regard to this one little life. He had answered both of our prayers and it was nothing short of a miracle.

That day marked the beginning of a new facet of life for me. Motherhood held its challenges as well as blessings, especially since Erin had special needs requiring special care. It was a responsibility and challenge I flowed in unreservedly. My husband and I were delighted and fulfilled now in all aspects of our lives.

It was six years before we pursued adoption again. During those years we moved to a bigger home in another town, I had a hysterectomy, we came to the Lord, and Eric began his own construction company. Life was really good and we felt settled – at least until we began feeling the prompting of God to seek training for full-time ministry.

Sarah was born in 1988 and joined our family at birth. Like Erin, the news that we were new parents came unexpectedly and without forewarning. The phone call came the day after she was born; but because she was premature, she needed to gain some weight before she could be released from the hospital. Much to my surprise, the day she was released my husband arranged for me to be wheeled out of the hospital in a wheelchair with her in my arms. How did he know that I secretly desired this experience? He didn't of course, but God did! I beamed the whole way to the car as I realized that motherhood bliss had again visited me.

Sarah was just eight months old when we moved to New York. We knew we needed training for ministry so Eric enrolled at Elim Bible Institute (EBI) in Lima. They had a wonderful one-year program on which we wanted to focus as we prepared to go to Malawi, Africa. Unbeknownst to us at the time, God would have us stay the full three years at EBI, Eric would graduate, and then step into the role of pastor at our own local church. Due to bizarre circumstances that would take the life of our beloved Pastor John the day after Eric's graduation, Eric would be asked to fill his position, and it is there that we remain to this day.

Six more years passed. It's true we had our hands full with a growing church and two daughters already, but we felt strongly that God wanted us to adopt more children. We wanted a larger family so this was good news! We weren't sure how it would necessarily come about or even the time frame, we just knew what was in our hearts. A friend shared a tape by Pastor Jack Hayford in which he spoke about "singing over the barren places in our lives." Feeling barren in no other area than children, I began to sing in what I called my "Faith Room." It was the bedroom just off the master bedroom in our home that was the perfect room for a baby. As I lay in my bed at night I could see right into that room at the spot where the crib would eventually go. I would go in early in the morning and sing to the Lover of my soul. Mid-day and evening I would sing too, thanking Him for His miraculous ways in my life and for the child or children who would occupy this room. They weren't particular songs, just whatever was on my heart. Some I made up. Others were favorites I had come to love during my Christian life. Sing. Sing. Sing. And believe. I trusted that God would do the impossible once again and we would, in fact, even at age thirty-nine, receive another son or daughter. We trusted His word and chose to hold on to our inheritance.

Within months Josiah joined our family. This was 1995. He, like his siblings who came after him, came with but a few days' advance notice. Hannah joined us in May 1996 and Nicholas in December that same year. Deborah was born in November 1997 and it was then I stopped singing! I say this in jest of course because I KNOW I am a blessed woman! Even during all those many years of my rebellion and promiscuity which eventually, I believe, led to my infertility, God had a plan. He saw my future and was in fact already there. He saw each and every one of our young birth mother's lives and the decisions they would have to make as a result of their own sinful choices. Hard decisions. Agonizing decisions. Decisions made from love and self-sacrifice. Decisions cloaked in God's amazing grace. God loved them and the children they carried in their wombs. And God had a plan all along. You see, He was in their future as well. He has always been in control.

Eric and I know that our children are on loan to us from God, as are all children born into this world. We have a sacred trust to raise them in loving, caring homes where Christ is honored and glorified so that their lives will make a mark on the world as we know it. God has purposes for each life that is born and we have a part to play in shaping and guiding that life that is entrusted to us.

God loves adoption. He made a way for us to become His sons and daughters through the spirit of adoption, and He has made a way for children born to others to be raised by people like you and me who couldn't have children in the natural sense. He brings two very different worlds together for the sake of the common good of one. He orchestrates events and places us where we need to be. He takes care of the details. We just need to be flexible and open to His direction.

My prayer for you today is that you never lose hope. I know the adoption process can be long and arduous. I know the wait time can be discouraging. But don't give up! God is just as interested in the process as we are the goal. Just add sugar – the sweetness of His presence, to each day as it unfolds. Relax, and enjoy your adoption journey. God is not on a time clock. Keep going. Take the next steps, delighting yourself in Him as you do. And don't be too surprised when the telephone rings. You never know who might be on the other end. And then your life can be filled with wild and crazy and wonderful stories to share about your family, just like mine.

With love and thanksgiving for all He has done,
Your sister in Christ,
Deby Scott

The High Call of Poopy Diapers

~ A Reflection on Anointing ~

"But you have an anointing from the Holy One . . ." (1 John 2:20).

ONE OF THE THINGS I admire most about mothers is their ability to change poopy diapers without skipping a beat. Diapers most men would cringe over. Diapers that would send some people screaming into the night. Diapers that represent a healthy little life.

"I can do that," I supposed, with relative assurance of my capabilities. After all, I had five siblings born after me and I had a lot of practice. I wanted the whole motherhood package – sleepless nights, doctor appointments, trips to Grandma's, baby paraphernalia in and out of the car, and yes, poopy diapers. To me the entire experience was the epitome of bliss – a little life to love and take care of – a baby who needed me.

When Erin joined our family the novelty of changing diapers quickly dissipated. At first it was, "Hey, look what she did!" Or, "Isn't this cute?" Of course my husband could never grasp the affinity I had for this sort of thing, but to me it was a sign that I was doing a good job. And I loved it. But as time went on the novelty became routine and second nature, much like combing my hair or brushing my teeth. I had a schedule and I kept it. The more I did it, the better I got. Why, I could practically change a diaper with one hand while the other searched in my purse for the car keys! I've heard it said that once you do something twenty-one times it becomes a habit. Changing diapers became a habit within two days of our receiving Erin. I would breeze through the living room with a dust rag . . . and change the baby. Grab the Comet on the way to the bathroom . . . and change the baby. Fold some clothes . . . and change the baby. Whether she really needed it or not, she got changed. My attitude was, "If it works, don't fix it!" And a dry baby worked for me.

There were some who questioned my decisions because I didn't pursue college and a great career. I knew what they thought, but I didn't care. I was answering the highest call of all. Jesus came as a baby. Mary, His mother, had to take care of Him and I'll bet that included changing a few diapers along the way. Mary was chosen for the task, and she took her job seriously. She stepped up to the plate, as it were, and swung the bat, even in the face of ridicule and chastisement.

Especially in today's society where "self" seems to be emphasized, there will always be those who won't understand your desire to be a mother, especially when your mode of having a family involves social workers, home studies and lawyers. "Why bother?" they'll say. But you know what God has spoken to you in the quiet. It is He Who instilled in you this desire. Just as Mary was chosen for a great task, so are you. Be faithful to that which the Lord has called you, even if you haven't seen the fulfillment of it yet. Pray for the child(ren) the Lord will give you. Pray for their birth parents, and their extended families. Remember, when God wants to accomplish something on the earth, a baby is born. And babies need mothers, like you and me, to care for and guide them through their years so they grow up well-adjusted and with full knowledge of His love and provision.

Yes, poopy diapers are a high calling. Motherhood isn't for everyone and that's okay. But for you who are reading this book, I suspect it IS for you. So I pray you'll rise to the challenge with the same intensity you would a high-paying job, if not more so. And when faced with obstacles and challenges that may, it seems, put you one step back in the process, remember the benefits that perseverance brings. You'll find it's definitely worth the effort!

Dear Lord, the sweetness of Your presence encourages me to persevere toward my calling. Thank You for holding my future in Your hands. In Jesus' name, Amen.

Whose Report Will You Believe?

~ A Reflection on Faith ~

"Commit your way to the Lord, trust also in Him, and He shall bring it to pass. He shall bring forth your righteousness as the light, and your justice as the noonday. Rest in the Lord, and wait patiently for Him" (Psalm 37:5-7a).

THE DOCTORS DIDN'T KNOW OUR God. The report had come back that "Erin would probably never walk, talk, read, or even ride a bike." In fact, she would probably never be normal. But like most things with which we beg to differ, we sought to prove just how wrong the doctors were!

True, Erin had been severely malnourished to the point of near death. True, she had been deprogrammed from smiling, crying, or even the slightest infantile cooings during the three and a half months of neglect prior to her adoption. But she was our special gift from God, and no one was going to tell us what she could and could not do!

We enrolled her in a special school at the age of eleven months. It was a wonderful school with marvelously gifted teachers. There she began the course of physical and emotional development that she had been deprived of for far too long.

She walked at seventeen months. She crawled shortly thereafter. She began to speak using simple words; and at the age of two and a half, she was completely potty trained! What EVER did those doctors mean? As far as we were concerned, Erin was now developing normally and this was nothing short of what we expected. To God be the glory!

Erin has learned many things since those first few milestones. She reads. She writes. She tells time. She even rides a bike, and quite well! She knows the importance of health and hygiene and can care for herself in that regard. She can count money; and she can carry on a conversation with understanding and reciprocal dialog. She also has manners, something many young people today don't have. She even graduated with an IEP diploma (Individual Education Program) at age twenty-one and has lived "on her own" in a Christian group home since age twenty-three.

Her years of formal education weren't always easy for her – or us. At times we had to coax her and prod her along, sometimes feeling like we were dragging her. At other times she caught on quickly. But we never let her give up or quit just because the particular task was difficult or she didn't want to do it. Once she achieved the goal we'd set a new one and then begin the work to help her achieve it. It has required focused determination on our parts, and a very strong will on hers to persevere, which she still has to this day.

She has truly defied everything the doctors said she would never be able to do and I attribute it 100% to the grace and mercy of God. He wasn't in that negative report! The Word of God in Jeremiah 29:11 states that He has not only a plan and purpose for our lives, but a future and hope as well which is always good! Walking that plan out may take some resolve and effort on our part. If we're diligent and keep our eyes rightly focused on Him, we're sure to not only make it but enjoy the journey as we do!

The Bible teaches us many things about our lives, but the one I always remember is that He's promised us "life, and that more abundantly" (John 10:10). Where would Erin be today if it were not so?

If He has spoken something to you, please believe it. If you're waiting on the fulfillment of a promise, don't give up. Remember, He is always faithful. At the appointed time you will receive what He's promised.

Erin is a living, breathing testimony to the goodness of our God! Thank You, Jesus, for YOUR report!

Dear Lord, I love Your Word which tells me You are always faithful. The sweetness of Your presence helps me to keep going when I sometimes want to quit. Thank You. In Jesus' name, Amen.

Raindrops and Angels

~ A Reflection on God's Truthfulness ~

"... rejoice in hope of the glory of God" (Romans 5:2b).

I LOVE THE SOUND OF RAIN as it taps on rooftops and sidewalks, especially when it's a heavy rain. I love it even more when I don't have to be out in it! The morning's downpour gave me a good reason to stay in my pajamas a bit longer than usual. It was Saturday anyway; and since I had nowhere I had to be, I took advantage of my background music while I sipped my morning coffee and read my Bible. Eric wasn't afforded the lazy morning so after packing his lunch and planting a couple kisses on his lips, Erin and I sent him off to work with hearty good-bye waves.

I was well into my morning devotions when the phone rang. I certainly expected it to be someone other than who it was. Keep in mind this call came the day *before* our eleventh anniversary.

Since we had wanted to adopt another baby we had spent the summer months leading up to this day meeting the requirements of the Christian adoption agency – attending classes, writing papers, and completing a home study. We finished the process at the end of October with somewhat of a heavy heart on my part because they told us that, even though we did all we were supposed to, it would be at least two years before we would be chosen as adoptive parents. Two years!!! This seemed like an eternity and certainly wasn't something we expected to be told.

One day shortly after we finished all of our requirements to adopt, Eric had been praying. He shared with me that the Lord told him we would have a baby *before* our next anniversary. "But how could this be?" I thought. Our anniversary was only two weeks away and there's *no way* this could happen, especially in light of what we had been told. I felt like Abraham's Sarah when I chuckled under my breath with an "Oh, yeah right" attitude in my heart! One part of me wanted to believe this man that I loved. The other part had nothing but doubt. After all, we were told two years, at best.

I answered the phone with my usual cheery hello. People often told me how nice it was to call our house because I always greeted them with such enthusiasm. This morning was no different. But as the person on the other end of the phone began to speak, I stood motionless as the phone lay plastered against my ear with a trembling hand. As I listened I hung onto her every word.

After hanging up the phone I quickly threw on a pair of jeans and grabbed Erin and the car keys. We had to go find Daddy and tell him the news! I wasn't quite sure where his construction jobsite was specifically, but I had a pretty good idea of his general location. Thankfully it wasn't that far as the windshield wipers on my loaner car didn't work worth a hoot. Having to stop periodically and rap the wipers against the windshield to get them going again made the journey to Eric's jobsite even more laborious. But I was determined to find him, and finally I did! I spied his truck atop a hill; and in spite of the thundering rain and inept wipers, I made it to him with nary a problem.

Eric saw me coming so he met me at the car. His first words to me were, "What is it? Boy or girl?" I was shocked, amazed and all out flabbergasted! How could he have possibly known? But I, without skipping a beat, shouted out with pure exhilaration, "A girl! It's a girl!" And then I recounted my entire conversation with the social worker at the adoption agency in full detail. I still couldn't believe that our daughter had been born the night before and that we were chosen to be her adoptive parents!

Eric really had heard from the Lord. And as much as I trusted the Lord and had grown in faith myself, I didn't have the faith to believe the words my husband spoke were from the Lord. In this instance, I believed the words of man, and not my God.

Eric loaded up his tools and came home as quickly as he could. We headed to the hospital to meet our new little addition, her birth mom, and birth mom's entire family! We wondered why she chose us. We also wondered what her situation was that she couldn't keep her baby. Sarah was born four weeks early so we also questioned whether she would be okay or not. It didn't matter that we didn't have answers just yet. We knew we had just experienced another miracle at the hand of our God.

We knew we wanted to take our birth mom a gift upon meeting her, but what do you take to the woman who just had your baby? Stopping at a gift shop we found the perfect Precious Moments porcelain statue of a mom and a baby that we felt was appropriate and would be appreciated. We hoped it would be a constant reminder to her of the fact that we would never forget her sacrifice. That, along with some flowers, would be a nice gesture of "friendship" even though those two items couldn't even begin to express what was in our hearts. Too, we hoped our bringing gifts would put her at ease and relieve any awkwardness she might feel.

Our meeting with her was anything but awkward. Lying in the hospital bed was a beautiful young woman who had just made the hardest decision of her life. The compassion in our hearts grew immediately as we embraced her and began our exchange of information and individual stories. Once again our joy was truly another woman's sorrow. Thankfully she had a loving and devoted Christian family who supported her in her decision even though it meant a loss to them as well. She knew she wanted two parents for her baby, something she couldn't give her at the time; so with her baby's future having far more importance than her own agony, she had perused the files of adoptive families and chose us. I can't tell you why we stood out over the others. All I can say is I'm glad we did.

As Sarah's birth mom chose us to adopt her baby, her entire extended family – parents, brothers, and sisters, adopted us! In fact, after we finished talking with the entire family and then holding our little four pound ten ounce daughter for the first time, we all went out to eat together which marked the beginning of a wonderful relationship that we still enjoy to this day.

I know that not all adoption stories are so cloaked in God's amazing grace. I've heard the stories, as you have, of birth moms changing their minds, the extended family being bitter, the ongoing struggles and battles, and so forth. But when God's in it, there's none of that. God was speaking and everyone was listening, even when it was difficult. And the end result was His plan for all of our lives.

Sarah came home that day, not literally (because she was premature), but figuratively and spiritually. She came home in our hearts. And we know that, just as when one lost soul finds Jesus and comes home to His kingdom, when God's plan comes together, the angels rejoice together!

If your baby has already come home, you don't need me to remind you to rejoice! If you're still waiting all I can say is, listen to the raindrops. It just may be that the angels are tuning up their vocal cords in preparation of all heavenly praise because of what God is about to do!

Dear Lord, the sweetness of Your presence is such a joy to possess! Thank You for Your promises that are always Yea and Amen. In Jesus' name, Amen.

His Banner Over Me Is Love

~ A Reflection on Belonging ~

"My beloved is mine, and I am his" (Song of Solomon 2:16a).

I CAN STILL PICTURE THAT DAY in my mind. I wore a little yellow crinoline dress that poofed from my waist to my knees. I had a petticoat slip on underneath that helped it to stay that way, white ankle socks, and black patent leather shoes. I skipped up and down the sidewalk in front of the big brick building that was the court house. It was sunny outside, and I was happy. My dad was becoming my dad for real. It was my adoption day. I was seven years old.

My parents had dressed in their Sunday best too. The other kids stayed in the care of my grandmother so my mom, dad and I could meet the judge at the Santa Ana courthouse as planned. I was excited about the day, and my mom tried to prepare me as best as she could.

We waited outside the big wooden door to the judge's chambers. I wiggled in my chair as my parents tried to keep me still. It was hard because I was so excited! I was REALLY becoming a Probst like the rest of the family!

Finally they called our names. My dad grabbed my hand and we walked inside the big office where the white-haired man sat. He took me to his big, long table and began to ask me questions.

"Do you know why you are here?" "Yes." "Do you know what adoption means?" "Yes." "Do you want Duane to adopt you?" "Yes." "Do you want him to be your daddy?" "YES!" In my heart he was already my daddy. He's the only daddy I knew since my mom and he started dating when I was two years old. And the only reason I knew he wasn't my daddy for real is because I had a different last name. My mom had explained the reason to me many times, and I did understand. But now, finally, I would have the same last name as the rest of my family and I was super happy!

The judge signed the papers and showed my dad where he needed to sign too. Afterward he shook my dad's hand, expressed his "congratulations," and we left his office. The best part was stopping for ice cream on the way home!

That day I became an official member of the family – and we had the paper to prove it! Years later my brothers would tease me about being only half their sister because Dad wasn't my "real dad!" Oh, yes he was! I'd come right back at them explaining that Dad *chose* me, but he was stuck with them!

I'm here to tell you that we belong to a big, wonderful family! It's the family of God, and our names are written in the Lamb's Book of Life. Just as I was officially adopted that day by my earthly father, our Father in Heaven made a way for us to be adopted into His family. From the moment we were born, He waited until that glorious day when we bowed our knee to His Great Name and became His child officially.

Aren't you glad that you belong to Him and bear His name? I sure am. As far as I'm concerned, there's no greater privilege. If for no other reason than that, let's rejoice in the fact that we belong in His family!

Dear Lord, thank You for my adoption – both in the natural and in the spiritual. The sweetness of Your presence reminds me that I belong to You. In Jesus' name, Amen.

The Fat Lady Can't Sing

~ A Reflection on Trust ~

"I would have lost heart, unless I had believed, that I would see the goodness of the Lord in the land of the living. Wait on the Lord; be of good courage. And He shall strengthen your heart; Wait, I say, on the Lord"
(Psalm 27:13-14).

THE SIX YEARS FOLLOWING SARAH's adoption brought a lot of change in our lives, not the least of which was a huge geographical move from west coast to east. I can't say I was totally prepared for the radical differences in temperature and lifestyle, but I was determined to make the best of it even though there were some aspects to the whole thing I didn't particularly like. Still, I knew we were right where God wanted us to be so it didn't matter whether I liked it or not. Our goal was obedience to His will no matter what the cost. So when He prompted us to again pursue adoption, we did so with the same gusto we'd always shown. If God said it and we believed it, then we were doing it! Praise God!

The laws in New York are different from those in California. For instance there are no "open adoptions" in New York, or at least there weren't at the time we were adopting. We would not be able to meet our birth mothers let alone know their names, unlike Erin and Sarah's adoptions in California. Likewise, all information relating to us would be kept confidential as well. Birth mom would only know the type of family we were, not who we were or where we lived. I was sad to learn this. I believe our children are who they are because of the people who gave them life as well as us, the ones who raise them. It's a triangle of connection and, in my opinion, the more information that's shared, the better off we all are. But that's not how New York State views it; and since they didn't ask me, we had to go along with their program.

A ministry in Buffalo came highly recommended. I was a bit taken aback when the very nice ladies on the phone told me to go ahead and send in our information, but declared that we probably wouldn't be chosen as adoptive parents *due to our age*. Our whaaat????? I didn't have one gray hair on my head and I was still quite active and physically fit! True, Eric had grown a few gray hairs by this time (the ministry has a way of doing that to a person), but he was still young too. What were they talking about? Thirty-nine isn't old! The gasp in my voice and heart was evident but what could I say? After Eric and I talked about it some more, we still felt the Lord was saying for us to go for it, so we did. We sent in all of our paperwork and waited. Finally a call came a few months later. It was those same nice ladies and they had good news!

We were told that we'd been chosen to receive a little boy that was about to be born. Birth mom was in labor and we should wait for the follow-up phone call giving us details of his birth and subsequent release date from the hospital. Eric and I were ecstatic! A son! We were really having a son! We tossed around names and eventually came up with a good Biblical one.

We got the phone call that he'd been born, but it would be a day or two before we could bring him home. No problem. That gave us plenty of time to get ready for our new arrival. Who needs more than two days anyway?

The next phone call a day later didn't bring the news we were waiting to hear. Instead, we were told that our birth mom had changed her mind and she was, in fact, taking her baby home. For some reason I wasn't completely devastated. I didn't cry for days. I didn't slip into a grave depression. For some reason I had the peace of God that passes all understanding. And for another reason I failed to understand, I knew it wasn't over. You've heard the phrase, "It ain't over till the fat lady sings?" Well, the fat lady hadn't opened her mouth, of that I was sure! God was still up to something, I just knew it. And so we believed and prayed as we waited for God.

One week went by, then two. No word. Then three weeks, then four. Still no word from them. Eric and I often wondered how the nice ladies were doing but we dared not call. We also wondered how birth mom and her son were doing. We prayed for all of them every day believing that God was on His throne and His will would be done, whatever that was.

One night, as week five began, the phone rang. It was them, the ladies at the ministry. My heart about leapt out of my chest as I listened to their story. Birth mom took her son home as expected, but then turned around and brought him back the very next day. She decided once again that she wanted him to have a mother and a father. Since she wasn't in a stable relationship at the time, the best option for her was placing him in a loving Christian home.

The ladies didn't tell us right away because they wanted to allow her time to really be sure. They agreed to keep him until such time as she was certain. And once she was, they called to say we could come get him the next day!

The timing couldn't have been worse! This whole thing happened the night before I was to go to Michigan to visit my sister. She had just been diagnosed with breast cancer and needed me to come. I was leaving in the morning and wouldn't be returning for a week. Needless to say, I was very happy to be going to her, but I was still looking forward to getting home too!

So our dear little friends at the ministry kept Josiah another week. With my feet barely planted back on New York soil, we headed for Buffalo and picked up our son! The fat lady couldn't sing because the story wasn't over!

I almost titled this story "(Almost) Losing Josiah." But that wouldn't have been an accurate picture of what was going on here. We didn't almost lose anything. God just delayed Josiah's homecoming so our precious birth mom would have peace with her decision. We would've wanted nothing less.

It's hard to be so certain of something, then watch a turn of events bring about an unexpected outcome. I know. I've been there and it's not easy or fun. In fact, it's hard and uncomfortable. But that's where faith kicks in. Isn't that what the Christian life is all about anyway?

Trust God for your final outcome. As you wait for Him remember, you WILL see His goodness in the here and now. He loves you and will continue to guide you as you place your confidence in His character and Word.

Dear Lord, thank You for Your gift of faith. I stand on Your Word as the sweetness of Your presence comforts me in the hard places of life. In Jesus' name, Amen.

A Mother's Day Package

~ A Reflection on Possibility ~

"Every good gift and every perfect gift is from above, and comes down from the Father of lights, with whom there is no variation or shadow of turning"
(James 1:17).

LIKE HER SIBLINGS BEFORE HER, Hannah's arrival into our lives came with but a few days' notice. By this time we'd become pros at putting a nursery together in record time. Diapers. Check. Formula. Check. Onesies, socks, blankets, jammies, burp cloths, crib bedding. Check, check, check, check, and check. We were ready for the day we were to yet again drive to Buffalo and pick up our little darling.

Hannah was born just sixteen months after her brother, Josiah. We had told the sweet ladies at the ministry that we were open to receiving any child the Lord wanted us to have so "please keep us on the list of potential adoptive couples." They were in awe of God's hand in our being chosen the last time (because of our age, remember), so the fact we'd been chosen again just reminded them that no "norms" can or will hinder God. He will do what

He wants when He wants, and our job is to go along with His program. No problem there.

We had gotten the call telling us that we'd been chosen because Hannah's birth mom was older and wanted an older couple to parent her daughter. This is a time I praised God for my age even though I still didn't feel or act "old." In my book, forty wasn't old; but if it helped to get chosen, then so be it!

Hannah was born on Friday; but since she wasn't due to be released until Sunday, we had to wait to get her. Dressing the older children in their "Mother's Day Sunday Best," we sped off down the road after church to our new favorite place. This ministry home had become so special to us because of the hearts of the people who worked there. Not only did they minister to young (and older) women in crisis pregnancies, they also cared for aged people in their twilight years, giving them a comfortable, Christian home filled with lots of love. Both ends of life's spectrum were ministered to there, and we loved them for their hearts of devotion and service.

Hannah didn't look a thing like I envisioned. She was much pudgier than I expected, and oh, that head of hair! It was full of beautiful, soft curls. Actually she looked more like an Eskimo than a bi-racial baby, but she was still cute as a button! After each of us had our time holding and feeding her, and yes diapering her, we swaddled her in a cute pink blanket, fastened her in her new car seat, and headed for home.

The older kids chattered endlessly all the way home. Eric and I smiled at each other with the sober realization that once again we'd have lawyer bills to tackle. But it didn't matter. Just like we knew that Hannah was His plan for our growing family, we also knew that He would give us the means with which to pay the expenses that came with the new addition.

This was truly the best Mother's Day present I could have ever been given. Eric is fabulous in remembering special days with nice gifts (he's been well-taught!), but even he couldn't have done any better! Hannah was God's special gift to me. And on a day when mothers all over the country were being remembered and honored, it was a day of declaration and praise that what is impossible with men IS possible with God. Several years earlier I had been told by doctors I would never have children. How wrong they were! I may not have had them in the physical sense, but I definitely birthed them in my heart.

If you're reading this book, you may have been told something similar too. Well-meaning friends and family members, even doctors and lawyers, only have so much information. But you know what the Lord has spoken to your heart. Keep standing on His promises. Keep believing what He said. You will get your own Mother's Day present when you least expect it because our Father delights in giving His children good gifts. And babies are the best gifts ever! Let me be the first to wish you a Happy Mother's Day. I don't know when that time will be, but God does.

Dear Lord, I have an expectant heart because I believe Your Word. The sweetness of Your presence gives me hope and joy. I love You. In Jesus' name, Amen.

Jack

~ A Reflection on Rejection ~

"Blessed be the God and Father of our Lord Jesus Christ, who has blessed us with every spiritual blessing in the heavenly places in Christ, . . . to the praise of the glory of His grace, by which He made us accepted in the Beloved" (Ephesians 1:3-6).

I ALWAYS KNEW MY DAD WASN'T the one who fathered me, but I didn't think about it much until I was about fifteen. It was then that I decided I wanted to meet my mom's first husband, if for no other reason than to see what the man looked like. Did I look like him? I mentioned my curiosity to my mom and she scheduled a visit. We didn't say a whole lot as we drove to his sister's house where the meeting would take place.

We pulled up in front of the house and sat there for a few brief seconds. By this time she had become as nervous as I was. Out the door bounded a man whom I would not have known as my father if I tripped over him. He greeted us both with a big grin and a hug for me. Was I supposed to embrace him in return? I felt very uncomfortable with his gestures, even though I thought they were sincere. My crossed arms across my chest told him just how much. And that was pretty much my posture during the whole visit.

My aunt (his sister) had prepared a very nice lunch for us all. While the grown-ups sat catching up on the last decade of their lives, my eyes pierced Jack with questions in my mind as to why he never wanted me. My mom had told me that during the divorce proceedings, he told the judge he didn't think I was his child which totally devastated her. This was an attempt to get out of having to pay child support (nice guy, I know!). It didn't set well with her at all, or me when I found out years later. Many, many years later when I met him again after this visit, he told me that this was his biggest regret in life; in fact, he would rather have admitted murder! I was glad he now felt bad about disowning me.

I was in my early thirties before I talked with Jack again. Apparently he had tried to get in touch with me several times after that first meeting, but my mom ran interference to our connections, telling him I didn't want to have a relationship with him. After a few attempts to reach me, he quit trying. Since I didn't know he had tried to get in touch with me, I felt abandoned and rejected – probably pretty much like my mom felt when he walked out on her. My face registered an "I don't care" attitude. But deep inside my heart were the longings for my "father's" love and acceptance.

My mom passed away in 1984 and our family quickly became disjointed. The glue that held us together was gone; and it seemed like my dad (who raised me) lost all ability to relate or connect to us "kids." I can't really explain how or why that happened, it just did, and none of us liked it. It was at this point in time that I decided to try, once again, to find Jack as I had a real parental void and need in my life.

My sister had my mom's phone book so I called for any information she might have. I was surprised to find that she had my grandmother's phone number and address, not because she had it, but because my grandparents didn't move to this new place until *after* my mom died. I can't explain it and I'm sure you're sitting there scratching your head too! But after a wonderful talk, my grandmother gave me Jack's number in San Diego.

I called Jack with no small amount of fear and trembling. Would he want to talk to me after all these years? Would he even care that I called? I cannot even begin to explain the sheer excitement I heard coming from his end of the phone when I told him who I was! He was in the middle of a prayer meeting with a bunch of men who were also estranged from their kids, praying that they'd be reunited! Talk about answered prayer! We chatted for some time when we decided we had to meet, and next week would be perfect as Eric and I were taking Erin to the San Diego Wild Animal Park. We'd go to his house afterwards.

Jack opened the door with the same giant grin I had remembered from our first meeting in 1970. This time, however, my arms reached for him right back. And I loved his wife, Maria, who was as beautiful on the inside as she was on the outside. She was wife number six, I found out.

We spent the evening getting acquainted with one another and catching up on days gone by. Jack had accepted Jesus after wife number five, and he and Maria shared an adventurous marriage until his death in 2003. He and I loved each other, it's true, but we often times found it difficult to express our hearts and really be ourselves with each other. To me at least it always seemed like we had to prove our worth in having the other in our lives. I don't know if it was further fear of rejection on both of our parts, or what. But as I said, we loved each other and we were grateful we had been reconnected.

When I found Jack in 1988 I also found that I had more siblings – two sisters by wife number two, and a sister and brother from wife number three. Thankfully I've had the opportunity to meet each of them, though I don't share a relationship with three of them. I am fairly close to my sister, Bridgette (nicknamed Bunny because she was born on Easter Sunday), but the miles between Idaho and New York prohibit time to be together. In our hearts we're sisters and we know it. We keep in touch by text and Facebook. But it would be so much better if we lived closer to really have that connection. As to the others, they have their own lives and are doing their own thing. They never knew me growing up and they haven't learned yet what they're missing by not having a relationship with me now! Someday, I hope.

As you might imagine, I've struggled with rejection through a big portion of my life. And every now and again it tries to rear its ugly head and drag me down, and always when I least expect it. But I've learned to take authority over that thing when it comes – in the name of Jesus – and send it packing. I know who I am. I know that I am worth loving. And I know that my God is always by my side – and He loves me more than everyone I know put together!

Getting free of rejection is usually not as simple as saying a prayer or two and washing your hands of it. It can be, of course, but my experience has been that it takes time. It's a process that involves forgiveness, love, and God's guiding hand.

I know I'm not the only one who has ever dealt with rejection. Some of you reading this may have too. My prayer for you is that you let God lead you through the process of healing. You won't be disappointed as you get free and come through on the other side.

Dear Lord, thank You for never rejecting me or disowning me. The sweetness of Your presence reminds me how much I am loved. In Jesus' name, Amen.

Are You Sure, God?

~ A Reflection on God's Grace ~

"My grace is sufficient for you, for My strength is made perfect in weakness"
(2 Corinthians 12:9).

BEFORE I BEGIN, LET ME just say that I'm not complaining. I don't wish we had said, "No" when we said, "Yes." It wasn't an option. Jesus was given all power and authority in our lives from the moment we invited Him in as our Lord and Savior. We have always believed He knew what He was doing so, like all the times before, we didn't question what He was saying to us.

Hannah was just seven months old when we got the call about Nicholas. The ladies at the ministry knew it was a little soon, but "would we consider another baby?" We knew in our hearts that this was God's will, His green light if you will, so we did what we knew to do. We prepared the nursery with again only a few days advance notice and headed off down the road to collect our little inheritance. Truly we had become experts at it by now.

I have some Native American blood in me because my biological father is part Cherokee. Nick is one-quarter Cayuga which, we've come to learn, is part of the Seneca nation. I'm not sure we were chosen to parent him because of my Native American blood, albeit small, but I'm sure it was a fact considered as birth mom was making her choice. His Indian name of "Pathfinder" should have been a clue as to what we were getting into.

We suspected that this little boy would not be an ordinary child who would eat, sleep and poop at regular intervals. From the moment we first strapped him in his car seat, we knew we were going to have our hands full. The enjoyable afternoon with the ministry ladies prior to our departure was the proverbial calm before the storm.

We knew there would be normal things like more bottles to warm and diapers to change, and more nights with less sleep than needed. But we had absolutely no idea what was in store! He fussed and fumed the whole way home. Nothing we did soothed him. He wiggled and squirmed until we were worn out. We wondered what had happened to the sweet little child we had just met.

Over the course of days that followed, we found he didn't like to sleep at all, night or day. No amount of rocking or walking helped to bring on much-needed zzz's for either of us. He had powerful lungs too that he liked to exercise often, setting us all on edge when he decided to let loose. And the fact that his whole body never seemed to rest from bouncing all over the place gave us clear indication that he was going to be a "little active!" Unless you've had an overactive child in your home, or one with special needs on top of the hyperactivity, you can't quite begin to understand the energy and stamina it takes to make it through a day.

He bypassed walking altogether and started running at nine months. Along with this feat he conquered climbing which meant he'd frequently escape the confines of his crib by climbing over the rails. He learned shortly thereafter that his toes were also powerful leveraging tools to help him scale the cupboards in the kitchen. I can't tell you how many times I found him sitting on top of the counter with a Cheshire cat grin of accomplishment on his face! I doubt he sat plotting for the right moment when I'd look away and he'd make a run for it. But, I do know if the passing thought pleased him, he acted on it. I, of course, was always hot on his trail once I realized he was out of eyeshot. You'd think I'd be skinny as a rail with all the running I did after him! Sadly, I'm not.

One time I had the audacity to use the bathroom in the middle of the day. He seemed pretty content with his toys so I slipped away for only a couple minutes to relieve my distending bladder. When I came out of the bathroom I didn't find him where I left him; rather, I found him climbing the *inside* of the refrigerator! Ah, uncharted territory! I could see the gleam in his eyes as I removed him from his perch. It didn't matter to me at the time how he got the fridge door opened. I just couldn't help but wonder what was next – the roof?

As he's grown, his behavior has only intensified. To say he's "into everything" is an understatement. Literally we cannot take our eyes off of him for a second! Some things never change. His learning disabilities require that he have a special classroom setting. His social skills are severely lacking even though we've done our best to teach him about proper relationships. It's sometimes hard to get a sitter to come back a second time because he wears her out, even though he's not doing anything out of his ordinary.

On the other hand, he can be quite sweet and charming. This same energetic kid is always thinking about his older brother. Even on his birthdays, Nick asks for something for Josiah too so they can play together. When it comes to his sisters though, he teases them mercilessly, but don't let anyone else pick on them! He frequently remembers how much I love flowers and brings me a hand-picked bouquet from our yard of dandelions. He loves babies, and animals too, and has proven to be quite sentimental when it comes to both.

Like most little boys he can do without baths, brushing his teeth, or changing his underwear. If I don't stay on him about it, it doesn't happen. However, he does remember to track dirt or snow in the house regardless of how many times I've reminded him to wipe his feet.

Nick is all boy in some senses. Some of what I've shared is just normal kid stuff, I know. But the constant tape loop, (and I mean *constant*), of "Don't do that . . . Put that down . . . Get off that . . . Stay out of other people's business . . . Yes, you may have a snack . . . No, it can't be a cup of sugar . . . You're right, people shouldn't smoke . . . Yes, you may have a sheet of paper . . . No, you may not bring a snake in the house . . . No, knives are not good toys for little boys . . . Didn't I ask you to stop doing that? . . . No, you may not start the fire . . . No, you can't go in your sister's room . . . Yes, you are a good boy . . . No, you can't have that . . . Yes, you have to go to school today . . . no, you can't stay up past your bedtime . . . Yes . . . No . . . Yes . . . No . . . Stop!" on top of everything else is a daily summons for Eric and me to join the ranks of others who have succumbed to the funny farm!

Sometimes I wonder if God made a mistake by choosing us because we feel like such failures. Sometimes we wonder if we can make it through another day without drooling on ourselves.

Through it all we remember that we were bought at a very high price. Our invitation to be a member of God's family cost Jesus His very life. Though raising this little boy does not compare to dying on a cross, it is a daily dying to self and a constant reminder of just how much we need a Savior. If we don't stay connected to the "Heavenly Umbilical Cord," I dare say the men in the funny white coats would come looking for us!

We try to keep our lives in perspective. Jesus has never given us more than we can handle, though at times we've thought we were going over the edge. It's our joy to try to be a good mom and dad to our precious son because it's what the Lord requires of us. I can honestly say that many rough edges in our characters have been worn off due to the job God gave us. Like I said before, God knew what He was doing.

We may not know what Nick's future holds, but we do know Who holds his future. And we can absolutely go to the bank with that one – if we can find him. Did anyone see which way he went?

Who stretches you to the end of your endurance? Could it be that this person was put in your life as much for you as it was for them? God's grace is amazing and wonderful and we need it, sometimes moment by moment. Let's not be afraid to speak up when it's been "one of those days" and call on His name. His grace is sufficient for our every need.

Dear Lord, I cherish the sweetness of Your presence as Your grace fills my life. I honor You for being my Lord and Savior. In Jesus' name, Amen.

Plan B Is Good

~ A Reflection on Planning Well ~

"God is faithful, by Whom you were called into the fellowship of His Son, Jesus Christ the Lord" (1 Corinthians 1:9).

I REMEMBER SO CLEARLY THE DAY I called my dad (who raised me) to tell him we were adopting another child. With an obvious questioning chuckle as to our sanity he did express joy for us as we told him the story. But underneath the "good for you" and "when do you get to bring her home," I knew what he was thinking. "Do they know what they're doing? Aren't they busy enough?" I reassured him that God knew what He was doing and our only response could be, "Yes." It was our joy and privilege to receive another little life into our family.

God had been preparing us for this day. True, I was up to my eyeballs with diapers, formula, car seats, cribs, and high chairs, and by this time, fifteen year old attitudes. In addition to Erin who was my fifteen year old, I had an almost nine year old, almost three year old, a one-and-a-half year old, and an eleven month old who I couldn't take my eyes off of for a second! And on top of it all, I had just turned forty-two! At a time when most of my friends were becoming grandparents, I was still adopting babies. But a long time ago I had decided that the most awesome thing I could ever do with my life was to invest my love, time, and resources, such as they were, into the lives of others. I didn't care how old I was, and apparently neither did the ladies at the ministry or our birth mother. Deborah was coming home to us!

Prior to the phone call I had been planning a special getaway for Sarah and me. Her birthday was coming up; and since she had been wanting to get her ears pierced, I had planned to take her out for lunch and then to the mall to get her ears fully adorned with cute little birthstone studs. That particular story with all of its drama is penned under the section, "The Surprise."

The ministry lady's phone call required that our day default to Plan B. We had to manage a trip to Buffalo before Sarah and I could go about our day. Normally the whole family would go together when we brought home another baby, making it a special event with lots of love and celebration. But in addition to the two hour drive there and two hour drive back, we would need another two hours for the usual family hoopla, making it nearly impossible to still take Sarah for her birthday surprise. This time was going to have to be different.

Eric and I decided we'd ask a friend to stay with the gang while he and I raced to Buffalo and back. Perfect. The kids weren't all too thrilled with the idea but they liked Cindy and knew they'd have a good time with her in our absence. They knew what we were bringing home so they were happy as they could be in spite of the fact that they couldn't go with us.

Five little noses were pressed against the window as we drove in the driveway that afternoon. Had they been puppies their tails would've been wagging, I'm sure. Cheers of glee filled the house as we entered with our newest little bundle all swaddled in pink. Each sibling took a turn holding their baby sister with the curly brown hair and big eyes. We took pictures for posterity, called everyone we could think of to share our wonderful news, and then I did the unthinkable! I left Eric for the rest of the day with not only the bigger kids, but the two day old baby as well! Sarah and I headed for Rochester and our birthday plans – an hour's drive each way. I knew my Super Husband-Dad could handle it. He had become an expert at crowd control so I left with complete confidence that he wouldn't be a blithering idiot when I returned home.

We could've told Sarah that her special day we'd been planning had to be postponed for a while, but we didn't want to take that away from her. To this day she remembers the events of Deborah's homecoming on HER birthday with great detail. She recalls it with fondness of course, but how raw a memory would it have become had we not followed through with our promise and the day she'd been so looking forward to? We could've waited several more days to pick up our daughter also, but that wasn't an option any more than not taking Sarah. We needed a win/win scenario.

God gave us the wisdom we needed to handle both situations. Now I know that this story is somewhat trivial in light of some of the things we face in life. Trust me, we've had to renege on promises we've made to our kids since then because of the magnitude of other pressing situations that held no other solution. But it truly has been our goal to be "parents of our word" to the utmost degree possible. And our kids have come to learn that sometimes things don't work out quite like we had planned.

If you're faced with decisions on how you're going to accomplish all that you need, ask God to give you wisdom. He'll show you the best plan of attack, just like He did the day we brought Deborah home. It's His joy to give us strategies and plans with which to accomplish our goals, even if it is just a birthday shopping trip. He cares about the things that concern us. Let's put our confidence in Him to show us the best way to get done what needs to be done. I am so glad He's always faithful, and I know you are too.

Dear Lord, I submit my plans for the day to You, knowing You will help me prioritize the important things. I love the sweetness of Your presence as You walk with me through every detail. In Jesus' name, Amen.

Food Fight!

~ A Reflection on Abandon ~

". . . and a little child shall lead them" (Isaiah 11:6).

I GREW UP WITH A DAD who was a comedian, or at least he thought he was. We kids did too, though my mom was a little less enchanted than the rest of us and truly found him annoying at times. As I've gotten older I understand why this was, but at the time we were routinely treated to a good laugh or two at one or another's expense. And more often than not, my dad was usually behind it!

My mom ran a tight ship when it came to kids, house, chores, curfews, and other good stuff. I take after her in that regard because I like standards too. And while my mom usually ended up laughing at his antics along with the rest of us, this one night left her at wit's end.

We sat down to eat dinner at the regular time – 6:00 p.m. Dad was home by 5:30 p.m.; we ate at 6:00 p.m. Sometimes there were exceptions to this norm but that was how we did things. We all knew we had to be in the house, sitting at the kitchen table, when Mom put dinner on the table.

I had done my laundry earlier in the day so I had one of my favorite dresses hanging in the kitchen doorway to dry. It was white with three gold buttons down the front, very cute and stylish. I loved it so I took very good care of it.

I also had a date coming around 7:00 p.m. so I needed to eat and get myself ready. It wasn't my night for dishes so I was good to go as soon as dinner was over and I had changed my clothes.

I come from a large family so when we all sat down for a meal together it was more like hogs at a feeding trough trying to get a word in edgewise as we ate. This night we were enjoying the meal my mother had prepared when all of a sudden, from across the table, my dad calls to me, "D e b y y y ..." As I looked up from my plate I saw what appeared to be mashed potatoes flying in my direction – potatoes launched from HIS spoon! Less than a second later they were hitting me square in the face! My dad laughed hysterically. That was the cue that a major food fight was ON!

My brothers and sisters and I dove on the butter, the corn, the 'taters, everything that was in arms reach, and started flinging them at one another. We were a mess, and so was the kitchen. So was my white dress which soon was covered in catsup!

My mom (bless her heart) calmly and politely pushed herself away from the table and walked out of the room in silence. She didn't need to tell us we'd have to clean up the mess when we were through flinging food around. We KNEW!

Why am I sharing this story with you from so long ago? Do I want you to feel sorry for Eric knowing what he married into? Certainly not. I'm sharing it because when we were kids, we knew how to let go and just be – to seize the moments at hand. We knew that kids, and walls, and tables, and dresses could be cleaned (hopefully the dress!). It's the lives of the people making a memory that really matters. And oh, what a memory this event has been! It's a story we've retold time and again that has garnered as many raised eyebrows as chuckles. (It's always the sourpusses that don't think it's very funny!).

As kids we're spontaneous, sometimes acting before really engaging our brains. But, there's a sense of freedom to just be and do, with little care or concern about what others might think, even our mothers. As we get older we become more "dignified," a lot of the time losing that sense of carefreeness. I'm not suggesting that we should all go out and have a food fight at home. But I am suggesting that we could all use a little loosening up!

Think of David. Didn't he dance before the Lord with just a linen ephod on (2 Samuel 6:14)? And didn't Saul's daughter, Michal, despise him for it (2 Samuel 6:16)? Because she chastised him for his behavior she was barren until the day she died (2 Samuel 6:23). But what was it that grabbed David that day as he danced half naked down the street in front of "maids of his servants, as one of the base fellows shamelessly uncovers himself" (2 Samuel 6:20)? Was it his childlike abandon and love for his Lord?

I dare say that if we danced half naked down a street there would be plenty of people ready to call the men in the funny white coats to come take us away. Again, I am not suggesting we try it. But I would like for us to examine our own hearts and ask, "What is it that keeps me from being totally surrendered in worship to Him?" "Am I concerned about what others will say or think?" It's true that there are plenty of judgmental people around, even in the church. If you stood on your head and whistled "Dixie" they'd undoubtedly have something to say. But our relationship with the Lord is vertical – between Him and us. What matters is what He thinks about what we're doing.

I encourage you to let yourself go in your worship. Raise your hands. Dance. Sing. Rejoice. It doesn't have to be in the front row of your conservative church. But if it is, so what! Maybe God will use you to pour a little of what David had into the people you worship with.

Be a kid at heart! Let yourself go! Enjoy life! Enjoy His presence! You'll never be disappointed. If a food fight happens to break out, so what. Just go with the flow and enjoy the moments.

Dear Lord, the sweetness of Your presence helps me live my life with child-like abandon. Thank You for all the enjoyment You put into it. In Jesus' name, Amen.

No Imposters, Please!

~ A Reflection on God's Love ~

"Before I formed you in the womb I knew you; before you were born I sanctified you" (Jeremiah 1:5).

ONE OF ERIN'S FAVORITE THINGS as a little girl was a blanket puppet in the shape of a bunny. She absolutely adored this bunny. It was the first thing she reached for in the morning and the last thing she held onto while falling asleep at night. It went everywhere she did; and when it needed a washing, I'd have to unwrap her entwined fingers from around it while she slept.

Erin knew her bunny's smell and its texture. She knew the places that were "loved too much" which sported worn spots after a time, and the type of satin ribbon that edged its bottom. She knew the size of the satin cheeks on its face as well as she did the pattern of the plaid flannel which was its body, something I myself couldn't remember exactly. How amazing was her then three-year old recollection of her beloved friend.

I thought my idea to buy a second bunny to have "just in case" was a good one. You know those "just in case" cases that come along when you least expect (OR need) them – just in case it was still in the washer in the morning – just in case we couldn't find it at home – just in case we left it at Grandma's, or worse yet, at a store – just in case!

My pantry is proof of the fact that I like to be prepared for the unexpected, so having an extra bunny is nothing out of the ordinary. Extra toilet paper and napkins. Extra jars of peanut butter and jelly. Extra toothbrushes and cans of Comet. Extra bottles of soda, juice and snacks. And of course those extra boxes of noodles and cans of spaghetti sauce for a quick fix meal when unexpected guests show up at the house. Extra bunny? Of course!

How interesting was Erin's reaction when I introduced the "imposter" to her! She recognized it immediately for what it was and determinably would have nothing to do with it! She took one look at it, felt it, smelled it, and promptly threw it on the floor! I got the message. Nothing but the "real deal" would do.

How unfortunate then when it was left at the Lake Elsinore State Park after a great afternoon picnic with family members. Erin had carried it around with her everywhere she toddled. I am sad to say we didn't notice that she had dropped it when we were packing up to go home. Her cries upon our arrival home signaled the truth of the realization. Bunny was gone!

The imposter was refused again. She cried and cried to the point she was physically worn out, and so were we. We knew we had to try to find it. Daddy was elected to go back to the park, even at the late hour and now chilly temps. His brother decided to accompany him because he couldn't handle the wailing of our three-year old. So, with flashlights in hand, off they ventured back to the park. After explaining their plight to the park attendant, who didn't have to let them in without paying a second time but did anyway, they were on their way to being Erin's heroes. Their mission – FIND THE BUNNY!

The only thing that kept Erin quiet was the promise that Daddy would find her most precious possession. I couldn't allow myself to dwell on the "What if he can't find it?" question, even though that was a real possibility. Erin had never known her father to fail before so she was certain he would come home a proud and mighty victor which meant her being reunited with her favorite friend. Praise God that's exactly what happened! We were all so happy!

He came through the door with the bunny perched on his head like a hat. She grabbed him around his tree trunk leg and squeezed with all that her three-year old body could muster. It didn't matter that her bunny had purple, yellow, and brown stains from the soda she drank earlier, the potato salad she had eaten, and the earth it had been dragged through. She didn't care that it smelled; she was just glad to have it home. Off she toddled with a smile on her face and joy in her heart that radiated through her whole body. The rest of the evening was peaceful, but you can be certain that from that day forward we kept a pretty good eye on that bunny!

Awww. The comfort of the one you love. The joy of a special friend. The peace of knowing you have all you need.

The story of Erin's bunny really isn't significant in and of itself, as children lose things all the time. Adults do too, more than we'd care to admit. The reaction to losing something varies, depending on our emotional attachment to it. If it's something really special like Erin's bunny, our reaction can be total devastation. If it's not really that important we take it like eating cake with no frosting – we don't like it but we eat it anyway.

Until we acknowledge Jesus as our Lord and Savior we're like that lost bunny – stained with sin, a little worn in spots, and feeling a bit like we've been dragged through the dirt.

Our Heavenly Father has known us from the very beginning of time. He knew who our parents would be, what color our cheeks would be, and how valued we'd be in life. He knew the places we'd go, the experiences we'd have, and how tattered we'd get along the way. He also knew the designs of the enemy to keep us "hidden from God" while we tried to live a life apart from Him. But, oh, how He rejoiced with the angels when we found our way home!

I say this to remind you that you are loved. It doesn't matter where you've been or what you've done. He sees you as He sees Jesus – perfectly clean! And He wants you to be with Him forever. He never wants to let you go. When morning dawns, it's you He reaches for. When darkness signals day's end, it's you He wants to wrap His arms around so that you're safe and secure. There's no other you. And certainly no imposter could ever take your place.

Erin outgrew her bunny eventually. I have it tucked away for the perfect moment in time when I'll give it back to her to keep in her own keepsake box. And when I do, I'll tell her again about how much she is loved and how wonderful it is to belong to Him, the Keeper of her heart!

Dear Lord, I love how You love me. The sweetness of Your presence reminds me just how much. In Jesus' name, Amen.

Lord, We Thank You

~ A Reflection on Gratitude ~

"We give thanks to You, O God, we give thanks! For Your wondrous works declare that Your name is near" (Psalm 75:1).

WE DROVE TO REDLANDS EVERY day to see Sarah since we learned she was our new daughter. Because she was a preemie she had to gain at least a pound before the hospital would release her. Babies weighing less than five pounds were too small yet, according to the doctors. So we visited and prayed and visited some more until we got the green light. The day after we visited Sarah in the hospital for the first time, we were blessed that her birth mom and her family wanted to have a dedication service right there in the hospital. Everybody was there – birth mom, her parents, grandmother, brothers, sisters, their spouses, the adoption social worker, nurses, and Eric, Erin and I. The room was jam-packed with people for this simple, yet loving service where this precious mom dedicated her baby to the Lord and to us. I was moved to tears – in fact, several of us were. It was a beautiful time. Love and God's grace permeated the room. I'm sure all of our lives were touched that day in a powerful way.

I wasn't expecting her to come home on day number six. I was just making my regular trek in to see her when I was met with the news that we could take her home! I was delighted of course, but I hadn't come prepared. No car seat. No diaper bag full of necessities, just a willing heart. So I called Eric and gave him the news. He wasted no time in loading up from work, gathering up the list I gave him, and heading out. Redlands was nearly an hour's drive from home, especially during heavy traffic. Eric arrived in record time. We talked and smooched as we celebrated Sarah's "going home day."

But then it dawned on me. Birth mom would be going home alone without her baby. And just as she had made her baby's hospital dedication so special, I wanted to make her departure from this phase of her life also special. I called and asked if she would like to come and dress Sarah before we left, and to have some time alone with her. She choked back the tears as she responded affirmatively. Before long she and her mother entered the room and I gave them their time together to say their good-byes. It was a God moment for sure.

I can't tell you how grateful I have been for not only God's presence in the whole situation, but also for birth mom and her family's acceptance of us. It never was and still isn't a situation where they felt like we "took" something from them. In fact, they believe as we do that we were God's answer to their prayers. It has been a beautiful experience.

As a side note, Sarah was just recently re-acquainted with her birth mom and siblings on Facebook. (Birth mom and birth father ended up getting married and have three more children together.) They've texted by phone and chatted online but only by those means so far. Sarah is taking it slowly. One day Sarah will make a trip out west to meet her "other" family, and when she does, I'll go with her. I again want to thank this amazing woman for the precious gift she gave us. My presence will give Sarah the comfort and assurance she's going to need as they meet for the first time since that last day in the hospital. I expect it to be just as glorious as the first.

More than once during our lifetime Eric and I have built altars to the Lord where we laid down all of our own goals and ambition and embraced God's will for our lives. They have been times marked with prayer and admiration for all that God had done in the past, and expectation for what

He would do in the future. Inevitably, they were landmark times where we remembered that God had always been faithful and we could trust Him. Sarah's hospital dedication was one such landmark.

I think it's important for all of us to remember those times in our lives, if for no other reason than to remember that God has our lives under His control. He's always been faithful so we have no reason to fear or be afraid. Even though the new season may seem hard at first, once we're in the midst of it we'll be reminded yet again what an awesome God we serve!

I am forever grateful for all that He has ever done, and I know you are too!

Dear Lord, thank You that You provide moments in our lives that will help us remember Who You are! The sweetness of Your presence gives me joy as my heart fills with gratitude. In Jesus' name, Amen.

Death by Beef Stroganoff

~ A Reflection on Laughter ~

"A merry heart does good, like medicine" (Proverbs 17:22).

EVEN THOUGH I'M FAIRLY GOOD at it, I can't say that I particularly enjoy slaving over a hot stove. I cook because we need to eat but it's definitely not my favorite pastime. When I was a young wife I'd pour over my cookbooks looking for new and tantalizing dishes with which to surprise my husband after a long, hard day's work. His rave reviews during and after the meal gave me the encouragement I needed to keep trying new things. I was hitting home runs; and being the perfectionist I tended to be at the time, I intended to keep it that way. Sure, I had little slip-ups here and there, like the time I forgot to put the tuna in the Tuna Casserole. But for the most part, none of the "woopsies!" were significant enough for him to notice until the night he believes I tried to kill him. (He did notice the tuna-less Tuna Casserole though!).

I have no idea how it happened. I have no clue what I did wrong. I thought I followed the recipe to the very letter, not guessing at any measurement or ingredient. But my Beef Stroganoff didn't look good, smell good, or taste good. It was absolutely horrible! (So he says! I didn't bother to try it myself!).

We had already begun our after-work conversation when we both sat down to the table to eat. The smell and appearance of the stuff I'd just prepared should've been our first clue to skip it altogether and go directly to Plan B. I served it up anyway and he took a big bite. The look of horror on his face as he tried to quench the gag reflex was all it took to tell me it was worse than I thought. Tears rolled down his face as he tried to decide what to do with this yuck in his mouth. Swallow it? Perish the thought! Spit it out in the napkin? Maybe. Run to the bathroom and flush it down the toilet where it belongs? Best plan by far! I was mortified as he pushed himself away from the table and headed down the hall.

I sat there staring at my plate as I rehearsed the meal prep steps in my mind. What on earth did I do? And with all the drama that was coming from the bathroom, I was absolutely certain that there was no way to salvage the situation. The damage was done, big time!

It was all I could do to choke back the tears. "Good thing we hadn't invited friends over tonight," I thought to myself. My pride was deflated as I got an F in cooking class that night.

Eric's comedy routine now in full tilt finally shook me out of my self-pity. I knew he wasn't dying, but you sure couldn't tell from his theatrics! I began to laugh . . . and I mean belly laugh. You know – the kind of laugh where your sides and stomach hurt so badly that you think you're going to die if it doesn't stop! Well, I laughed, and then I cried as I laughed, and then I laughed some more. Flat out hee-haws! I was so sorry, but it was so funny now! By this time Eric lightened up on me and laughed too – at me, with me, and for me. It's exactly what we both needed. Yes, the meal was a disaster. No, it wasn't intentional. But laughter kept everything in perspective. It really wasn't a big deal. It was a flop, so what? Eric chuckled all the way to the pizza parlor that night to pick up our replacement. And I promised to never make Beef Stroganoff ever again, and I haven't.

I'm sure most of you have had similar experiences in the kitchen. Good plans sometimes go terribly wrong. But don't let them get you down! Don't take yourself so seriously that there's no room for error. Try hard and do your very best. More often than not the outcome will be near perfection.

But when it's not, thank God for the story-in-the-making that will be retold for years to come if your husband has anything to do with it! The playful bantering will be a wonderful reminder of from whence you came. And it'll help you to appreciate where you're going too.

Beef Stroganoff is certainly one of the most memorable meals I've ever fixed, but definitely not because of its ability to tantalize the taste buds, in a positive way anyway. With the mere mention of the two words our eyes roll practically in unison as we recall the night you would have thought I poisoned my husband on purpose!

Remembering that night long ago also reminds me how powerfully God spoke to me about perfectionism. He showed me how excellence is one thing but pride is quite another! I had some things to learn for sure.

What's your story? What crazy thing have you done that will go down in the annals of your history? Are you able to laugh about it now and thank God for the experience and lesson learned? Such freedom waits once you do!

Dear Lord, thank You for the wonderful gift of laughter. The sweetness of Your presence enables me to keep things in perspective. In Jesus' name, Amen.

Head Wall and Head Strong

~ A Reflection on Youthfulness ~

*"Remember now your Creator in the days of your youth,
before the difficult days come" (Ecclesiastes 12:1a).*

ERIC LEARNED TO SKI AS a pre-teen when he lived near Hunter Mountain. He'd hike up the hill by his house, strap on his skis, and go as fast as he could down the hill only to walk back up and do it again. Hour after hour he'd stay out in the cold repeating the process until one day, when he was a full-fledged teenager, he actually got to ski the "big mountain." He loved the thrill of the "controlled fall" and it's been a favorite winter pastime for him ever since.

It seemed only natural then when we moved to our current house that eventually all of us learn to ski too. We live only seven miles from a ski resort so it's pretty easy to get there and back, even on weekdays. I had only been on snow skis once prior to this time (it was NOT a pretty sight!) but I decided to give it a whirl anyway. Erin had no interest in learning whatsoever, but Sarah was game and so was Josiah. Josiah!? He was only three! Dad thought we should let him try even though he'd be the youngest person on the hill.

I agreed that he could but only if he took a few lessons . . . especially since he wanted to SNOWBOARD! Since neither his dad nor I would be able to offer any training in the snowboarding department, lessons were that much more important.

Of course Josiah did well in those lessons. Of course he hounded us after they were done to let him go to the TOP of the mountain. Of course his father gave in. And of course I trailed behind as Dad and son prepared for the run of a lifetime!

Dad cranked down his bindings and reminded him of everything the instructor had told him. "Make lots of turns." "Don't go too fast." "Watch out for other people on the hill." "Remember to lean." My heart beat hard in my chest as I prepared for this. We were actually strapping our THREE-YEAR OLD's feet onto a board, and sending him down a really slippery mountain slope. What were we thinking? Was he ready for this? Even if he was, I wasn't.

He made his way to the edge of the head wall and, bloop, he disappeared from sight! Eric and I rushed to the edge to see how he was doing. The hill looked daunting to me. I could only imagine what it must've felt like to Josiah.

Our hearts raced as we saw our precious son zooming down the hill like he was an arrow shot out of a bow! Turns? He didn't make a one! Speed? Oh, yeah, he had PLENTY! Eric raced after him as I sat on the top trying to figure out how I was going to get down. I was new at this too and had one thing going for me – I knew when to be afraid! Josiah, on the other hand, hadn't a clue that he was rocketing towards disaster. The ride down may have been fun; but I knew it was the landing that would get him . . . especially at that speed!

Josiah made it down in one piece, thank the good Lord. Eric met him at the bottom and gave him a good talking to. Josiah wanted to go right back up and do it again but Eric had a few choice words first. It took several of those heart-to-heart talks with his dad after more runs like the first, which eventually led to a threat. "That's it. If you won't make turns and keep your speed under control, you're off the hill!" Eric was on Ski Patrol and had more than just fatherly authority to wield. Josiah got the message and decided he'd better do it the way he was supposed to or his snowboarding days were over.

Our son has become quite the good snowboarder through the years. I doubt he really remembers those first years when he was just learning, or the heart attacks he almost gave me, or his father's intense lectures (well, he probably remembers those!). But one thing's for certain – as he's gotten a little older he's become more aware that he's not so bullet-proof. Not only has he had a few good crashes, he's seen others around him experience some pretty spectacular ones too.

I think that's one of those traits that mark our maturity. We no longer have an "I can do anything and not get hurt" mentality. Life experiences add an element of caution. At least it gets us to consider all the "what ifs." It doesn't mean it will stop us; but we do put on extra padding if there's a question as to the outcome.

I love youth. I love their carefree spirits and attitudes. They'll try new things just for the sake of trying. Don't you wish you had just a hint of their enthusiasm for life? I do. It's not that I want to check my brain at the door and do something stupid. That's not what I'm inferring. But just because we age chronologically we don't have to stop having fun. What about riding a bicycle built for two? Or jet skiing on a lake? How about paragliding – that's one I'd like to try! How about doing the sixty mile walk for breast cancer? I did that once with a friend and it was awesome! I wasn't sure I'd make it, but I did!

I think I'm going to look over my list again and set a new goal. Why don't you do the same? What a story you'll have to tell once you've done it!

Dear Lord, thank You for giving me life, and that more abundantly. The sweetness of Your presence is all I need. In Jesus' name, Amen.

What's In a Name?

~ A Reflection on Importance ~

"A good name is to be chosen rather than great riches" (Proverbs 22:1a).

WHEN I WAS GROWING UP and planning my family in my mind, I always had great names for each of my children, names I was certain I would use when the events actually happened. But I can say with all certainty that NONE of those names were given to any of our kids, not because they weren't great names, but because we had become Christians and decided we wanted names that represented God's heart for each of them – the type of personality they'd have, the mark they'd leave on society, and so on, so we sought the Lord for His opinion on the matter. We hashed out each possibility amongst ourselves until we knew we had the right one!

When we were informed of Hannah's birth it didn't take long for us to decide what her name should be. "Hannah" means "handmaiden of the Lord," a perfect name for a life who would submit herself to the Lord for His use in practical, yet meaningful and necessary ways. We also believed she would be a joyful person, having deep joy within her that couldn't help but spill out on all whom she met, so Joy was her perfect middle name.

We really heard from God on this one. She is one of the most joyful young ladies I know; and as a result, she has lots of people who want to be her friend. It's true. All of us desire to be around positive, uplifting people who lighten the dark places in life. We're drawn to them. We like them. We want to be like them. This is our Hannah Joy.

We weren't Christians yet when we adopted Erin, but we named her Erin Denay because Erin was close to her daddy's name, Eric, and Denay because my two sisters' middle names were Denise and Kay, thus Denay. When we became Christians we also became aware of the fact that Erin is the female form of Aaron and that was a strong Biblical name for sure!

Sarah's given middle name by her birth mother was Christine. We kept it because it was a feminine variant of Christ; and since we were new Christians when she entered our world, we wanted her to have His name. Sarah Christine. God's princess. Our princess.

We were actually going to name Josiah 'Austin James.' But at the same time we were discussing what his name should be while trying to discern the mind of Christ, the name Josiah Daniel ran across each of our brains at the *exact* same time like ticker tapes. That was really weird! But we knew that God had already decided . . . and we liked it! Like Josiah in the Bible who became King at age eight, our son tells us he is a king, and plans to never give up his throne! Daniel suggests strength and that's exactly what and who he is. He's a definite leader who hasn't yet realized the full potential of this gift God has given him.

I've already talked about Hannah. Next is Nick. Honestly, his name suits him perfectly because every Nick, or Nicholas, we've met has exactly the same disposition! Busy, busy boys – active, curious, not able to leave well enough alone. In the Bible in Acts 6:1-7, 'Nicolas' was one of the first deacons chosen to serve alongside Stephen and the other five. I'd say it's pretty safe to say that 'Nick' was a pretty busy guy as he served the people God had entrusted to him! His middle name is Duane, after my dad, who is himself another busy guy! Does that mean "double trouble?" I guess so!

Then there's Deborah Grace. What a lovely little girl with a perfectly lovely name. It was awesome that we were naming her after me AND a prophetess in the Old Testament! We knew she'd be strong and courageous and set apart from the rest. We also knew her life would be marked by God's amazing grace and so our Deb Grace, as she likes to be called, was born and embraced.

As you consider what to name your child or children, make sure you consult the Father Who may have a few ideas of His own. Whether it's a still small voice or a ticker tape across your brain, He'll tell you. He's one of the best communicators I know!

God bless you as you seek the throne and hear from heaven.

Dear Lord, I submit all of my wonderful blessings to You for Your care and consideration. The sweetness of Your presence helps me to hear from heaven, and for that I am grateful. In Jesus' name, Amen.

Let's Rock This Neighborhood

~ A Reflection on Abundant Life ~

"I have come that they may have life, and that they may have it more abundantly" (John 10:10b).

OUR NEIGHBORHOOD IN RIVERSIDE, CA was fairly normal as far as neighborhoods go. Young couples with new families lined both sides of the street with a few oldies thrown in for good measure. Many of us knew each other to some degree, so it wasn't uncommon for us to stop and chat in garages with the dads, or to be invited in by one of the moms.

There were three of us who had children about the same time. The couple across the street had a baby boy a few weeks before we adopted Erin, and the couple two doors down had a baby boy a few months before that. The boys' moms were doting and cautious. I understood why but found it odd when they took it to extremes.

Once the babies were old enough to be propped up in strollers, our three families would take walks around the block. The boys' moms typically walked in front with the strollers, chit-chatting, while the dads trailed behind, engaged in their own conversation.

I, on the other hand, commonly walked empty-handed with the women. Eric pushed our stroller and typically gave our daughter the ride of her life – zooming up and down the sidewalks, across peoples' lawns, jumping off curbs, doing wheelies – anything for a thrill. I'm not sure who it was really for – her or him. But it was familiar routine; and the older Erin got, the more she loved it. Her dad knew how to show her a good time!

Even though this was many years ago, I smile as I remember those warm, sunny afternoon walks. I chuckle as I think about the other moms, whom I fondly remember and appreciate, gingerly caring for their sons as they would precious cargo. I laugh as I recall Eric's antics, making the goal a thrilling ride for his daughter – also precious cargo!

"What does this have to do with anything," you might be thinking? Well, to me it's a great comparison with our lives. How can two people experience the same walk in life, yet one enjoy a much more adventurous time of it? I think it boils down to this. We get out of life what we put into it. If we're cautious and guarded, then our lives will be the same. If we're a little more carefree (not careless), then our lives will also be the same.

I think today would be a good day for us to examine our lives – what we like and what we'd like to change. Do we miss adventures (memories in the making) because we're excessively guarded, or maybe too sedentary? Or do we throw caution to the wind, too often giving those who love us excess stress? Both scenarios are on life's continuum, and both are easy enough to fix if that's our desire. Thoughtful examination and planning will always lend itself to a satisfying life which will end with minimal regrets. The important thing is to get started. Set goals, and then start walking towards them. Whether it's a calm and serene life you desire, or one that looks for adventure around every corner, the life you desire can be yours if you put your mind and will to it.

Dear Lord, thank You for my life. The sweetness of Your presence helps me live it to the full, with guard rails as well as excitement. In Jesus' name, Amen.

Stick a Candle In It and Eat It!

~ A Reflection on Disappointment ~

"Being confident of this very thing, that He Who has begun a good work in you will complete it until the day of Jesus Christ" (Philippians 1:6).

NICK HAS ALWAYS BEEN A climber. His little toes have always been put to good use from the time he started to crawl. I am amazed that climbing is still one of his favorite things to do – trees, hills, roofs, automobiles . . . just about whatever fancy strikes him. He's the one kid in the family who's kept our doctor in business in a big way.

He was turning one, a huge reason to celebrate, and I wanted to make him a really special cake. It wouldn't be any ordinary cake. It would be a chocolate bear cake with fluffy chocolate frosting. Finding the perfect pan at the store, I bought it and the supplies I'd need to make it the creation of his lifetime.

I got a pretty good start on it while the kids napped in the morning. I felt pretty confident I'd get it done in time for the evening's celebration. I worked on it all day in between all the other things I had to do, like retrieving Nick from the bookcases, cupboards, and other places he wasn't supposed to be!

Finally, it was finished! I was so proud of myself. It had actually come out pretty cute considering I had no talent in the cake decorating department. The ears were defined; the eyes were the right proportion; it was perfect! I left it sitting on the kitchen counter away from the edge and little prying fingers. Daddy would be home soon; so after dinner, we'd celebrate Nick's milestone!

Nick disappeared from eyeshot for a bit longer than I was comfortable with so I set out to look for him. Why couldn't he stay in one place like the other kids? I was a bit frazzled that I had to get up and go look for him *again*, but I did it anyway because I knew what kind of trouble he could get into if I didn't. I found him about the time I heard the crash in the kitchen!

I raced through the doorway only to find Nick sitting on the floor with a mischievous grin on his face. Sitting next to him was his cute, fluffy bear cake, *upside down*! The chocolate was smashed and smeared all over the floor! I shrieked out of disappointment and disbelief! My son, bless his heart, didn't know whether he should sit there or run away. He knew he had done it again this time, and that Mom was not happy!

My cake! My darling little bear cake! What was I going to do now? I was in shock and had to think fast about how to handle the situation.

I grabbed my spatula and started scooping the cake off the floor in chunks. I tried arranging those chunks, some with frosting and some now without, back into the shape of the cute, fluffy bear; but by the time I was finished, it was anything but that. It was a hopeless, miserable mess, and one that looked very much like it had been in a horrible wreck!

Daddy came home and was as shocked as I was! He had been hearing about this bear cake for some time as I planned for Nick's special day. My pride was dashed and I was heartbroken, but what could I do? I didn't have time to make another cake, regular or otherwise. I was in a bind so I did the only thing I knew to do.

I stuck a candle in it and we ate it! And it tasted good – definitely much better than it looked. But I learned some things that day. One, little boys' curiosity sometimes gets the best of them. Two, chocolate yumminess was too much to resist for this particular little boy. And three, chocolate cake, even if it's off the floor, tastes pretty good.

Birthdays are for celebrating, so we do. Fluffy, chocolate, cute bear cakes were never meant to be, so we haven't had them since Nick's first birthday disaster. And I'm okay with that . . . now.

Disappointment comes in all shapes, sizes and forms. It comes when we least expect it, and when we had no reason to hope for anything different. But I know the One Who never disappoints! And you do too; His name is Jesus, the Christ. Even when people fail us and events don't pan out like we expect, our Savior is the One who will always have our back and come through for us every time. We can count on Him!

Dear Lord, the sweetness of Your presence is the reason that I always have hope. Thank You for always being true to Your Word. In Jesus' name, Amen.

All Praise Be Unto God

~ A Reflection on Worship ~

"(S)he who dwells in the secret place of the Most High, shall abide under the shadow of the Almighty" (Psalm 91:1).

MUSIC HAS BEEN A BIG part of my life since I was old enough to get a radio and eventually an eight-track tape deck in my teen years. I've always enjoyed belting out a hearty song mostly with accompanying music, but when no one was around, without it as well. I don't have the voice of an angelic songbird and I know it. I'm not offended that you know it too. But I know the One who does enjoy hearing it; His name is Jesus! And so I continue to sing.

When I got saved I was introduced to the whole wonderful world of Christian music. I loved it all, some more than others, true; but I loved the presence of God it brought into my life as praises filled the atmosphere surrounding me. Praise and worship music became the backdrop for most everything I did. And I always wanted more when it was time to quit. I shouldn't have been surprised then when my little namesake, Deborah, developed her own love for worship.

She was just a baby when we first noticed it. She'd be sitting in her high chair with her head flung back *again,* with her eyes closed and hands raised. When it first started happening we thought she was struggling in some way, unable to breathe, maybe with something lodged in her throat. We'd stick our fingers in her mouth to check for foreign objects only to find nothing there. Our intrusion into her mouth with our prodding fingers made her laugh and giggle so we decided something else must be going on.

One day it dawned on us. Deborah was worshipping the Lord. She had watched us do it over and over again. She'd been saturated in His presence at the prayer meetings we had in our home, at church services and Prayer & Praise meetings, and other events that ushered in the Holy Spirit. Even at her young age of one, not even walking yet, Deborah was meeting with the Lord *right there in her high chair!* We were in awe of this whole concept.

To this day Deborah is the most spiritual of all the kids. She's also the one who's been attacked the most by the enemy, battling bad dreams, overcoming fear, and struggling to build confidence in friendships. She's the one who always likes to go to church, and youth meetings and women's meetings with me. When it's time to sign up for Christian youth camp she's the first one to ask to have her registration form filled out. And she's also the first one to lay hands on another in need of prayer, just like she's not afraid to ask for prayer when she's facing a test at school or not feeling well. As she heads upstairs to bed each night, her last words are always, "Will you pray for me?" She loves the Lord with her whole heart and it's evident in her mannerisms, speech and yes, in her worship.

I had no idea that a baby could worship the Lord. Since it wasn't like I sat her down and said, "Ok now, this is how you do it," I knew that it was real and straight from her heart. He instilled that desire in her. He beckoned her and she responded in the only way she knew how. Hands raised. Eyes closed. Tuned out to everything around her, but Him.

I give glory to God for the good seeds planted in her young life that will no doubt grow and lead her beside His still waters as she becomes a young woman. She's learned to trust Him – something many adults have yet to experience. She reads her Bible and asks for help when she doesn't understand a particular passage. And now, as a teenager, she takes her Bible to school and reads it during free time, often telling her friends about the wonderful promises of God. I can only imagine the joy He receives from His times together with her.

Our children want to be like us. They're watching us and, to some degree, are modeling what they see in us. It's important to cultivate godly characteristics in our kids. If they are going to demonstrate the Fruit of the Spirit in their lives, then we need to exude those qualities as well – "love, joy, peace, longsuffering, kindness, goodness, faithfulness, gentleness, and self-control" (Galatians 5:22).

Today is a fresh new day, filled with amazing opportunities to praise our Maker. Because of His life, we possess all of His riches in glory. Let's not hide our lights under a bushel, as the song says. Let's show the world just how much we love Him.

And when that day comes that you find your precious little one having an intimate moment with God, rejoice with the angels for that day will mark the beginning of an extraordinary life in Christ. God will be pleased, but so will you!

Dear Lord, I love the sweetness of Your presence in my worship! Thank You for inhabiting my praises. To You is all the glory, honor, and power forever. In Jesus' name, Amen.

Chainsaw Massacre

~ A Reflection on Being Christ-like ~

"For we through the Spirit eagerly wait for the hope of righteousness by faith"
(Galatians 5:5).

AT ONE POINT IN OUR lives, we had a very spirited neighborhood. An assortment of blue-collar workers lined both sides of the street, with a Marine band leader and his family living on the corner across the street, a biker and his family living next door, a "crazy" woman living on the other side of us, and a very "interesting" family living kitty-corner across the street.

Tom and Roberta (not their real names) were a blended family. He was Caucasian while his wife and her children from a previous marriage were of Mexican descent. He spent a lot of time in his garage; I believe this was to avoid the nagging of his wife. He was an alcoholic and the more he drank, the more she harped on him. The more she harped, the more projects in his garage he'd find to do. It was a sad, vicious cycle that usually ended up in all-out warfare, sometimes with objects being thrown. They flung four-letter words at each other like none I'd ever heard. And without fail, one of them, if not both, would end up threatening to leave. Why neither of them actually did remains a mystery. Perhaps it was out of desperate hope that things really would change and be better the next day. I don't believe they began their marriage with the goal of hating each other by the time they'd been married as long as they were. I'm sure they had dreams for their future as they said their "I Do's." But since they never changed or submitted to one another, their lives only got worse as the years went by. It was a slow erosion that finally deteriorated their relationship to the point of them barely being able to be in the same room together, even when he wasn't drinking. Too much damage had been done and it seemed it was easier to keep going forward (even though it was backwards) than to turn around and go the other way. My husband always says, "If you always do what you've always done, you'll always get what you've always gotten." He couldn't be more right. What they got was more of the same heartache from endless fights, broken promises, and a general distrust and dislike of the other.

Tom and his wife had determined that their problems stemmed from his drinking so he vowed he wouldn't drink anymore. Each day proved it was an oath he wasn't able to keep. She was justifiably angry and upset; but as much as he meant it each time he said it, his addiction drew him further and further away from the man he wanted to be! When he wasn't drunk he was very personable. Everybody liked him. Once he started drinking he became an obnoxious, antagonizing man that his family couldn't stand, neither could his friends who were sober.

One early afternoon he started on a six-pack of beer, and then graduated to other liquor. He was totally wasted, and her anger now turned to rage. She had had enough of his lies and decided to take matters into her own hands.

Predictably he wandered out to his garage so he wouldn't have to listen to her, which only made her more furious. She followed behind him and, once he was far enough inside the garage, she pulled down the garage door, closed it, and locked it from the outside! She taunted him from the other side of the door, and didn't budge one iota no matter how he thundered inside and demanded that she unlock the door and let him out. Tom, by this time, even though he was totally inebriated, decided she was not going to have the last word.

Keep in mind that all the neighbors within earshot could hear the yelling and ranting back and forth that indicated another doozy of a fight was in progress. We weren't quite sure what was going to happen once he managed to get out, but we were certain it wasn't going to be pretty!

As we watched from across the street and the safety of our own home, with disbelief we heard a familiar noise coming from inside the garage. It was Tom's chainsaw! He attacked the garage door with force as he shoved the chainsaw right through the middle of it, cutting up one side, over, and down, making a doorway through which he could escape his confines. When she realized what he had done she ran for cover! He was madder than a wet, drunken hen who wanted revenge.

The next thing we heard was more yelling and name calling as he tried to stumble in the house after her. Then we saw canned vegetables come flying out of the house in his direction! He picked them up and flung them back at her, but she disappeared behind a now locked front door. It was like a bad movie playing out right in front of our eyes. We were young and newly married so we didn't know what to do. We just knew that the police were eventually going to have to be called, and they were.

That wasn't the last fight that Tom and Roberta had. But it was the last time she locked him in the garage!

They ended up moving shortly after that nightmare, though I heard they didn't stay married. He finally left her and sank even further down in the abyss of alcoholism. And she remained angry and alone.

Do I believe that their marriage was too far gone for the Lord to intervene and help, even when they stooped to such obvious lows in getting even with the other? I do not. Do I believe they could have been saved? I absolutely do.

The Bible is clear about marital relationships and what is expected from both. Ephesians 5:21-33 spells it out plainly. Husbands are supposed to love their wives (v. 25). And wives are supposed to respect their husbands (v. 33). BOTH are supposed to "submit to one another in the fear of God" (v. 21) and that means mutual consideration of the other's needs and desires.

Tom and Roberta had a lot of problems before they got married that they carried into their relationship when they became husband and wife. Obviously, he brought a drinking problem that was ready to spiral out of control, and she had rejection and trust issues from her previous marriage. Both had tempers that went unchecked; and when they went off at the same time, there were fireworks. They didn't know the Lord and neither did any of us at the time so we were no help. Several did recommend counseling though, but they never pursued any support.

I wish they would have made it! I wish they had a story to tell today of how God had redeemed their lives and saved their family. Instead they ended up a casualty like so many others do. The devil won when he should have lost.

I'm sure it is your goal to live by the Word of God, doing the "do's" and not doing the "don'ts." That's my goal too. I want to hear Him say, "Well done, thou good and faithful servant" when I stand before Him on that day. I want no regrets for the things I should have or shouldn't have done.

I love my husband even when he's being persnickety, which isn't very often. I respect him always, even when he's disciplined the wrong child, or handled a situation poorly. He deserves my respect if for no other reason than God demands it. There are a whole lot of other reasons to respect him too for he is truly an honorable man.

In return he loves me the way I need to be loved – with time and attention, and whatever else I may need. Even when I'm not being particularly loveable, he loves me anyway. But why should he? Shouldn't he withhold his love when I'm being ugly? The world may say so, but not God. God never said "if" she's being loveable, or "if" he's acting worthy of respect. He just says, "Do it."

I believe that doing it God's way is a choice. No excuses are good enough when it comes to disobeying His Word. It is my desire to sow good seeds into my relationships that will produce life, harmony, and growth. I don't want to end up like Tom and Roberta. I don't want to live apart from my husband and be angry and alone with wrath seething under the surface. I want God to show me the areas I need to change so I can change them. Habits that are contrary to God's likeness have to go. No amount of sin is acceptable.

My prayer for us today is that we would recognize our shortcomings and set about to change them as He enlightens the process. I want our testimony to be, "Look what the Lord has done!" As we submit our lives to His tutelage, He can't help but make us a work of art. And that's the whole idea!

Dear Lord, Your Word teaches me how I should live. The sweetness of Your presence pushes me to pursue righteousness, and for that I thank You. In Jesus' name, Amen.

School Is In Session

~ A Reflection on God's Gifts ~

"But God has chosen the foolish things of the world to put to shame the wise,
and God has chosen the weak things of the world to put to shame the things
which are mighty; and the base things of the world and the things which are
despised God has chosen, and the things which are not, to bring to nothing the
things that are, that no flesh should glory in His presence"
(1 Corinthians 1:27-29).

ERIN WAS THREE YEARS OLD when her dad and I got saved. Even though God gave her to us prior to our knowing Him, He knew it wouldn't be too long before we fully surrendered our hearts and lives to Him and His master plan which also, unbeknownst to us, promised eternal life. Prior to coming to the Lord our lives were much like a rollercoaster. We had love and harmony in our home one day, and anger and harsh words the next. Up and down, day after day. Eric was as frustrated with me as I was with him. And yet, the mystery remains as to why we stuck it out and stayed married. Heaven only knows we had days when we both wanted to run away! We can only attribute it now to God's staying hand on our lives even when we didn't know it existed. Once we opened the door to Him and His abiding presence though, our lives were forever changed. That's not to say we haven't had our off days since, because we have. But we've never looked back as we've pursued our Lord with all that is within us. And from the day we let Him in, we've truly been united as one.

I doubt any of us can remember our toddlerhood so it's safe to say that those first few years of Erin's life are nothing more than general facts to her. She was born, adopted, and raised by a mom and dad who loved her. She doesn't remember the days before Jesus when our home was in turmoil, and we're thankful for that.

Our Christian home was much like most, I'd guess. Prayer before meals. Church on Sundays. Prayer & Praise gatherings on Thursday nights. Bible studies. Youth Group meetings that we led. Outreaches into the community. Prayer meetings that lasted well into the wee hours of the morning. Homeless people "showing up" at our door and us feeding and clothing them, and buying them bus tickets home. Helping strangers on the street. Hanging out with the pastor and his wife. You know – normal stuff.

We were so enjoying our Christian lives with all of the wonder and excitement people have when they first meet Jesus. We were learning new things all the time. Because our lives had so dramatically been turned around, there were times when I actually would kiss my Bible because it was so sweet to me. God had done so many amazing things for us that I was filled with excitement and expectation for more!

One particular evening when Erin was about four, God showed me how it was never too early to get started in the things of God. We were at one of our prayer meetings at a friend's house. Normally we would host these meetings but this night found us in Santa Ana at a friend's home. In fact, it was the very same night that both Eric and I were water baptized in the fountain in the middle of the city there! (Shhh ... don't tell anyone! I'll share that story with you later.)

The people were energized as they spoke casually of what the Lord was doing in their lives. Encouragement was given for those facing tough times, and the Word was "fitly spoken" (Proverbs 25:11). Thanksgiving was offered for answered prayer with claps, songs and shouts of praise! We weren't special people but rather ordinary folks who loved to get together and praise His name!

It came time in the evening for more focused prayer when everyone bowed their heads and began to really intercede. Prayer for our nation. Prayer for our churches and pastors. Prayer for our families. Prayers of petition, praise and thanksgiving. Erin usually sat quietly next to us playing with her toys or lying down on her blanket and falling asleep. She was neither a disturbance nor a distraction.

This night, though, as everyone began to pray, she didn't pick up her toys or lie down. She bowed her head like the rest and began to pray quietly *in tongues!* Eric and I were amazed because we had no idea someone so young could receive this gift. And we definitely had no idea SHE had it! Then, without warning, she jumped up off the floor and went around the room, person to person, laying hands on them and praying – both in her limited vocabulary and in the spirit! We were shocked. She was so young. How could this be?

When she was finished she sat down next to us with complete calm and quiet. Tears rolled down my cheeks; and as I looked around the room, I found I wasn't the only one. The presence of the Lord was there. We were experiencing an extraordinary holy moment.

What amazed me the most was the absence of any inhibitions in regard to her "ministry." True, I was shocked she prayed in tongues and that she went around the room praying for each and every person. But the most remarkable thing was that she did it with complete assurance and authority!

I didn't know God could use someone so young. I didn't know He could use someone with intellectual disabilities. And I definitely didn't know she was old enough to respond to His promptings, or that she would! But His presence was ushered in that night in a profound way by a little girl who didn't know much about anything. Come to find out, her mom didn't know much either.

I was in school that night. And God used my own daughter to teach me an important lesson. My prayer for all of us is that we never choose recess over classroom time. God will use whomever He chooses to teach us the lessons we need to learn. It is our job, then, to stay open and receive all that He has for us, even when it comes through a little girl.

Dear Lord, thank You for teaching me Your truths. I want more of You, God. The sweetness of Your presence beckons me on. In Jesus' name, Amen.

Streaker!

~ A Reflection on First Impressions ~

"A man who flatters his neighbor spreads a net for his feet" (Proverbs 29:5).

S ARAH WAS NORMALLY A VERY happy, polite and predictable little girl, at least when she was quite young. For the most part we were pretty safe in our beliefs about her behavior. She was a good girl who never did anything outrageous.

How Eric became the pastor of our church is very humbling. Our pastor, John, who was changing a light bulb before service one Sunday morning in 1992, fell off the ladder he was standing on, hit the newel post on the stairs, and bled internally until he died the next day. The doctors didn't catch it. But his passing put Eric in the driver's seat at the church, and we were trying to figure out how and what to do. Remember, he took only mission courses at Bible school!

We had just enjoyed the ministry of some of the leaders from the governing organization through whom Eric is ordained and I'm licensed. They had come to check out the church and to see if there was anything they could do to help us. Our goal was to show them we had it pretty much together even though we had no clue what we were doing! We had also invited them to our home for lunch with our family.

We had just finished our meal together. The kids were happily playing in the yard, and we were watching them as we enjoyed the sunshine and conversation with our guests! All of a sudden, Sarah ran by stark naked! When did she have time to take off her clothes? WHY did she take off her clothes? Not only did she streak on by, she climbed the door of THEIR car and promptly sat herself down inside! We were mortified! What on God's green earth was she thinking?

She was only about three at the time. But she knew better, so we were quite surprised by her impulsive behavior. Our visitors were just as stunned especially since they were driving their first new car! I don't think they expected to see what they did!

They didn't get a word in edgewise as we offered our apologies and explanations for our little princess's actions. We could only believe this incident left a bad impression on them. Couldn't we control our child?

All of our fears were put to rest when they began telling us stories of their kids. What Sarah did this day was nothing compared to what they'd had to explain. But it just goes to show you that if you're looking to impress your friends, don't expect your kids to help you!

Everything turned out okay as you can expect. We have enjoyed a long and lasting friendship with these people who actually have come back to our house since.

I don't know about you, but I like to leave good impressions on people. I want people to like me, not because I'm a fabulous hostess or a good enough cook, though those are good reasons too. I want people to like me for me, the person I am, and the genuineness of my heart. Since I'm no different than most, it's probably true of you too.

Sometimes I find that I try too hard to impress someone who is older, wiser, more educated, or more experienced. And sometimes, like the events of this story, my efforts backfire, leaving me embarrassed and wishing I hadn't tried so hard.

If our hearts are inclined in the right direction, and if we have the ability to laugh at ourselves when things go awry, then it won't matter if we appear less than perfect. Even hopeless perfectionists will tell you that they have "off" days! I think the best thing we can do is be real to the people around us, letting them see our flaws, as well as our little kids who streak by in the nude and then hop in their new car! I think its times like these that help us to connect on a real and personal level.

> *Dear Lord, the sweetness of Your presence helps me to shed my tendencies toward perfection. Thank You for the gift of laughter which aids in the process. In Jesus' name, Amen.*

Ex-Lax Meatballs

~ A Reflection on Desperation ~

"For our light affliction, which is but for a moment, is working for us a far more exceeding and eternal weight of glory" (2 Corinthians 4:17).

I LOVED OUR NEW HOUSE IN southern California. It was modern, fresh, and nestled in the middle of a recently-built subdivision. I liked the new neighbors as well. The family across the street moved in right after we did. The husband, we soon learned, worked construction like Eric, so our conversations usually centered on jobsite activity.

The families on either side of us were living there when we moved in. To one side was a childless couple a little older than us. They kept pretty much to themselves, though we did enjoy some casual conversation while watering our respective front yards. On occasion they would come over for coffee, but since they both worked long hours, those times were few and far between.

To the other side of us was a nice, growing family whom we absolutely adored. They had a couple of young daughters who looked just like their mom. We really enjoyed them! I was one of their favorite babysitters too, so the feelings were mutual. We didn't know it at the time, but they were a

Christian family. As I think back to that time in our lives, I understand now why we were drawn to them. They were always positive and encouraging, even in the face of a medical crisis with one of their daughters. Nothing seemed to get them down. I don't know why they never shared their faith with us. Maybe they tried at one time or another and we rejected what they had to offer, I don't know. I just remember that it was a surprise to us when we became Christians to find they were as well.

The homes in that development were "zero-zoning" which meant that the side of our yard butted right up to the fence in the neighbor's yard. Their yard butted right up to their neighbor's fence, and so on. They were fair-sized houses on small lots but we were comfortable so we didn't complain, at least not until our neighbors got Doberman Pincers.

Even though we were assured that the dogs were friendly, they were quite intimidating so we steered clear of them. To be truthful, I couldn't understand why they got them. Hadn't they heard about all the Dobermans who turned on their masters? Weren't they concerned about their kids? They were watchdogs more than they were family pets. The dogs' owners both worked during the day while the kids went to school; and they were gone a lot at night, so the dogs were left alone in the back yard day after day. I didn't have a problem with it until the dogs started barking at all hours of the day and night, day after day, week after week, with no let up. Constant barking! It's like barking was the only thing they had to do! No one played with them, that was for sure. Bark! Bark! Bark! It drove Eric and me crazy, but I had a harder time because I was home and had to endure the noise more hours than he did. It was when we started losing sleep that I decided to take matters into my own hands.

If our nice neighbors weren't going to handle the situation, I would! Who would know anyway? I had heard that Ex-Lax rolled up in ground beef made for yummy treats that packed a punch! The dogs certainly wouldn't be able to resist them! The more they ate, the more the "medicine" would work! Aha! That's exactly what I decided to do! I didn't want to kill them. I just wanted them to wish they were dead by the time I got through with them!

(Don't hate me now. I'm just getting to the good part! And if you're a member of the Humane Society, I believe there's a Statute of Limitations on such acts!). Erin and I made a special trip to the store for several boxes of the "secret ingredient." Once home, I put her down for her afternoon nap and began making my concoction of delectable goodies that I couldn't wait to feed the noisemakers. What is it that witches are supposed to chant while they stir their brew? "Bubble, bubble, toil and trouble," or something like that? Well, that was me to a "T" – adding, mixing, and stirring, until my potion was complete, taking great delight in my finished product! I know that sounds sinister . . . because it was! But I felt justified. I had had enough and these dogs were going to pay! I felt like the Wicked Witch of the West! "I'll get you my pretty!"

I grabbed a step stool as I headed out the door to our mutual fence. They were already waiting for me, barking of course! I peered over the fence and threw one meatball, then another, then another, until they practically sat on command as they waited for their next treat! Inwardly I was rejoicing because I knew what was awaiting them in, oh, about an hour if all went as planned.

When the bowl of meatballs disappeared, so did I – into the house. I went back to my chores until I heard the tell-tale signs that my mixture had taken affect, which made me laugh with great delight! (You can clap; I did!). As much as they tried to bark, all they could muster was a muffled whimper – and then they would squat! The plan had worked, so much so that this went on for over an hour. I was so proud of myself! Yes, sirree . . . they had messed with the wrong girl! And if they didn't want dessert they'd better get a clue!

My husband came home from work and couldn't believe his ears as I recounted my every move. He thought for sure I had lost my mind but agreed, without defense, that something had to be done. He just hadn't planned on me resorting to such drastic measures.

Once the dogs made it through their afternoon and evening misery, they laid pretty low for about another week. I heard neither bark nor whimper from them at all! I'm sure they were still recovering from their ordeal. I was a little concerned one day late in the week because I hadn't heard them at all so I peeked over the fence to make sure they were okay, and they ran to the other side of the yard! Ha! Good for them (and me)!

Our neighbors commented on how calm the dogs had been and, "had we noticed?" "Oh, yeah. We had noticed alright!" But we didn't let on as to why.

I'm sure my confession would have made them pretty angry (I can't say that I would've blamed them) and that wasn't something either of us wanted.

Now, I'm not saying that what I did was right. I'm not condoning my behavior in the slightest. And that's why I won't tell you in great detail about another time when I actually duct taped a neighbor's barking dog's mouth shut! It was several years earlier in another city but as in this instance, I had had enough! I wasn't completely heartless; I didn't tape it completely shut. I did leave a partial opening so he could breathe, drink, and pant, but he definitely couldn't bark and that was the whole idea. I knew I had to tell the owner that time because the tape wasn't something he could easily miss when he went to pet his pooch. He wasn't pleased, not surprisingly. It wasn't long afterwards that we moved.

Desperation CAN drive people to do things they wouldn't normally do. I'm the perfect example of that. In my defense, I didn't know the Lord at the time so I used the only tools I had in my toolbox – my culinary expertise and duct tape!

Desperation SHOULD drive us to our knees, crying out to God for help in the situation and wisdom for how to handle it. If I'm walking around waving duct tape in the faces of everybody who irritates me, then that's an obvious sign that I'm in crisis and need an intervention. So please feel free!

My husband scratches his legs for at least five minutes every night when we get in bed. He puts on his glasses, grabs his William Johnstone novel, and reads and scratches. Scratch. Scratch. Turn the page. Scratch. Scratch. I don't know why all of a sudden his legs are so itchy, but it's as predictable as it is annoying. I try to tune it out and roll over, but sometimes I find it difficult to fall asleep. To date he hasn't figured out just how much of a bother it is so I think I may need to whip up another batch of meatballs! (Settle down. I'm just kidding! I AM saved now, remember!). In his defense, he recently told me it's a nervous condition that also makes his legs go numb at times. And that's something I never knew!

Ask the Lord to give you wisdom on how to handle those desperate situations. Talk to the people involved. And, for heaven's sake, don't do anything you'll be sorry for later. That's the point of this story.

Dear Lord, in desperation I cry out to You for help. The sweetness of Your presence reminds me that You are always near and have already planned a way of escape. Thank You, Lord. In Jesus' name, Amen.

Monkey See, Monkey Do

~ A Reflection on Being a Good Example ~

". . . being examples to the flock . . ." (1 Peter 5:3).

Iᴛ'ꜱ ᴛʀᴜᴇ ᴛʜᴀᴛ ᴄʜɪʟᴅʀᴇɴ ᴡᴀɴᴛ to be like their fathers and mothers. It's also true that some of the habits they pick up are not necessarily ones that parents appreciate, like bad language. More often than not, kids merely mimic their parents' behaviors. So it didn't surprise us when we found our kids in the pool baptizing one another.

It was a hot day and we had the kiddie pool filled with water within a few inches from the top. The kids weren't even in bathing suits but rather underpants or a diaper, depending on their ages. Eric and I kept a pretty good eye on them as they splashed around and played together.

Josiah hollered to us to watch him. He had one hand on Hannah's head and the other on her arm as he pushed her under the water. I jumped up ready to rescue her when he said, "I baptize you in the name of the Father, and the Son, and the Holy Ghost!" Hannah giggled as she gurgled and came up from under the water. She then offered to baptize Josiah which he thought was a great idea too! Afterwards they both baptized Nick and then Deb, but they had instructions not to hold them under the water quite so long! We wanted them very much alive once they'd been afforded the sacrament!

We thought it amusing that our kids liked to "play church." Not only would they baptize one another, they'd also take turns being the Sunday school teacher or pastor. Josiah liked that part best. He'd get out the briefcase that Dad had given him, take out his Bible that was tucked inside, and a note pad. He would then pretend to preach, feeling slightly awkward under our smiling gazes. If only he knew how much we loved it!

When Josiah hit the fifth grade he was told by his school counselors and teachers that he had to start thinking about what he wanted to be when he grew up. (Can you believe it? FIFTH grade! How many of us knew in fifth grade what we were going to do? How many of us knew in tenth, or twelfth grade? Give me a break!). Do you know that on the list of possibilities there wasn't one Christian job for him to consider? When he told them he wanted to be a pastor just like his dad, they told him to choose something else. You can bet your bottom dollar we had a few choice and pointed words to say to those educators at the school!

Then the day came for Josiah to give a presentation to his class on the career of his choice. He opted for his good suit and shoes instead of his jeans and t-shirt. His dad helped him tie his tie. As he grabbed his briefcase, Bible and note pad, he told us he was ready for his presentation. We beamed as he shared his desires to be just like his dad. And those counselors and teachers, well, they all of a sudden had nothing to say! They knew where we stood and it was inappropriate for them to discourage our son from being what he wanted.

We're not sure if Josiah will actually become a pastor. We hope so, as we believe it's God's will for his life. If not, we will support him in whichever direction the Lord leads him.

It's important that we encourage our kids to go in the direction of their dreams. Dreams change from age to age, I know. But dreams give us something to reach for. They fuel our passions and launch us, hopefully, in the right direction.

There is no greater feeling than knowing your child wants to be just like you. It's our job, then, to be the best examples we can possibly be! With God's help, we will be!

Dear Lord, the sweetness of Your presence helps me to be a good example to my children. I love You with all that is within me. In Jesus' name, Amen.

Cover Girl

~ A Reflection on Growing Up ~

". . . and let beauty preparations be given them" (Esther 2:3).

I REMEMBER SNEAKING INTO MY MOM and dad's bathroom and getting into my mom's make-up when I was a kid. I did it a lot more than I got caught, that's for sure. As I entered my teen years my mom was insistent that I wear NO make-up until I was sixteen. Sixteen!? Really? Why did I have to wait so long when all of my friends got to wear it at thirteen? It just wasn't fair!

I couldn't help but defy her. I was the oddball and wanted to fit in. I wanted to be like my friends. I would leave for school clean-faced and return the same way, but that's not exactly how I remained during school hours. I got off the bus in the morning and headed right into the bathroom where my friends were waiting to doll me up! They became quite adept at putting the stuff on my face in the blink of an eye, and getting it off of me in the same measure! I didn't feel particularly good about deceiving my mom like that, but I wanted to wear make-up, so I did it anyway. I figured I'd deal with the fall-out if and when I ever got caught.

One day I was called into the office for a reason unbeknownst to me at the time. Seeing my mom standing there with my lunch bag made it all too clear. Oops! I was as surprised at seeing her as she was at seeing me! It wasn't going to be a good scene when I got home. She wasn't happy and I knew I was in for it.

I was quite tender towards my own girls when they got into my stash of make-up. One day when Hannah was about four years old, she met me outside with the bluest eyes and cheeks of anyone I'd ever seen! It was obvious what she'd been doing in my absence. At first she tried to deny that she'd done anything wrong, but when I showed her the mirror and the bathroom, which was as blue as her face, she admitted that she had been in my stuff. It was okay. She was so cute I couldn't help but understand.

Hannah didn't have to wait until she was sixteen to wear make-up. When she turned thirteen I had a make-up party for her and her friends. My friend, who was also a Mary Kay consultant, came over and gave the girls tips on keeping their skin healthy and the appropriate use of make-up application. I did the same for Sarah when she turned thirteen, and Deb too when she hit that magical age.

What is it about make-up that intrigues little girls? I think it's a couple of things – curiosity, for one. The biggest reason, I believe, is because they want to be like us, their moms. That's why they play house and dress up. That's why they pretend to talk on the phone, and cook dinners, and change babies. We're their role models. And that's a good enough reason for me to be the best me possible!

I remind Hannah on a regular basis that she doesn't need to wear any make-up because she's a natural beauty. She just rolls her eyes, as if my comments are going to change her mind.

She's growing up and I need to let her flourish. As she experiments with different clothing and hair styles, I see a little glimmer of "I'm beautiful" even though the words aren't spoken. I'm just glad she's decided she doesn't like blue eye shadow anymore.

Kids are going to be kids. They're going to do things that drive us crazy, and other things that make us laugh. And there's going to be a whole lot of other stuff in between that makes us shake our heads with disbelief. It's okay.

It's their job to do those things. It's all part of the process of growing up and finding their way to become the person God intended for them to be.

We should be the kind of person our child wants to become. We should be good-natured and have giving hearts. We should be hard workers and people of our word. We should be fair and just and open to reason, while holding fast to our convictions of faith. We should also never wear blue eye shadow.

> *Dear Lord, thank You for the sweetness of Your presence that gives me grace to let my children grow up. You love them even more than I do, even though I can't imagine it. In Jesus' name, Amen.*

And Then There Was None

~ A Reflection on Finality ~

"Death is swallowed up in victory" (1 Corinthians 15:54).

A S YOU READ IN MY Introduction, the only thing I ever wanted to be when I grew up was a mom. I desired no fame or fortune – just a bunch of kids. I desperately wanted to experience the whole pregnancy thing, but as the days, weeks, months, and then years came and went, and still no baby, we knew we had problems. Doctor after doctor, and then test after test, proved there would be no baby for me. Even though I was completely devastated, I still held out a glimmer of hope because I believed in miracles, even though I hadn't established a relationship with my Lord thus far. Since I still had my "internal baby carriage," my uterus, I believed that somehow, some way, it would happen, if for no other reason than I wanted it to so badly.

From the time I had my first menstrual cycle at age fourteen I had problems. My periods were always quite painful, whether they were irregular, too heavy, or too light. Even when I didn't get one at all I was in pain. They never settled down and became normal. The fact that I became promiscuous in later years didn't help in the slightest, because then I had emotional issues on top of the physical ones which didn't help my hormones one bit!

I was twenty-nine when I got the news that I needed a hysterectomy. I had been diagnosed with Severe Dysplasia, a pre-cancerous condition. Considering my history and ongoing problems with my reproductive system, my doctor suggested this was the best treatment option to keep me healthy. I couldn't believe what he was saying. I didn't want to believe it in fact, yet I knew he was right. But that also meant that I would never, ever carry a baby in my womb. That was the hardest pill to swallow and the one, above all else, that I had to come to terms with.

A hysterectomy is so final. It takes away all hope of a better and promising tomorrow when a baby is what we're longing for. But when one is necessary to prevent a life-threatening disease, we have no choice.

If you are reading this, you or someone you know has faced infertility, which puts a question mark behind the dream of having kids instead of an exclamation mark. If you or they have experienced a hysterectomy like I have, that question mark has been exchanged for an axe that has put to death, once and for all, that dream. Oh, the pain of loss!

Praise the Lord, though, that doesn't have to be the end of the story! Think of Easter and the reason we celebrate. Jesus died on the cross, was buried, and then rose again. Because He died, He experienced resurrection. That same promise is for us today.

I realize that we didn't ask for death to come. But I also realize that because it did, we get to experience resurrection life to our dreams by adoption. We may have to wait a little longer for our children, or jump through more hoops than most, but what a joy when we get the news that the baby we've held in our hearts for so long is finally coming home.

Adoption is not second-best; it's just another path to follow when chasing our dreams. Jesus showed us the way. I remind myself all the time that, had I been able to conceive and deliver babies, I would never have known the children I have now, and that makes me so sad. I am blessed, and you will be too as you embrace all that God has for you. You might be experiencing an amount of death to your dreams, but fear not! Resurrection day is on the horizon, and new life is being born. So let's celebrate what God is doing! God bless you.

Dear Lord, thank You for Your resurrection power! The sweetness of Your presence gives me faith to believe that my dreams are not dead, but alive! I love You. In Jesus' name, Amen.

Blow!

~ A Reflection On Wisdom ~

"If any of you lacks wisdom, let him ask of God, who gives to all liberally and without reproach, and it will be given to him" (James 1:5).

NICK HAS ALWAYS BEEN ONE to learn things the hard way. I don't know why, but that's the way it is. Just as he has learned that touching a hot stove results in burned fingers, and throwing rocks can result in a broken window, and riding his bike over too high of a jump can end in a crash, he's also learned that inhaling Kix cereal can result in Mom's tweezers up his nose!

Nick was a toddler sitting in his high chair waiting for his morning snack. He had just eaten breakfast not too long before, but that didn't matter. He was still hungry. That pretty much sums up his appetite even to this day! ("I'm STILL hungry!") And I'll show you my grocery bill to prove it! Anyway, he was waiting patiently while I got him a bowl of Kix. He had never eaten Kix before so I was exploiting the virtues of the little round morsels and how much I thought he'd like them!

Now, I knew he smelled everything before he tried it. It wasn't just food he smelled though. He liked to smell other things too – dirty socks, the remote, dish towels, and pretty much everything else with which he came in contact. We thought it was a little odd but considering the quirkiness of our son, we didn't give it a whole lot of extra thought. It was just the way he was! And this act had saved him many times from later regrets!

I had no sooner given him the bowl of cereal when I remembered he would undoubtedly stick his nose in the bowl for a good whiff. Just as I was saying the words, "Don't smell it, Nick," he stuck his nose as far down in the bowl as he could and inhaled deeply. I tried to get to him but it was too late. A Kix went up his nose and lodged. I was a little freaked out by the whole ordeal even though he didn't seem to mind that one side of his nose was blocked. But all of my anxiety was quickly eased once I was successful in clearing his nasal passage. It's amazing how far tweezers can go up a little boy's nose IF he holds still!

Truth be told, it came out pretty easily. And lest you think that prevented him from eating the whole bowl afterwards, think again. Apparently he liked what he smelled so he proceeded to eat the entire bowl full, wanting more afterwards.

I believe that wisdom makes all the difference in the world. We need to know the type of friend that will be good for us, and the type to stay away from. We need to know if we should be involved in certain behaviors or activities *before* we do them! I believe the only way to know for sure is to take time to "smell" the choice, to evaluate it, and to determine its worth and benefit in our lives against the Word of God.

Let's not ignore Wisdom when she speaks. She will save us a lot of heartache if we embrace her Truth.

Dear Lord, thank You for Your Wisdom. The sweetness of Your presence helps me to embrace Her every day. In Jesus' name, Amen.

Do I Have To?

~ A Reflection on Doing God's Will ~

"Serve the Lord with gladness; come before His presence with singing"
(Psalm 100:2).

MY SISTER'S SON HAS ALWAYS been a finicky eater. As a young boy he turned his nose up at new things, leaving only a very small variety of foods that he'd eat without complaint or resistance. I always commended her for keeping him healthy in spite of his eating habits. I'm not sure I would have had the tolerance if he were mine. I'm not passing judgment, just being honest.

How disconcerting when Deborah decided she no longer liked oatmeal. How can she NOT like oatmeal? There's really not much to it. It's kind of bland actually. Why the change all of a sudden? And how can this be when she used to love it? I didn't understand.

I tried every trick in the book to get her to eat it. Airplane spoons. Surprise bites. More brown sugar. More milk. Less milk. But nothing worked. Her clinched lips and hands pushing the bowl away were obvious signals that she was having no part of it. I finally decided it wasn't worth the headache trying to coax her.

This is kind of like doing God's will, isn't it? We may be travelling through life just fine, obeying the Lord, serving at our church, flowing in our gifts, with hearts fully surrendered to His will, when all of a sudden we resist what we usually found pleasurable. Maybe God has asked us to continue doing something we don't want to do anymore, or go somewhere we don't want to go. Maybe we don't like who we've been asked to mentor, or who's supposed to mentor us. Maybe we've entertained sin and that's preventing us from hearing and obeying the Lord fully.

If we find ourselves resenting our walk with the Lord, or wanting to get off the conveyor belt of service, let's ask God what has changed in our hearts. Maybe we already know; maybe we don't. But He will be faithful to show us how to get back on track because He wants us happy and blessed. And the only way to be that is to be fully surrendered to His will. As He brings wisdom and deliverance, let's walk in discipline with grateful hearts for all He's done.

And while you're at it, please eat your oatmeal. It's good for you! Don't you know there are lots of starving people in other countries who wish they had oatmeal to eat? That's what I tell Deborah all the time. Be honest. You tell your kids the same thing too!

Dear Lord, I love the sweetness of Your presence as I serve others in Your name! It is both an honor and privilege! In Jesus' name, Amen.

Be Ye Baptized

~ A Reflection on Timing ~

"And now why are you waiting? Arise and be baptized, and wash away your sins, calling on the name of the Lord" (Acts 22:16).

IT WASN'T LONG AFTER OUR salvation that we realized we needed to be baptized. Eric had been baptized as a baby but I hadn't. Neither of us had been baptized since we believed on the Lord Jesus Christ.

We were at one of our regular prayer meetings when the power of God fell for healing and deliverance. The praise reports and prayers were awesome that night! (See "School Is In Session." It was THAT night!). We were having a glorious time in His presence when the pastor stood up and started preaching on baptism and the importance of it for all of us. He asked if there was anyone desiring baptism, and Eric and I responded affirmatively at the very same time! We knew the Lord was speaking to us through him and we didn't want to wait a moment longer!

But we were in the middle of Santa Ana and no one nearby had a pool. We thought of the bathtub but didn't really want to go that route, even though it would have been perfectly okay. Then someone thought of the city fountain! We could go there, get baptized, and be gone before anyone noticed. It didn't matter that it was illegal for us to get in it. It seemed like a logical place for a baptism at the very late hour. How would anyone know anyway? It was pitch black outside and most everyone would be in bed. We thought the lights went off at midnight anyway.

Upon our arrival a twinge of discouragement set in as we spied the fountain with the lights very much ON and brighter than we remembered! And if that wasn't enough of a deterrent, there was a police car nearby with two policemen inside! For sure we wouldn't be able to escape their gaze!

We prayed and decided to do it anyway. We could be quiet. Maybe they just wouldn't see us. From the moment we made that decision, the fountain lights went off making it impossible to see your hand in front of you much less a few people "swimming" in the fountain. Even though that's not what we were doing, we knew we wouldn't be able to explain it should we get caught.

It was a great experience and I'm glad we did it! Just as the lights went off, they came back on the moment we stepped out of the fountain. Better yet, the police officers had no clue that we had been there! We were quiet as church mice in the dark, true, but I believe He shielded their eyes and ears from seeing and hearing what was going on. His sovereignty and majesty was overwhelming. He had done this for us!

I would never suggest that you break the law as we did to fulfill God's command. But I will suggest that if you haven't been baptized since you believed, do so right away. As the old (wo)man dies and the new (wo)man is raised to new life, you won't be able to help yourself, as your heart fills with appreciation for all He has done. Young or old, rich or poor, tall or short – be ye baptized!

Dear Lord, the sweetness of Your presence encourages me to do the things You command. Thank You for the gift of salvation, and my declaration of it through baptism. In Jesus' name, Amen.

The Gospels According to Erin

~ A Reflection on Truth ~

"And you shall know the Truth, and the Truth shall make you free"
(John 8:32).

ERIN WAS TEN YEARS OLD when we assumed the leadership of our church. At the time our church's name was Elim Gospel Church of Mt. Morris (EGC). It wasn't until we moved to our new location in a neighboring town that we changed it to what it is today, Celebrate! Family Church (CFC).

When our pastor fell off the ladder and died the next day, our hearts were broken and our world a bit shattered. Surely we didn't know how we'd manage with such a devastating blow, but we knew God was in control and we trusted Him.

During the eighteen months preceding our pastorate we spent a lot of time with our pastor and his wife. We had moved to the area to become the parents of the county's foster home so we also decided to make EGC our church home. If there was one thing we knew, it was that the pastor needed help! He had a big job and any support we could give him was greatly appreciated.

So it was that we did many things with the pastor and his wife. We had meals together, spent free time together, and did the "work of the ministry" together (Ephesians 4:12). We were their right arms, so to speak, and were happy in that role!

Erin had gone to Sunday school since she was three, and she learned a lot of wonderful Bible stories from that time forward. At home we focused on memorizing the books of the Bible in order, the Old Testament as well as the New Testament. Erin actually did well until she got to the Gospels in the New Testament. "Matthew, Mark, Luke, John, and Lois." "No, Erin. Lois is not one of the Gospel books. There are only four." She tried again. "Matthew, Mark, Luke, John, and Lois." Again she added Lois' name. Over and again we'd tell her that Lois was not one of the four, and again she would add it. We didn't understand.

Then it occurred to us! Pastor John's wife was named Lois. Lois went with John as much as John went with Lois. She was having a hard time imagining one without the other. She likes things just as they are. In her mind, it was John AND Lois. She eventually got it, of course. We laugh as we remember the effort it took to convince her that the Apostle John did not have a wife named Lois, even though Pastor John did.

It's a fond memory of a little girl who was, and is, simple in her thinking. The big things in life really aren't that big. She takes things at face value and accepts them, and others, just as they are. There are no preconceptions with our Erin. What you see is what you get, and what she believes is, well, what she believes. There's no changing her mind no matter how hard you may try. And that's okay. We wouldn't want her any other way!

So what deep spiritual truth can this story offer? I can't say there is one, really. But I can say that Erin's simple thinking and acceptance of others should be a model for the rest of us. Let's not make things harder than they need to be. Let's accept others as they are, without any preconceptions. And if someone insists that the Apostle John had a wife named Lois, don't lose sleep over it. You know the truth, and the truth indeed sets you free!

Dear Lord, Your truth sets me free. The sweetness of Your presence helps me share it with others. In Jesus' name, Amen.

Running With No Feet

~ A Reflection on Confidence ~

"I can do all things through Christ who strengthens me" (Philippians 4:13).

S ARAH WAS ABOUT FOUR YEARS old when we moved to the house on the hill. It was a nice house with a great view on a large plot of land, tucked up and away from the other houses on the street. It sat securely nestled in what seemed to be its own little world. We loved it there. We had peace and quiet in a beautiful setting which, we felt, was a great place to raise our kids and entertain guests. It was also a great place to fly kites because of the wonderful afternoon breezes!

We had just moved from the therapeutic foster home we parented for the county so this new dwelling place was a welcomed respite from the whirlwind of activity we experienced daily for eighteen months straight. But the calm of our new little sanctuary didn't last long. It was the "calm before the storm," you might say. The honeymoon period at the church where Eric was the new pastor ended within a few weeks of our moving in, and we found ourselves immersed in the lives of people with all sorts of problems – problems that we never would have dreamed would be in the church!

He was the twelfth pastor in seventeen years which immediately tells you that the church had issues. The longest period any of the former pastors stayed was two years. Our church had a history, that's for sure, but not necessarily a completely positive one. I don't believe it was intentional on anyone's part, but it's the way it was just the same. And now this was our lot in life!

Just as we knew God sent us to the foster home, we knew He had sent us to the church to begin a work that would change not only its image and reputation, but the future of the people who called it home. We were the ones who were blessed with the privilege of "messing up their hair" while preaching the Truth of God's Word, leading by example, and challenging them to think outside the box. Our wisdom wasn't always or easily embraced which meant we met resistance a lot of the time. But over the ensuing weeks and months the people came to love us, trust us, and count on us to be the real deal and tell it like it was, knowing we had their best interests at heart.

Keep in mind we hadn't trained for this position. Eric didn't take one pastoral ministry class at Bible school, only classes with a mission emphasis. We knew nothing about pastoring a church or dealing with the quirkiness of individuals, much less how to get them to do the work of the ministry (Ephesians 4:12), especially when they didn't want to! In their minds the pastor was supposed to do everything, which is probably part of the reason the pastors didn't have the desire to stay put very long. Helping people to understand and embrace their ministry was hard work. We had our hands full for sure.

I was the woman behind the man. All the energy and encouragement I could muster towards my beloved on a daily basis, I did. As we prayed and sought the Lord for wisdom on how to build up His people, our days turned into longer days, and our nights became blurs. "How come ministry is so hard?" I wondered. "Didn't people know the freedom they had in Christ?" "Why did they have so many problems?" "Didn't their new life in Christ mean they'd changed their habits and ways?"

We were finding that we had to be on guard at all times. Just when we thought we'd heard it all, seen it all, and done it all, another bizarre situation would unveil itself. Why, one night we came home after a busy day only to find a woman *from the church* hiding in our bushes with a really big knife!

What she had planned to do with that knife only she and God know to this day. But this event, like so many others I could share, caused us to truly wonder if God knew what He was doing by making us "shepherds" in this place!

Not everyone was weird. In fact, most were not. But we did have more than our fair share of weirdness! People with all kinds of dysfunctions seemed to congregate in our midst (lucky us!), and it was our job to straighten 'em out! Good grief! "Why us?"

Often times it felt as if we were just running from thing to thing, person to person, crisis to crisis! People who think preachers only work on Sundays couldn't be more wrong. Ministry is more than preparing and delivering a good message once or twice a week. It is a job that will consume all of your time seven days a week if you let it.

It seemed like we quit every Monday back then. We just didn't think we could do it anymore. Sundays were glorious; it was the rest of the week that wreaked havoc on our lives. But every time, without exception, God would pick us up, dust us off, and set us back on the treadmill a little better equipped and encouraged than the day before. We knew that we could, with His help, do a good job if we leaned on His everlasting arms.

One day our little curly-haired, brown-eyed Sarah was romping around the house, playing quite gleefully. She was bouncing everywhere. She hopped and skipped and did cartwheels (normally not allowed in the house). As she ran down the hall (also not allowed), she exclaimed to her dad, "Look Daddy! I can run with no feet!" She'd run and jump landing but a foot or two from where she launched. In her mind she was accomplishing something grand. You and I both know she was merely jumping from one spot to another. What struck us though was the notion that she THOUGHT she was actually doing something no one else had ever done.

Whether we think we can or think we can't, we're right. True, pastoring a church is no picnic. It's hard and time-consuming. But the joy and satisfaction we receive when one life is changed forever – when value of eternal proportion has been added – makes it all worthwhile. The same is true when we mother our children. There are joys unspeakable but there are also times we want to pull our hair out by the roots!

God never asks us to do something for which He hasn't equipped us. He doesn't lead us where He isn't prepared to give guidance. He always provides for us so that we can accomplish His purposes on the earth. It's all about His love for people and the fact that He uses ordinary people like you and me to do His bidding.

You and I can do anything God sets before us – adopt children, pastor churches, even run with no feet! Understand we're going to have obstacles and trials. But we must be determined! We need to set our hearts like flint and then just start. Before long we'll be doing it. We can have an overcomer's attitude – one filled with determination and perseverance, or a victim mentality which never accomplishes anything and, in fact, blames others for the way things are! The choice is ours to make.

Trust me, we had a lot of people telling us we shouldn't bother trying to adopt for one reason or another. We had an equal number of people telling us we wouldn't last at our church because no one else did. We chose instead to listen to God and push forward.

You do the same. I promise you, you won't be disappointed. You too, my friend, can run with no feet if you believe it!

Dear Lord, the sweetness of Your presence reminds me that I can do anything I set my mind to do! Thank You for encouraging me and leading me onward. In Jesus' name, Amen.

Never Say, "Never"

~ A Reflection on Submission ~

"For the Lord God is a sun and shield; the Lord will give and glory; no good thing will he withhold from those who walk uprightly" (Psalm 84:11).

YEARS AGO I WAS A perfectionist/clean freak/control freak. I had issues, I know. I liked my domain tidy and my family members looking their best so I went to great lengths to keep them looking picture-perfect. My house was immaculate at all times, day or night (not so today), my schedule always under control (where did that ability go to?), and my husband's work t-shirts ironed (ridiculous). I wore myself out, of course, trying to keep everything together. There were things I was willing to do and places I was willing to go, and others that I was not. At the time I thought I was flexible, but even as I write this story, I am reminded just how inflexible I really was. I wanted things my way! I think that would make me a diva, if there was such a thing thirty years ago, because I was queen and liked to think I ruled the roost.

I most definitely had to learn a few things after I got saved. Life was not all about me and what I wanted – it was all about Him! Slowly He began smoothing off the rough places of my personality and character, and I loosened up. I had to. It was either let Him change me, or I'd never grow into the person He wanted me to be. And that would mean that Eric would become this wonderful Christian and I'd be stuck in my rut. I didn't want that! I wanted to be a wonderful Christian too! It was a painful process, let me tell you, and one I'm still working on. But He has done a good work in me so far – I am not the same person I was then. Praise God!

I remember so clearly declaring one afternoon before God really got ahold of my heart, "I will NEVER drive a station wagon, I will NEVER live in a grass hut, and I will NEVER live in an igloo!" My husband's eyes rolled as he heard that statement burst forth from my mouth. He has always been a smart man. He knew when to keep his mouth shut and not say anything, even though everything inside of him wanted to put me in my place. He knew God would have His way and I'd be learning a few things in the near future. As a faithful follower of Jesus Christ, you never say, "Never!" to God.

We got saved in 1985, October to be exact. At the time I drove a brand new Nissan 300ZX, 5-speed, T-top, white with red interior. It was extremely cool, and fast. (Don't ask me how I know!) I loved that car! It definitely turned a few heads as I drove it. But then, after we adopted Erin, we decided it wasn't the best family car and we needed to get something more practical. It couldn't very well accommodate all of the baby paraphernalia we needed to carry around.

We decided to find a used car so we wouldn't have a car payment. We looked and looked but couldn't find anything suitable that matched our criteria. Sure, there were lots of cars that we would have liked to own, but we passed on each of them as we stuck to our desire to be car payment-free. And then, there it was – the car that fit all of our criteria! It was small enough so as not to cost an arm and a leg in gas. It was roomy enough to carry everything but the kitchen sink. The only problem was – it was a station wagon! I could not believe that we were even considering this vehicle! Hadn't I just said not that long before, I would "never drive a station wagon?" My mom drove one of those big Ford station wagons, white with wood-grain looking sides. It was atrocious, but perfect for hauling our large family around. I did not want to be relegated to old womanhood – I was young and hip and had my act together (not!). Eric insisted we trade in the Z car for that champagne-colored family mobile. My heart sank as we said good-bye to the sports car and hello to the wagon. One of my worst fears had come upon me.

It wasn't but a couple of years later that we got the call to the mission field. We were headed to Malawi, Africa just as soon as we could sell our house and business, and make it through a year of Bible school. Oh no! Worst fear number two was coming upon me! I was going to be living in a grass hut!

Recalling what I had said very early in my walk with the Lord, and realizing that two of the three "NEVERs" either had, or were going to, come to pass, I quickly repented and asked the Lord to forgive me for telling Him what I would and would not do. Good thing I did – the northeast is plenty cold enough; I can only imagine what the weather conditions must be like which would require living in an igloo!

There's a difference between a volunteer and a servant. A volunteer says, "I will do this or that," while a servant says, "What do You want me to do?" Do you see the difference? A volunteer dictates what she will do and how far she will go, but a servant says, "I am Your's – do with me as You want."

We can certainly love God and still possess volunteer attitudes. I see it all the time in the church. When it comes right down to it, it is only what Christ wills for our lives that really matter. Our will must be surrendered to His. We must never say, "I will never _____ (you fill in the blank)." Be open. Remain pliable. And let the Master Craftsman mold you into a beautiful vessel, destined for honor. I was so foolish when I declared very matter-of-factly that I would never drive a station wagon, live in a grass hut, or live in an igloo. How arrogant of me! "Oh, yeah?" questioned the Lord.

God has good plans for each and every one of us. Let's let go of our preconceived notions of what those plans will be, and hang on to the promise that He will never lead us where His grace can't keep us. He is a good God. He loves us, and wants only His best for us. So, let us walk uprightly before Him – in all His ways. We won't be disappointed.

Dear Lord, the sweetness of Your presence beckons me to be with You every second of every day. Thank You for helping me to get over myself, and for giving me the grace to walk in all of Your ways. You alone are worthy. In Jesus' name, Amen.

No, I Didn't!

~ A Reflection on Admitting Mistake ~

"Do not lie to one another, since you have put off the old man with his deeds"
(Colossians 3:9).

JOSIAH TOOK TO MOTORCYCLING AS he did snowboarding. From the moment he strapped his two little feet onto a snowboard, he was a natural and quite able to maneuver the hills and back terrain of our local ski resort. Once he slung his leg over the little Honda 70 we bought, and kicked it over, he zoomed off with as much thrill as flying down the snow-covered slopes. The kid is fearless and definitely not afraid to try new things, though he's not the daredevil that his brother is. Josiah has much more common sense than Nick. He knows if he gets too crazy he can get hurt. And that's not something he's inclined to do!

The back trails of our property are perfect for little kids to learn to ride. There are just enough obstacles to maneuver around or over as there are adequate turns to learn the principles of offensive riding. The more time Josiah had on the bike, the faster he rode. The faster he rode, the more his dad would remind him about safety, and the more I would pray. I grew up riding dirt bikes so I knew what could happen. More often than I care to count I crashed on one of my family's bikes, or got into a situation I had to get myself out of – even though I was scared to death – like being too high up a hill and having to figure out how to turn around to get down. I didn't want my son to have to learn the hard way. Boys will be boys, though, and he was going to push the limits to the degree he thought he could handle and he assumed we would let him. We weren't surprised that he did so well. He had a good head on his shoulders even if he was only six. Around and around he went, wearing rough spots in our grassy yard that led to and from the woods. The last time he came around the lower garage, his Dad called to him yet again, "Remember! Don't use the front brake!" Josiah nodded in agreement as he passed by, not quite projecting an "I know!" attitude, but close. He didn't think his dad needed to tell him this *again*. After all, he knew what he was doing! Kids can be such know-it-alls sometimes – and periodically to their detriment!

On his last pass he landed in a heap on the driveway with the bike on its side, spinning wildly with him still on it. For some reason he did what his dad had just reminded him not to – he gripped the front brake when he should have stepped on the back, and his momentum sent him sailing – only he refused to let go of the bike. As the bike, with Josiah still on it, did donuts in the driveway, his dad came running from one direction while I came from another. "I told you not to grab that front brake," said his dad. "I didn't, Dad!" said Josiah. "You had to," said his dad, "or you wouldn't be on the ground right now!" "No, I didn't!" "Yes, you DID!"

Josiah never liked admitting he was wrong. From the time he was a very small boy it had been a very hard thing for him to do, even though we always insisted. When you do something wrong or incorrectly, say so, ask forgiveness if you've wronged someone in the process, and be done with it. But that was a hard pill for Josiah to swallow. He would rather not say anything than admit he wasn't perfect. I don't know if he thought it made him look bad, or what. But you and I both know that admitting mistake or failure is as much a part of life as rejoicing in success. He has, of course, done much better with it as he has gotten older, but back then it was like pulling teeth! It was hard and very painful!

As he and his dad talked about the situation, Josiah finally admitted he had gripped the front brake *by mistake*. That's the key word – mistake. He didn't do it on purpose. That mistake landed him in a heap in the driveway. It was okay. Life was going on.

We're never going to be perfect at everything we do. We may have done something a hundred times, but that doesn't mean that the one-hundred and first time will be just as seamless. I remember, after riding my Sportster for months and months, dumping it in the middle of the driveway by doing the very same thing as Josiah – grabbing the front brake as I turned in, which sent me flying over the handlebars. All of our kids and their friends were in the front yard to see it so we all had a good laugh at my expense. But you can be sure I always think twice about what I'm doing when making a turn and braking at the same time.

Today's encouragement is to remember that none of us are perfect. We would all like to be, but there's only One Who is. We're all going to blow it from time to time. Let's not get mad or try to cover it up. Let's learn from the experience. Let's purpose to be lifelong learners that never embrace an "I know it all" attitude which doesn't allow for teaching or correction. And when it comes down to it, confess to your dad that he was right all along. He'll already know it, but he'll be so proud of you for admitting it too!

Dear Lord, thank You for the teachers you have put in my life to help me grow and learn. The sweetness of Your presence reminds me that I will continue to learn new things as long as I am open to wisdom. I love You, Lord. In Jesus' name, Amen.

Put A Sock On It

~ A Reflection on Habits ~

"I will go before you and make the crooked places straight" (Isaiah 45:2).

PACIFIERS ARE GREAT LITTLE INVENTIONS that have preserved many a parent's sanity, mine included. When our kids were little and needed a little soothing or calming, we'd find the binkie and all would be well. I didn't mind that they had them even though it bothered others. Those who were the most vocal about their dislike of the little rubbery things I tuned out. After all, they didn't have to live with these babies.

Hannah, on the other hand, was the only one of our kids who didn't like a pacifier. We offered it to her several times but each time it was refused, in deference to her thumb. Why would she want that when she had her nice, soft, attached *left* thumb? I guess I can't argue with that one. The ladies at the adoption ministry told us that Hannah's birth mom's sonograms revealed that this was a habit she developed in utero! That being the case, you can imagine the effort it took to break her of the habit!

When it was time to break the other kids of their binkies, we talked to them ahead of time for days, preparing them for the actual event of walking to the garbage can and throwing it out. As the date approached, we talked it up even more, exclaiming how much of a big boy or girl they would be once they didn't need it anymore. They would plead for us to let them keep it a while longer; and even if we agreed, it wasn't for very much longer. The event usually ended with cheers of accolade and an ice cream cone.

Hannah, on the other hand, couldn't quite shake off her left thumb! So it took a lot more coaxing and planning on our part to get her to stop. We had to be creative!

We talked to her of the virtues of not sucking her thumb anymore. Her momentary successes were quickly surrendered to the body part which had become her best friend. We rewarded her for keeping it out of her mouth. We reminded her constantly. Even so, she'd default to the thumb that quickly became our worst nightmare the older she got! We resorted to putting pepper and hot sauce on it after all else failed, but even that didn't work! We finally resorted to tying a sock around her wrist so she couldn't get to her thumb. That seemed to work after a very long while. It took persistence and concerted effort on both of our parts to make Hannah successful, all of which were worth it!

I have bad habits that I'd like to break. How about you? I bite my nails if I don't keep them painted so I either have to keep them cut short or keep them polished. I like food so I over-eat which has resulted in weight gain. I get impatient when drivers in front of me don't drive the speed limit. And I sometimes procrastinate to keep from doing things I don't enjoy.

When I'm really serious about being free from the bad habits, I will take action. I will put measures in place that will help me be successful. I'll keep my hands away from my face, say no to second helpings, and leave a little earlier so even if I do get behind slow pokes, I will still be on time. And I'll set goals for the things I don't like to do so they get accomplished. I won't say it's easy to break bad habits, but I will say it's easier when you have a plan to succeed. With God's help, we can do it!

Dear Lord, the sweetness of Your presence helps me to overcome the bad habits I want to change. Thank You for helping me through each day. In Jesus' name, Amen.

The Huddled Mass

~ A Reflection on Embracing Life Experiences ~

*"He has shown you, O man, what is good; and what does the Lord require
of you but to do justly, to love mercy, and to walk humbly with your God?"*
(Micah 6:8).

ERIC AND I HAD NO idea what we were getting into when we sold our house in California, gave away our business, and moved to New York. We hadn't the slightest clue that we were headed for some hard experiences, ones that would grow us up in the Lord, enlarge our faith, and enrich our lives with unbelievable testimonies to His faithfulness as we walked humbly with Him day after day. It's not that we had rose-colored glasses on. It's just that we didn't expect to sink to such desperate lows.

We had gone from business owner – overseeing several employees and making a good wage, to "bean bagger and wife," making a hundred and fifty dollars a week for a living. The money we had when we came to New York ran out after the first few months since we were required to pay a whole year's rent up front. The landlords said it was because we were from out of state, had no job at the time, and no references. But we believe it was more than that. They saw an opportunity to make some money and took it. They had us over a barrel. We needed a place to rent; there were none anywhere close, and if we wanted the house, such as it was, we had to pay. So much for the on-hand money we thought we'd have to live on. The first lesson we learned was that things don't always turn out like we think they will.

Eric got the job at the bean-bagging plant so we could eat, plus he went to Bible school full-time. I stayed at home with Erin and Sarah who were little still, six years and nine months respectively, at the time. The house was a big, old farmhouse on a nice country road but it left a lot to be desired. It had old, single-pane windows that didn't fit well. During the cold, wintery months air would blow in around the windows, moving the paper as you read it if you happened to be sitting by the window. We couldn't afford heating oil so we burned everything we could get our hands on in the wood stove, including parts of the walls of the garage that we didn't think the landlords would miss. The second lesson we learned is that things can always get worse.

The smell from the farm next door was overpowering during the hot, summer months. The manure brought millions of flies that seemed to like to congregate on our ceilings, which totally disgusted me. My father-in-law didn't like it much either. Every time he came for a visit he got out my vacuum and sucked as many of them off the ceiling as he could. It was a hopeless battle though. Another lesson we learned is that some battles aren't worth the energy to fight.

One particularly cold night in the throes of winter, with no heating oil for the furnace and nothing to burn to keep us warm, our family of four decided we needed to huddle together to keep warm. The only room that had carpet for padding and a space heater for heat which could easily accommodate the four of us was the bathroom upstairs. We grabbed our sleeping bags and pillows, huddled together in the middle of the room, and tried to get our kids to make-believe we were camping out. They bought it, of course, but Eric's and my life flashed before us as we laid side-by-side on that bathroom floor. Had we left California – our home, job, friends, and family . . . for this? Somehow in the midst of that freezing cold night, we managed to keep warm. We also believed that even though we were especially low emotionally, and we hit impasses everywhere we seemed to turn, we had heard from God. We were right where we were supposed to be so we knuckled down and purposed to endure to the end.

We made it through that night, and the ones that followed. There were times when we cried out to God for His provision as we either had no money for food, or no money for heat. Each time, money from an anonymous source would show up in our mailbox at the school, a load of firewood would be dumped in our driveway, or bags of groceries would be left in our car. Time and again we were provided for by the very hand of God. It had to be Him because we never told anyone besides Him what our needs were. We learned through those experiences that God is always faithful and will always provide for our needs.

We've had many such experiences throughout our walk with Christ. Each time He provides in a miraculous way, we are surprised, blessed, and filled with wonder again. We marvel at His ways because they certainly aren't our ways. I feel much more comfortable having my ducks in a row before I need them. Eleventh hour timing gives me anxiety. But sometimes that's exactly how He chooses to meet us.

Each one of these experiences could have sent us packing back to whence we came. We could have given up, thrown in the towel, and called it a good effort. We certainly had reasons to quit. But each time we had to go back and remember the last time we heard His voice. In the midst of the cold, stink, flies, empty pockets, and everything else we had to endure, including eventually selling the only vehicle we had, we had the only thing we really needed – Him. He took care of everything as we trusted and waited. The overarching lesson we learned during this period of time was that God is always faithful and on the job, even when we find ourselves in seemingly impossible circumstances. It's when we can't see Him that the eyes of our faith are opened and tested.

I believe God was testing us during those times. I further believe that it was more for our knowledge than for His. He already knew what we were made of. He wanted us to know it too. We did have the determination and wherewithal to go the distance, through the good times and bad, during lean or plenteous times, and with or without heat. He was also teaching us about faith. I can't even begin to tell you how many times we've challenged others by sharing our testimony.

Not all of life's experiences are wonderful. Many are tough and leave scars. But if our goal is to follow the Lord and His path for our lives *no matter what*, then it doesn't really matter what obstacle we face. He will either show us a way around it, or walk with us through it. Either way, He's always with us. Of that we can be certain.

Have you decided to follow Jesus with your whole heart? Have you set your sights on His will for your life? If so, then you know about those lessons that are sometimes learned the hard way. If not, and you want to, then buckle up. You're in for the ride of your life. "Let go and hang on," as I say. Even though the road may get a little bumpy, one thing to remember is this – He will never leave you or forsake you (Hebrews 13:5). If you find yourself huddled on your bathroom floor just to keep warm, the thought is definitely going to cross your mind, "Is this worth it?" Let me be the first to tell you, "It is, sister, it is!"

Keep your eye on the prize. You'll never be disappointed. And like me, you too will have testimony after testimony of His unfailing love and provision just when you needed it, if for no other reason than to remind yourself that you have what it takes to endure to the very end.

Sometimes we quit just before our prayers are answered, and we miss out on the blessings. I can't tell you how many couples quit Bible school because it got too hard, or how many couples divorced because one or the other didn't want to change. Many are the pastors who quit the ministry because the work is difficult. You don't want to be among the quitters. If God is telling you to quit, that's one thing. But if not, you have no other choice than to hang in there and keep going. Be reminded that He is worth every step you take.

Dear Lord, the sweetness of Your presence is my joy in life. Thank You for showing me Your will for my life, and for giving me the grace to stay its course. In Jesus' name, Amen.

Don't Do It!

~ A Reflection on Mom's Wisdom ~

"Train up a child in the way he should go, and when he is old he will not depart from it" (Proverbs 22:6).

NICK HAS NEVER BEEN A good listener. No matter how long or hard, or how many times you try to explain to him why he shouldn't do something, he's going to do it anyway, especially if he's already set his mind on it. The end result is always a lesson learned the hard way, and sometimes those lessons have an accompanying injury or, as in this case, a rash of the worst kind. Praise God he didn't get splinters too!

The house we live in wasn't always as nice as it is now. To my way of thinking we would've been better off putting a stick of dynamite under it and starting over. But my husband, the perpetual optimist and visionary, saw the potential it had in spite of its condition when we first saw it.

The furnace had backed up so there was black soot everywhere and on everything. The floors were bits and pieces of old linoleum stuck together. The carpeting in the rooms that had it was old and frayed and mismatched from room to room. The walls were dull and browned from lack of paint and probably the furnace issues. And the drapes were those old vinyl plastic-y looking things that let no light in whatsoever.

I was quite depressed as we prepared to leave our other house. I had worked for many years to get it the way I wanted and now I was going to have to start over, only this time it was going to take a lot more time, effort and money, of that I was quite sure. Everywhere I looked it needed work. "How could the people before us live in this?" I wondered.

Well, that's just it. They didn't. They moved a year earlier to a much nicer house in another town after living in this one for over forty years. The former owner wasn't very good at fixing things either. The lawn hadn't gotten mowed in that amount of time and unwelcome varmints decided to take up residence on the inside. Besides several dead mice, there was a dead squirrel in the laundry room which left the scent of death in the air. It was not a pretty picture at all.

One of the first remodeling projects we did after fixing the furnace was enlarging the staircase. It was a narrow flight of stairs that was hidden behind a door right off the dining room. The boxed-in stairs meant even less light for the downstairs hall. It was so dark, in fact, that a fluorescent light had to be left on at all times – even in the middle of the day – or you would be in total darkness!

Eric did a beautiful job on the new staircase with oak handrail. It was now open and wide – perfect for little boys to climb up to get a quick ride down.

Unfortunately, one night after his bath but before any diapering, Nick decided to hop on the handrail and slide on down. I pleaded with him not to but he was determined. He tuned out my pleadings and did as he pleased, beginning his descent.

He wasn't a foot down the rail when he realized what he was in for. A look of horror stretched across his cute little face. He screamed as his genitalia burned. But what could he do? He couldn't get off quite as easily as he had gotten on so he had to continue down the handrail until he reached the bottom.

At final touchdown he hopped off in total distress! His eyes were now filled with huge flowing tears. He grabbed his privates and ran in circles hoping we could do something for him. Poor little guy! We did feel sorry for him and wished we could take away the pain. Since we couldn't, he had to bear the pain himself, though we did offer copious hugs and sympathy. If only he had listened in the first place!

Isn't that how we are with God sometimes? His wisdom details the rules and guidelines for a happy, safe, productive, satisfying life and yet, because of our own rebellion or selfish desire we choose another road. We tune Him out and ignore His gentle nudges and outright pleadings. More often than not, the choices we make that do not honor His will usually end with regret, disappointment, and sometimes marks on our soul that don't heal easily.

It is my prayer that my children will learn to listen to wisdom as it calls to them amid the many other voices in today's culture that also vie for their attention. Nick's burning genitalia was the consequence of him not listening to Mom's wisdom. And while we felt bad for him at the time, we knew it was one lesson we wouldn't have to teach again. It left an indelible mark on his memory – he didn't want to do THAT again! And to date he hasn't . . . well, not unclothed anyway. And for that we rejoice.

I'm sure you can easily remember the people who spoke into your life while you were growing up. Aren't you glad they told you the truth – the way it was for real? They didn't candy-coat the issues but told you like it was with the hope that you would learn without having to do it the hard way – like Nick.

Today's a good day to say a prayer of thanks for all the mentors you've ever had, do have, or will have in the future.

Dear Lord, thank You for the people in my life who have been the voice of reason and wisdom. The sweetness of Your presence allows me to honor them as Your divine placements. I appreciate them, Lord. In Jesus' name, Amen.

Tattered and Holey

~ A Reflection on a Security ~

". . . there is a friend who sticks closer than a brother" (Proverbs 18:24b).

IT'S TRUE THAT KIDS SOMETIMES get attached to things. Blankets. Stuffed animals. A favorite toy. Mom's car keys. Whatever it might be, the child feels safe and secure with that favorite object, and wants to know its whereabouts at all times.

Deb's favorite "best friend" was a blanket we gave her as a baby. She immediately took to it over the others, but why, I can't rightfully say. As she began crawling she'd drag it behind her wherever she went. When she learned to walk it also accompanied her, usually held tightly in her fist nestled next to her head. She loved the feel and smell of the thing which we couldn't quite understand. But we knew of its importance and so we kept a close eye on it – like we did Erin's bunny.

As Deborah has gotten older she still likes to snuggle with the now tattered and holey blanket – while doing homework on her bed, or watching TV, or reading a good book. Often times we'll find her and *it* together in the same place doing absolutely nothing. Why, I even saw her pack it for camp one summer, though she insists she never took it out of her bag the whole time. My suspicion is that she has taken it every other year she went to camp too, even though I didn't happen to see her pack it. I honestly don't mind. As a person who values things with sentimental worth, I understand. And I want her to stay a child as long as she can.

I'm glad that Deborah has found a small semblance of bliss in this inanimate object of her babyhood. I'm glad it holds fond memories for her. But I'm even gladder that she knows Who her real security is – and that is Jesus Christ. We've taught her to pray, to stand in faith, to hope without wavering, and to believe even when there's really no reason to, except for what God's Word says on the matter. She has a lot of time to really test those waters as she experiences life and grows to womanhood, but we believe she's got a good foundation on which to build. We know she's one who will truly live a faith-filled, faith-built life – on God's love.

Of all her possessions her blankie ranks right up there in the top spot, I'm sure. But even more important than it, more important than her own life, more important than her family and friends and those whom she holds dear, she cherishes her Savior.

We are so proud of our daughter. And we know that God is too. He knows He has His rightful place in her heart.

Dear Lord, thank You for capturing my heart and being my best Friend. I love the sweetness of Your presence. In Jesus' name, Amen.

The Bat from Hell

~ A Reflection on Conduct ~

"When the enemy comes in like a flood, the Spirit of the Lord will lift up a standard against him" (Isaiah 59:19).

THIS SITUATION COULD'VE COME RIGHT out of a scary movie. But instead of there being a bad guy on the other end of the phone cutting the lines, it was my husband (bless his heart) trying to figure out what the heck was going on at home!

As he had done several years in a row, Eric volunteered to be a counselor at youth camp. He loved the kids and all of the activities that a week at camp brings. True, he was tired when he got home, but it was well worth it considering the young lives that were touched by the Lord with, hopefully, an everlasting impact.

Like clockwork he would call home during free time to make sure the house was still standing and that I was still in my right mind. Being sole caretaker of six wonderful but active kids for a week sometimes sent me over the edge, especially when one of them rattled my cage by doing something totally bizarre – like flushing a ball down the toilet (I'll bet you can guess which kid!). The toilet doesn't work too well when that happens; and Mom's nerves don't fare much better either.

The day had been pretty calm so far and we were enjoying a quiet afternoon of play in the living room. Out of the corner of my eye I spied something buzzing overhead but I wasn't quite sure what it was. About the time it dawned on me that the flying object was a bat, the phone rang. It was the realization that we had a bat in the house that sent me whirling and twirling and flailing like I was doing some sort of break dance!

The screams are what bothered Eric. He couldn't figure out if a mass murderer had just broken into the house and we were all being victimized, or if something else was going on. And since I couldn't get the words out due to insufficient oxygen because of my screaming, he had no way of knowing how to handle the situation . . . or me.

It appeared that the bat liked the hum of the cordless phone, so whenever I moved, it moved with me. Finally I had the presence of mind to run to the kitchen where I could slam the two doors that led out to the other areas of the house and calm down, just long enough to inform Eric that it was a bat in the house and no, we weren't being murdered.

I was so out of breath and hysterical. It was Eric's question, "Where are the kids?" that brought a manner of lucidity back into my mind.

The reality that I had saved myself and left them to fend for themselves snapped me to attention. What kind of a mother was I? When I finally emerged from the safety of my kitchen to check on them, I found them all under blankets that their sister had thrown over them to keep the bat from landing on them. Good. She thought of others beside herself. I trained her well. ("Do as Mommy says, not as Mommy does!"). Even so they were all either crying or on the verge of crying because: 1. They had no clue why Mommy was acting like a nutcase, and 2. Mommy left them in their darkest hour of need!

I hustled them all back into the kitchen and slammed the doors yet again. We were all together and safe at last! After a few kisses and apologies I then called our neighbor, Tadd, as Eric instructed, to come and deal with the nasty intruder.

Tadd came armed with a smirk on his face and a tennis racket in his hand which eliminated the bat with one hearty whack! I was so grateful.

Even so, I slept with one eye open to make sure there weren't other creatures lurking around.

If this story doesn't remind you of the enemy of our souls, I don't know what does. This bat stole my peace, killed my sanity, and destroyed a perfectly good afternoon with my kids. We have all power and authority over the enemy in Jesus' name. Weird flesh is another matter, like my conduct in this story. I can't honestly tell you why I totally lost all presence of mind when the bat decided to fly over, and why I saved myself and not my kids. It makes some people furrow their eyebrows in judgment of my behavior . . . even though my kids were perfectly fine. It makes others laugh with me at the craziness of the event, including my husband who knows me better than anyone! I choose to not beat myself up, but rather take it in stride as "one of those days" that'll go down in the memory books for a long time to come.

I do keep tennis rackets and racquetball rackets on hand should any friends or relatives of the "one who got whacked" decide to show up too. Thankfully we've only had one other bat in the house that I know of and my amazing HERO husband took care of it for me with one well-placed swing of a racquet. He did whack it in my direction, however, giving me a faint heart attack. He had told me to "Stay in the bedroom and keep the door shut," so it was my own fault. It whizzed past my head, slammed into the bedroom door I had just opened, and fell dead on the floor. It gives me shivers just thinking about it!

May we all remember that Jesus is for us! May we also remember that our family is too, even when we act like a crazy person. That's good news, I'd say.

Dear Lord, sometimes life gets a little crazy and I do things that are a surprise. The sweetness of Your presence brings right thinking and calm when I feel out of control. Thank You, Jesus. In Jesus' name, Amen.

Snip! Snip!

~ A Reflection on Compassion ~

"I have shown you in every way, by laboring like this, that you must support the weak. And remember the words of the Lord Jesus, that He said, "It is more blessed to give than to receive" (Acts 20:35).

ERIN WAS BALD AS A billiard ball until she was two years old. Even though she was dressed in pinks and purples, innocent onlookers would comment, "Oh, what a cute little boy!" I got really tired of it so I started taping bows to the top of her head. Even though she was bothered by the tape jobs, I insisted she wear them so people would know she was a GIRL! I thwarted her attempts to pull the bows off as much as possible; so until we saw signs of hair growth, they were as much a part of her outfit as her shoes and socks. Looking back now all I can say is, "Poor thing! Mommy is sorry!"

I had lots of bows, bands and clips ready when those first signs of new hair showed themselves. As soon as I could get enough hair into a rubber band she wore pig tails. And as it grew longer, we tried other "do's," too.

When her hair came in, it really came in! Like her biological mother she was blessed with thick, long blond hair, and lots of it! I messed with it daily for as long as she would let me. When she was a pre-teen she demanded I leave it and her alone!

Our appointments at the beauty parlor were events we made special; and sometimes we'd both come home with painted fingernails as well. My friend, the beautician, was great!

As Erin grew, so did her hair. It got longer and longer which meant I was spending more and more time trying to get the knots out. She didn't like the ritual any more than I did, but she did look cute and coiffed.

It was during her tenure at School of the Holy Childhood in Rochester, New York that she heard about kids who, due to their treatments for various diseases, had no hair and needed wigs made from human hair. The facts hit her hard – some kids have NO HAIR! She was told that in order for these kids to get wigs, other people needed to donate their locks. How moved her dad and I were at the notion that this was something she wanted to do.

It wasn't a decision she entered into lightly. She thought about it for days, asking questions, weighing it out, until one day she decided for sure! Yep! She wanted to donate her hair to Locks of Love so one of these kids could have hair. We obtained all of the important criteria for sending donations, and I made the hair appointment.

In her limited speech she excitedly told everyone in the salon what she was doing and why. I believe they were as touched by her compassion as we were, as cheers and accolades followed her brief declaration. I suspect that a few were even convicted by this deliberate act of love by a developmentally challenged girl. For those who wanted more information about the organization, I passed on what I knew and we left feeling pretty good about ourselves.

We boxed up her twenty one inch pony tail, prayed over it, and sent it off. Erin was happy as a clam that she was blessing another child's life! We were pleased that she responded to God's invitation.

I believe it is God's desire that we bless others when it's within our means. Sometimes the opportunity will be an easy decision; sometimes it won't. When we give, He gives back, "pressed down, and shaken together" (Luke 6:38). We certainly don't give to get, but we definitely get as result of our giving because that's how His economy works. Our refund, if you will, may not come back in the same form as what we gave. More often than not what we receive is more of Him – more joy, more love, more peace, more grace, more confidence, and yes, more resources with which to carry on the #1 job He's given us – raising our kids in a God-fearing home.

Hair is hair; it'll grow back. In fact, it already has ten times over. Erin continues to wear her hair exactly the same way as she's done since she started taking care of it herself – parted in the middle and hanging loose. No more ribbons and bows, and rarely even a pony tail.

A long time ago she heard the Lord's voice. Without remorse or hesitation she heeded that voice and obeyed. My prayer for all of us is that we'd be ever so quick to respond when the Lord whispers to our hearts too. He has His reasons; He knows what's best. And since He uses ordinary people to accomplish His purposes on the earth, we have no alternative but to surrender. God is good all the time, and He won't ask us to give something without providing the grace that goes along with His request.

Dear Lord, I want to be faithful to do all that You ask me to, even the hard things. The sweetness of Your presence reminds me that I'll be blessed by being obedient. In Jesus' name, Amen.

Don't Cry, Mom

~ A Reflection on Letting Go ~

"Weeping may endure for a night, but joy comes in the morning"
(Psalm 30:5b).

S ARAH HAD REACHED THE MAGICAL age of seven when she was afforded the opportunity to go to summer youth camp. The minimum age was actually eight; but because we knew the directors and Eric had served on the camp's Board, as well as at the camp itself many times in the past, they let Sarah go a year early.

I think I was more excited than she! From the moment we got authorization for her to attend, we began making lists of what she'd need, shopping for those necessities, and packing her things. Then the day came.

Camp started on Sunday afternoon and ran through Friday night. She wasn't all that exuberant with the idea of going by herself, but I knew she'd do just fine and would, in fact, have a fabulous time! "What an opportunity!" I told her. "You get to go to camp when others your age aren't yet allowed!" Her partial smile and questioning eyes spoke buckets. She wasn't so sure she was ready.

We didn't hang around after church because we wanted to get home, have some lunch, and get on the road to the camp. Sarah seemed to be dragging her feet with everything she had to do. But I prodded her along until it was time to get in the car.

Sarah hung back while we registered and found her cabin number. Actually, she was in the gym that year as the cabins were full with the older kids (twelve year olds and under) which actually turned out to be a good thing. Her group of friends would be bigger. Surely she wouldn't feel alone.

We got her settled into her little area in the gym and then it was time to say good-bye. I knew this experience would be good for her, so we hugged and walked out to the car. Sarah was hot on our heels the whole way to the car! She didn't know if she wanted to stay; in fact, she thought she wanted to come home with us!

After some encouragement and a little help from her counselor, she agreed to stay. Getting in the car and driving away we saw her standing outside, tears rolling down her face, waving good bye. That sight made me cry too. What was I doing? Was she really too young for camp? Would an extra year make the difference? How could I leave my precious seven year old with a bunch of strangers in a strange place when she didn't want to be there? I thought about changing my mind and going back to get her! We had gotten this far though, why turn back?

Throughout the week I prayed for Sarah while wondering how she was doing. I knew that if she had any problems they'd call us. "All must be well," I thought, "because no news is good news!"

As expected, Sarah had a wonderful week with her new friends! She chatted all the way home about the crafts she did, the canoe rides in the lake, the games she played, the swimming, the worship services, and yes, the food – which actually wasn't too bad. She loved camp and decided she wanted to go back next year. I couldn't help but recall the transition from sad little face to happy little girl and "I want to go back!" What had happened?

I don't think it's ever easy to be in a new situation with people you don't know. I know I have a hard time sometimes. But in order to grow, we need to be stretched and step outside of our comfort zone. Kids are no exception. As adults we can be sympathetic with them because we've had to do it many more times ourselves.

The day we left Sarah at camp was a new day for her, and me. She learned how to make new friends with girls whom she'd never met before. And I learned that it was okay to leave her there when she really wanted to go with us. We HAD heard from the Lord. She WAS old enough to handle it. And she grew up a little as a result of the experience.

May we never hold on so tightly to our kids that we stunt their growth. Let's seize the opportunities that present themselves so they can move up a peg on the maturity continuum. It's kind of like camp food. They won't know if they'll like it until they try it!

Dear Lord, thank You for the experiences You allow so we can grow up a little more. The sweetness of Your presence comforts me when I might feel a little bit afraid. In Jesus' name, Amen.

Truth Trumps Fact

~ A Reflection on Identity ~

"The entirety of Your word is truth, and every one of Your righteous judgments endures forever" (Psalm 119:160).

I HAD A VARIETY OF NICKNAMES when I was growing up. My parents and siblings gave me some; my friends gave me others. Most of them I didn't mind because they were terms of endearment or just shortened forms of my given name . . . Deb, Debbers, DJ, Probst (my maiden name), to name a few. Others haunted me for years because of the damage they did to my self-esteem. When you're told something enough times, even though the person is "just teasing," you start to believe it if you're not careful. And it can have a negative effect on the rest of your life.

My brothers were normal, all-American boys full of life and spunk. Our house was a constant buzz of activity with friends coming and going on a regular basis. And like most brothers, when they thought they could get the best of their sister, they took full advantage of the situation. We girls were perfect targets because, more often than not, they got the reaction they hoped for!

I think they picked on me more than my sisters. Maybe it was because I was the oldest and they had more compassion on the younger ones, I don't know. But it did seem like I was the brunt of many of their jokes. So tease and taunt they did at every chance they got!

Bird Legs. Fried Eggs. DeBRA. Flat Chest. No Chest. Wish She Had a Chest. These were some of the things they called me when they wanted to get my goat. The latter ones are the ones that cut the deepest because there were bits of truth in each of them.

I was what you would call a "late bloomer." All of my friends got their training bras before I did; all of them got definitive breasts before my rose buds appeared; and all of them got their periods long before I did! My brothers picked up on the fact that it bothered me. What a mistake on my part!

How well I remember the "special" entire fifth grade health class. Moms came to sit with their daughters through the film about the birds and the bees. I had been out of school with rheumatic fever for a couple of weeks so my mom and I had to sit in the back of the auditorium. I didn't look at her once through the whole thing. "Do you understand what they are saying?" she'd ask. "Uh huh." "Do you have any questions?" "Nope." That was a lie because I had a lot of questions. I was just too embarrassed to ask them.

I could hear giggles and snickers throughout the whole hour-long presentation. I wondered how the boys were faring in the other auditorium with their dads. How embarrassing that they had to learn about us girls and our changing bodies, and SEX, at the same time we did!

The fact that I was deficient in this department made me think there was something wrong with me. My brothers' torture didn't help. I failed to realize that God made me just the way He wanted me, and it was a good me. Small, or shall I say, NO breasts didn't make me unlovable or of no value. But that sense of deficiency carried over into other areas as I got older, causing me no small amount of heartache and disappointment. I missed many opportunities presented because I just didn't think I had what it took to accomplish things set before me.

Words matter. Words are creative. What we think and believe about ourselves (and others) is a big deal. That's why in our home today we don't allow our kids to say negative or derogatory remarks to one another. Oh, they'll be kids and fling a few remarks in anger or during a competitive game on the Wii, but we quickly correct them, make them apologize, and make the offended one extend forgiveness. Sometimes we even make them hug to "seal the deal." We don't want any loose words hanging around in the atmosphere which the enemy can use to their detriment later. His goal is death in any way possible. Our goal is a healthy and positive self-esteem!

I came to the Lord when I was thirty so I had a lot of "junk in my trunk" that needed unloading. Thankfully, the inferiority complex that had become so familiar and part of my identity was one of the first things to go! I found such freedom when I began to see myself through His eyes. I wasn't deficient in any area! The fact was I was flat chested. The truth was, however, that He made me in His image, just the way He purposed, and there was nothing to be ashamed of! What a joy to truly get ahold of that!

Truth trumps fact every time.

In my parents' defense I'd like to say that I honestly don't think they knew about the teasing by my brothers, at least not to the degree it happened. They certainly didn't know the toll it took or the personal hell I was experiencing. As for my brothers, I forgive them. They also had no idea the extent of emotional turmoil I experienced by their teasing. They were just being boys.

A lot has changed since I was a young girl. Thankfully I finally got a chest, but even if I never did, I'd still have a good opinion of myself. My worth is not tied up in my bra size, nor is it based on what others think. My value and identity is in the One Who loved me enough to go to the cross on my behalf. All of the world's sin and sorrow died with Him that day so that we could live!

God's Word is the only truth that matters.

Dear Lord, thank You for Your Word which brings such freedom to my life! The sweetness of Your presence reminds me just how free I am. I love you, Lord. In Jesus' name, Amen.

Gurgle, Gurgle

~ A Reflection on Worry ~

"Which of you by worrying can add one cubit to his stature" (Matthew 6:27)?

OR YEARS WE HAD WANTED to take the kids to Disney World in Orlando, Florida. Since Eric's parents live about an hour's drive away from there, we decided to try really hard to make it a reality. The kids burst into laughter and started dancing when we told them we would be going. The deal was, however, that we'd only go to the Disney Park one day, and visit with Grandma and Grandpa the rest of our time down south. It was an amenable plan that all of us thoroughly looked forward to.

We had just bought a new-to-us family vehicle – a fifteen-passenger Ford van with which to haul our family around. Our drive to Florida from New York would be comfortable at least, even if we did have to take out the last seat in order to fit in the luggage. No one would have to sit directly next to another so there would be relatively little fighting about who touched whom. With potty, gas and eating stops, and stopping overnight in North Carolina, it took us two days to get there. The kids were great all the way; even so, we were glad to get them out of the van!

As expected, Disney World was fabulously marvelous! The sights and sounds of magical fun made the day the best one we'd ever had! We had locked our jackets in the car before taking the ferry across to the entrance, so we had to buy a round of sweatshirts when it started to rain. That set us back a few dollars! It was a wonderful day together though. We left tired, but that didn't stop the conversation the whole way back to Grandma and Grandpa's. Everybody talked about what ride they liked best, their favorite part of the whole day, and, "Can we come back again?" We knew they'd love it. We loved it too. We were so glad to be able to take this long-awaited family vacation.

We spent the week with Eric's folks and had a really nice time. Their house was not set up for little kids, though, so I was a bit frantic trying to keep the littler ones from touching anything they shouldn't. Mom and Dad were gracious and very accepting of our family that had invaded their otherwise quiet lives, but we suspect they were ready for us to leave when it came time. We were ready too. Vacations are fun and wonderful, but there's no place like home!

On our way back home to New York we decided, very spur of the moment, to take a little detour and add an extra few days to our allotted vacation. We thought we would take the kids to Virginia Beach so they could have some fun at the ocean. I grew up in southern California and loved the beach, but it had been a very long time since I'd been to one. Eric and the kids hadn't seen the shores in quite some time either, so what better opportunity than the present to enjoy a few days on the sandy shoreline! I think we tacked on about a thousand miles to our trip by the time all was said and done with sight-seeing and what not, but it was worth it. We had a most enjoyable and memorable time, even though the weather didn't cooperate. It had turned gloomy and overcast, and rained most of the time, but we made the most of it anyway.

The hotel we stayed at had a pool several stories up. That was the second best thing to the actual beach itself. The kids excitedly donned their bathing suits while Eric and I planned the next few days and got organized. We headed up to the pool with the promise of some fun, but found the pool to be crowded with people who also had gotten rained out at the beach.

We decided we would go in anyway. The kids had been looking forward to some swimming, and since the ocean was out, the pool was in – even if it was packed. Eric jumped right in while I took my time getting used to the water. Eric quickly got engaged in conversation with some of the other adults while I coaxed the kids to get in the water along with me. I, too, got distracted for a moment as another lady asked me a question about our kids and, "Were they ours?" (Oh, the dumb things people say sometimes!). While explaining to her that, "Yes, they were," Josiah decided to jump in the deep end of the pool. Neither Eric nor I noticed at the time because we were in the shallow end, but when someone shrieked, "He's drowning," we were quickly jolted to reality!

"Gurgle, gurgle." Josiah tried desperately to stay above the water and get to the side of the pool, but he only flailed around not doing either. The person who shrieked was by this time on her feet pointing to our son who was, indeed, drowning. Eric, being nearest to him, swam in panic over to save Josiah, who latched on to his dad with the look of fear in his eyes and gratefulness in his heart. My mind raced with the "what ifs" that could have happened. How could we have let this happen? I guess with so many people in the pool area, and so much commotion all around us, we just hadn't noticed that Josiah had jumped in. We felt horrible about letting that happen, but blessed that he was okay. It was a lesson learned though. From now on, no one goes in the water until our attention is gained! And they definitely don't go in the deep end! What was Josiah thinking?

You can bet we didn't stay in the pool very long after that. We gathered our kids and our things and headed to our room where we could relax and process what had just happened. It was a scary moment for us as well as for Josiah.

This story could have had another ending, and we all know what that ending could have been! We took our eyes off our son for just a moment – that's all it took – and he almost drowned! I doubt we would have ever been able to live with it if he had.

I beat myself up with the whole scenario again and again. I had sleepless nights and bad dreams when I did manage to nod off. It was like a tape loop that never ended. When Eric reminded me that it was worry, plain and simple, a light went on in my mind! I realized that I was worrying about something that didn't happen. The devil was beating me up and making me feel guilty over a mistake.

It is true that we were distracted when our son did something foolish. We weren't "Johnny on the Spot" on top of it at the moment it happened. But he was okay – the story had a good ending, and we (I), had no reason to fear or worry. God was watching Josiah even when we weren't, and he was fine.

God's Word tells us that we shouldn't worry, but we do sometimes, don't we? I know I don't mean to, and I try not to, but it happens. While I implicitly trust the Lord in all areas of my life, there are times when my trust is a bit wobbly at best. When I find myself in this state, I realize that I have transferred the burden of the situation to my own shoulders, and I haven't let Him handle it as He promised and I believe He will do.

This event was a wake-up call to us to keep our eyes on our kids a little bit better, especially around water. But it was a wake-up call for Josiah too; that "fearless leap" wasn't something he should do again. It was scary.

Today's encouragement is to "cast your burden on the Lord, and He shall sustain you; He shall never permit the righteous to be moved" (Psalm 55:22). Worry doesn't accomplish anything except to give us grey hair and high blood pressure. Let's be mindful to always walk in faith, giving Him our burdens, and not taking them back. We can count on Him.

Dear Lord, the sweetness of Your presence reminds me that I have nothing to fear or worry about. Thank You for Your angels that watch over me and those whom I love. In Jesus' name, Amen.

Mom!

~ A Reflection on Making Memories ~

"The righteous shall flourish like a palm tree ... they shall still bear fruit in old age; they shall be fresh and flourishing..." (Psalm 92:12-14).

I LOVE TO SHOP, AND SO does Hannah. Like me, she also loves to people watch, and finds it as entertaining as I do. We don't get to the mall as often as we'd like because we live an hour's drive away. When we do go, whether we buy much or not, we make the most of our time together and usually come home with more stories to share of whom or what we saw. Sometimes, we can hardly believe what we see – young beautiful girls with numerous piercings all over their faces, tattoos on old ladies, grown men in pajamas, kids screaming and crying with no one tending to their bad behaviors, and hairdos that even New York City salons wouldn't come up with had they tried! Yikes! It's fun to gaze upon all the "differences" out there, though Hannah always hits me when I stare too long. When she does, we giggle and go on about our business. We have a great time together.

Her latest love for the past few years is Black Friday shopping. I have to admit, I love it too. The multitude of people scurrying around, bumping into other shoppers, grabbing the last of something they have to have, the long lines, the incredible messes all over the place, energizes me as much as it tires me out. I know some of you are probably thinking, "WHY?" To be truthful, I don't know. No doubt it is rooted in the entertainment value I get from just being around people who aren't like me.

On those days Hannah likes to get up really early, get ready, and leave the house at the latest by 7:00 a.m. which, I know, is not early when it comes to shopping on Black Friday. Some stores are opening now at midnight, allowing them to capitalize on more revenue during the official start of the holiday season. It definitely gives shoppers a reason not to go to bed at all! Not this chickie, though! I need my sleep, especially if I plan on shopping the entire next day!

I've gone out earlier than 7:00 a.m. before. In fact, I camped out in a lawn chair at Wal-Mart two days in a row, just to be given a number so I could receive a Wii gaming system for the family. I think I left the house by 5:00 a.m. those days. The first day I missed getting a system by just a couple of numbers. The next day I was determined to be first in line, and I was! And that meant I got to bring one of the systems home for our kids to open on Christmas morning.

I love it that Hannah likes to shop and spend her days with me just wandering around the mall. I love it that she finds me enjoyable company, sometimes over her own friends. I think it's because she knows I like to have fun, and I always have her best intentions at heart. I'm not the pushover like her dad is when it comes to buying her things, but she knows every trip will become an adventure if we just put forth a little effort and seize the moments.

Sometimes our adventures aren't at the mall at all, but in other stores or places that we happen to find ourselves. There is a Staples commercial on TV where a guy is looking at an item in one of the aisles, and he yells in a really loud voice, "Wow! That's a low price!" Well, I convinced Hannah that we should do that – just for fun, so we drove to a Staples store with that being our sole intention. We walked in together, I gave her the nod, and she yelled with the loudest voice she could muster, "Wow! That's a LOW PRICE!" And then I did the same. We then laughed all the way out to the car. The cashier on duty nearest the door burst our bubble when she said,

"Yeah, we get a lot of that," as we rushed out past her, but that was fine. We had just made a memory.

One day while we were in Wal-Mart I grabbed a broom and started singing really loudly, "Baby, come back!" I was imitating a Swiffer commercial where mops were no longer necessary because of the new Swiffer. My bad singing brought the attention of everyone around me. It also made Hannah cringe and run around the corner and hide, but laugh – oh, how we laughed! That's one we still like to recall.

I encourage you to do silly things with your kids. Have fun with them. Parenting doesn't have to be full of "do's" and "don'ts" and what will happen if you do or don't. It's one of the things that will keep them coming around and *want* to be with you. As one of the characters in the movie, Stripes (I think it was the drill sergeant) said, "Loosen up, Frances!" When you can and do, you'll be teaching the younger generation that life will be what they make it, and that it can have memorable moments no matter what age they are. It's an important lesson they should learn early, before all the seriousness of life hits them. The best part is that it doesn't have to cost any money, which will be good to know when times are lean.

So today's mission is this – make a memory with someone you love. For each of us, it's going to be something different. Whatever it is, just remember that all eyes are on you learning how to be a grown-up. And that doesn't have to be a "four letter word," even though it's actually seven. You get my drift.

Dear Lord, the sweetness of Your presence lets me be myself in the presence of my children. Thank You for the gifts of spontaneity and laughter as we seize the moments we've been given and make memories with them. In Jesus' name, Amen.

I Need a Getaway!

~ A Reflection on God's Presence ~

"The Lord of hosts is with us; the God of Jacob is our refuge" (Psalm 46:7).

THE DAY STARTED OUT TO be like any ordinary day. I was in my bedroom putting clothes away when I heard one of my kids in the other room calling for me. I spun on my heels and headed out the bedroom door only to find a SNAKE slithering across the floor towards the cellar door. A HUGE snake! Being quick on my feet I jumped to new heights both literally and vocally. A "crescendo in flight" sums it up perfectly.

The snake slithered under the cellar door in panic from the increasingly loud noises that were flying overhead, as well as from the sounds of little feet pitter-pattering their way to the sound of my screams!

Opening the door to the cellar I found the snake crawling along the wall that separated the cellar and my bedroom. My heart raced. My mind pondered the "what ifs" in lightning fashion. I began to pace. "What to do? Oh, what to do?"

By this time the snake disappeared from sight. Quickly realizing there was a hole in the closet on the very wall the snake was slithering down – a hole big enough for a repulsive reptile to get through, I began plugging the hole with shoes, and lots of them. I was in total "I can't believe this is happening!" mode. The intense pacing continued.

Opening the cellar door once again, I was happy (Did I just say, HAPPY?) to see the snake in plain sight. The shoe-plugging had worked and in fact had deterred the snake from entering my bedroom! I thought fast. I screamed some more. And then I grabbed the broom! Yes, I could pin the snake against the wall with the broom until I figured out what to do next. But wait! I had a better idea. I called for my then twelve-year old who also had a high voice I soon discovered, and asked her to hold the broom on the snake against the wall while I raced to the kitchen to grab the barbecue tongs! Yes, the barbecue tongs would do nicely.

As I rummaged through the utensils drawer I heard from the cellar doorway, "Hurry, Mommy, hurry! It's getting away!" I raced to the doorway, my heart beating wildly and erratically, and grabbed the snake by the throat with the barbecue tongs! Sarah dropped the broom and jumped backwards. She landed on Deborah who began to wail due to the immediate pain in her feet from her sister landing on her. I had the snake by the neck in a death grip. Nicholas began chanting, "Kill it, Mommy, kill it!" (Didn't he know I was trying?). But wait, the snake wasn't going to give up so easily. It began whirling and twirling and winding around the not-so-long-now handles of the barbecue tongs closer and closer to my hands. I panicked again, and flung the snake, tongs and all, down the cellar stairs. We all screamed in unison. The snake and tongs both landed on the floor and the snake disappeared!

Disappeared!!! Oh, NO! Where could it have gone? There were so many cracks and crevices to search down there, but I hated the basement. Even so, no way could I let him get away! With my mind speeding out of control, I mustered up the faith to send Erin, my brave developmentally-challenged daughter, down the stairs to check things out. Once the coast was clear, I myself went down, but the snake was nowhere to be found, which created a whole other dilemma in my mind! Either the snake was hiding from my view intentionally, or it had crawled away to tell all its friends not to go up those stairs because a crazy woman would grab them by the neck with barbecue tongs and fling them back down the stairs! I prayed it was the latter but I knew in my heart otherwise. This meant that it was still around just waiting for the opportune moment when it could crawl back up the stairs and try, with a second attempt, to give me a heart attack.

I sent Erin back up the stairs. Actually I led the way and hollered for her to follow. (By now you think I'm a really bad mom, I know.). I don't know if she was more afraid of the possibility of seeing the snake or her mother, who by this time had begun to seem a bit schizophrenic. She bounded up the stairs and we closed the cellar door, posting watch until our rescuer, Daddy, could get home!

The rest of us looked for signs of more snakes throughout the house. Thankfully, there were none. I decided to check the basement once again. Mustering the wherewithal to sneak back down the stairs for a second look, I swallowed hard with bittersweet relief that I didn't find the snake. I did, however, find what looked to be a dead snake, all coiled up in the corner by the oil tank. Ahhh! In my opinion, the best snake is a dead snake. But that meant one thing. If "my snake" was very much alive when he was flung down the stairs, and this snake is very much dead and has been thus for some time . . . well, that means there were more snakes to begin with! That thought sent me into hysteria! And just how long would it be before they were adventurous enough to slither up the stairs to witness first-hand this nutcase who does business to unwanted guests with kitchen utensils?

I filled Eric's ear when he very innocently called from the office. I told him "I could no longer do snakes and that we were putting the house up for sale! The country life was NOT for me!" He did his best to calm me down, and then hurried home before I lost my mind completely.

What he found in the basement "dead" was not a snake at all, much to my relief. It was an innocent chain all coiled up and rusted. Even so, I couldn't relax no matter how hard I tried, which meant I had to get out of the house.

A trip to the mall calmed my shaken nerves. The two older girls and I enjoyed dinner out after some shopping. But when I came back home, I was immediately thrust back into "we have snakes" panic which my husband thought was pretty funny.

Bedtime came but I couldn't fall asleep no matter how hard I tried. I was so sure the thing I feared the most would either join me in my bed or bite me on the leg when I first got up in the morning. Eventually I managed to find relief in sleep, but it took days for me to be sure that I was going to be okay.

I wish I could say that that was our first and only snake in the house. Actually it was the third of four to date. The first two small ones were found within a couple months of our moving into this house. The house had sat vacant for over a year so several gross and detestable things had taken up residence inside. Both snakes died horrible deaths which didn't faze me one bit. The first crawled down a return air vent in the dining room and got burned up in the furnace. (Yes, I did insist Eric poke his head up through the furnace door to make sure!). I swept the second one out the front door with the broom and had my visiting friend run it over with her car. The fourth and last one, "else I'm surely moving," managed to get in while we were doing some remodeling in our family room. Thankfully I wasn't home to see that one. According to the kids, it was another big one! But our faithful protector, Daddy, came to the rescue and chopped off its head after hitting it repeatedly with, you guessed it – the broom!

Lest you think we still to this day have no clue what happened to the snake in this story, my husband did eventually find it wrapped around a pipe in the basement. My anxiety was killed when the snake was!

I'm not proud of the fact that I lost it in front of my kids and that I scared them half to death with my own fear and behavior. But I am glad I had a teachable moment afterwards wherein I could share with them our need for God in every situation. Even at their young age they knew what I was talking about.

My prayer for you today is that you consider God before reacting to the challenges you face. Don't throw your common sense out the window and opt for the funny farm by the time it's over and done with. Turn to His Word, take a few breaths, pray, and then respond. Let Him guide you as to how best to handle the situation. And by all means, don't be afraid to use your God-given power and authority in Jesus' name to send the enemy packing! Go for the "Big Gun" first! And when the storm has passed, thank Him for being your "very present Help in times of trouble" (Psalm 46:1). He delights in knowing we acknowledge His presence. And, it doesn't hurt to keep your barbecue tongs handy!

Dear Lord, thank You for always being with me even when life spins out of control. The sweetness of Your presence keeps everything in perspective. In Jesus' name, Amen.

That's Disgusting!

~ A Reflection on Limitations ~

"The righteous is delivered from trouble" (Proverbs 11:8a).

NICK HAS ALWAYS BEEN ONE of those persons who doesn't "go big" except every couple of days. When he goes, BIG isn't a large enough word to describe his deposit! Wow!

As a toddler we always knew when he went. It wasn't just the smell . . . it was the size of the droop in his drawers.

I had gone somewhere for a few hours and left Eric in charge of the home front which he was usually glad to do. It got me out of the house and kept me sane but he always prayed I'd come home before my appointed time. I can't really say that I blame him. Home was a place where you couldn't relax completely because you never knew what would happen next. Having six small kids all bounding around meant you really needed six pairs of eyes, maybe even seven, to keep watch. Two pairs could easily be used keeping track of "the boy!"

Eric had never been one to resort to drastic measures unless it was absolutely necessary. He's the level-headed one of the two of us, and the one who keeps his cool way longer than I do. I appreciate that about him because he possesses every good thing I don't. The converse is true too. The qualities he lacks (if there are any), I make up for in my persona. Opposites do attract. I think that's why God put us together.

Anyway, this one day Eric was putzing around with the kids in my absence when he "spied out of his little eye" something large and smelly dragging between Nick's legs. He knew it was going to be a bad one. Surely he couldn't leave it for me . . . he had to deal with it.

Eric decided he needed to take the situation outside. On his way out the door he grabbed a pair of scissors and a garbage bag. Standing Nick on the garbage bag he cut Nick's shorts and diaper right off his body. "Oooh, Mommy's going to be mad at YOU!" chanted Sarah as she watched him in disbelief. With the last snip you heard the ensemble "thud" on the ground, with the evidence of a well-fed life spilling all over. Eric gagged at the sight. The other kids ran. They didn't want any part of it either. Like their father, they knew their limitations.

With just as much finesse in cutting the "nasty" off, he quickly and determinably scooped up the garbage bag, tied it in a knot, and threw it in the garbage can!

But Eric wasn't finished with the situation just yet. He had to clean up Nick who now had evidence of the ordeal sticking to both of his stocky legs. He thought for a moment and then decided that the hose would do nicely. Yelling to Nick to stand still, He unraveled the hose and turned the cold water on. Nick's teeth chattered while Daddy hosed him down good. Daddy then ushered him in the house for a quick bath.

I wasn't too surprised when the kids tattle-tailed on their father when I got home. At least they weren't in trouble. To be truthful, I've seen him do far crazier things, even though cutting his son's clothing off his body is a little extreme! I knew it had to be a drastic situation for Eric to resort to such radical measures, so I trusted his judgment, even if Nick's shorts WERE NEW!

God knows our limitations even better than we do. If we find ourselves facing a difficult situation, the first thing we need to do is take a deep breath. Next, we need to enlist God's wisdom to show us how to handle the situation the best way possible. Once we have a solid plan in order, we can take care of business. Just be reminded that scissors work wonders in a pinch. Like duct tape, you won't know just what you can manage with them until you need to!

Dear Lord, thank You that You are my ever present help in times of trouble! The sweetness of Your presence calms my spirit as I wait for You to perform on my behalf. In Jesus' name, Amen.

A Keepsake Memory

~ A Reflection on Sowing and Reaping ~

"Those who sow in tears shall reap in joy" (Psalm 126:5)

DEBORAH WAS JUST A YOUNGSTER when we got the news about her birth mother. She was gravely ill in the hospital and needed everyone's prayers, including ours. God's army went to battle in the spirit, believing He would work a miracle on her behalf. My husband and I honestly didn't know what illness plagued her body, though we knew we needed to pray FOR life and AGAINST death. The enemy's curse had quite a grip on her, but we trusted God for her final outcome, believing that she would be healed. It was with very sad hearts a few days later that we learned she had passed away in the night. She fought the good fight. And while she didn't receive her healing on the earth as we would have liked, she did receive her healing in heaven where she lives today with her Savior. The Word tells us in 1 Corinthians 13:12 that we see dimly now – we don't see the full picture as He does. It's only natural then that we don't understand completely why things like this happen, especially when we had such great faith to believe that she would be healed and walk out of that hospital. In spite of the sorrow in our hearts, we had to trust that He is in control even when the whole thing didn't make sense.

Though we had never met her, my husband and I knew we needed to attend her memorial service. It was important that we honor her memory for she had given us so much. And we knew that one day it would be important to Deborah to know that we had attended. We were right.

When we arrived at the church where the service was held, love filled the room. Sorrow and sadness were there too because her family and friends were grief-stricken at her loss. But it was the bond of love for this young woman that captured our attention. It was obvious that she had touched so many lives besides our own. As we listened to each one recount memories, we got a glimpse of her life and the type of person she was. It's no wonder there were so many people there to remember her! Eric and I left that service with sadness at her passing, but with grateful hearts that we were privileged to be in attendance at such a special time together. Truly, she was remarkable!

Throughout her life she faced obstacles she was forced to navigate, making hard decisions on crucial crossroads – choices that would chart her life's course. She forsook her own life so that her daughter, our Deborah, would have a better life than what she could have provided on her own. She truly "sowed in tears" so that her daughter could "reap in joy," as the Scripture says. I know that this is a bit loosely translated from the intent of the passage which refers to the return of the Jews from Babylonian captivity after seventy years in exile, but I believe it fits just the same. It demonstrates a life poured out for another, even though it was difficult, with the promise of new life for both. Her tears were for the captivity she experienced as a result of her poor decision making, and her joy was found in knowing she had made a good choice for her daughter's provision.

I will always remember Deborah's birth mother. And I will always remember the service that commemorated her life. She, and the experience, lives in my heart. Every now and again Deborah and I purposely recollect the lady who brought us together. And each time we remember the reason why – her love.

My encouragement to you today is to remember the one who either already has, or who will, make it possible for you to be a mom. Bring her before the Lord in prayer, offering thanksgiving and appreciation for her as well as petitions that she would be abundantly cared for and loved. Ask that she be blessed beyond measure. May you never forget her sacrifice. Truly, your joy will be her sorrow.

Dear Lord, the sweetness of Your presence reminds me that my family is uniquely designed by Your hand. Thank You for the birth mothers of each of my children. Bless them, God, I pray. In Jesus' name. Amen.

The Week I Long To Forget

~ A Reflection on Victory ~

"Now thanks be to God Who always leads us in triumph through Christ, and through us diffuses the fragrance of His knowledge in every place"
(2 Corinthians 2:14).

IT WAS A SIGN. I should have hit the DELETE button on the week before it ever got started. The day I drove Eric to the airport it snowed – hard, but we ventured to the Buffalo airport anyway. Thankfully we made it there and back okay, but it wasn't without a few white knuckles along the way! This was **Monday**. The leak in the roof in one of my kid's rooms upon my return home was found by accident. It was nothing a few towels, buckets and continued attention couldn't handle.

Tuesday brought a distressed call from a friend that her mother, who was in critical care in a Rochester hospital, was being taken off life support with the probability she would not survive. Giving brief instructions to my sitter and throwing some TV dinners in the oven, I raced to the hospital sixty miles away but was five minutes too late! She had just passed. Gratefully I was there to embrace my friend and her family.

Wednesday brought a call from my (above) friend's husband that he could not lead the Bible study at our church in my husband's absence as planned, as now there were many details to handle and arrangements to be made for his mother-in-law. Needing to find someone else to lead the study, I made several phone calls to possible leaders, only to find that none were available and, in fact, one of the ladies was going for a heart test that very day! And "did I know that so-and-so was having mini strokes?" His wife couldn't stay home with him however, as she was the one needing the heart test which, gladly, turned out to be of no consequence, but which meant that someone needed to stay with the man who was having mini strokes. (Why is it pastors are the last to know such things?). Furthering my quest to find a leader for the Bible study but to no avail, and questioning the wisdom of racing to the church myself with four kids in tow, (breaking every traffic law in existence to get there on time), I made the command decision to cancel the meeting. After phoning every member of the group regarding the cancelled meeting, the situation was handled and I felt a release in anxiety. Then evening came.

I received a call from my friend who had just lost her mother asking if I would co-officiate at the funeral service. In my every-increasing pursuit to let joy lead the way regardless of circumstances or trials, as well as my desire to be a blessing to my friend, I responded affirmatively. Upon hanging up the phone, reality set in as to what I had just committed. The instant and obvious need to get with God right then burned in my heart! Having never done a funeral before, just how would I go about putting the service together? As I sought Him for wisdom, peace came (but I did wonder what He was doing Friday night instead)!

I was breathing a sigh of relief on **Thursday** with calm assurance that the storm had passed when all of a sudden the garbage man got his HUGE garbage truck stuck sideways in our driveway. Our long, snow-covered drive with a bit of an incline was too slick for Joe's truck. Joe didn't think to put more "pedal to the metal" as he began his ascent. Realizing his situation albeit too late, no matter how hard he tried to escape the inevitable, the truck slid sideways and we had an immediate problem. Running out to his rescue with two boards from the garage (my husband didn't REALLY need them, did he?), I graciously gave them to Joe to put under the wheels to aid in getting traction. Not only did the boards not work, the spinning wheels chewed up the boards and spit them out the back like bullets, leaving a splattering of wood everywhere and the situation ever worsening. Happily I had the foresight to move Eric's truck out of the path of the truck should it get traction and be thrust forward. As the kids watched from the house and I desperately prayed, Joe rocked the monstrous truck back and forth, back and forth, until finally his tires connected with terra firma and the truck began to move. Of course the big, gaping holes in the front where lawn was now covered by snow were sure to be a reminder of the experience for a long time to come. Waving good-bye to the garbage man, I came inside to find my two littlest ones enjoying a feast of grapes and chocolate chip cookies which they had been told earlier to stay out of. "What's a few squished grapes on our brand new carpet," I thought, and, "What was it again that takes chocolate out of the furniture?" They were smiling and I thought I'd better do the same.

It was only a few short hours later that I heard screams from the front yard, "Someone help me!" One of my sons who had been playing in the back of Daddy's pick-up truck had fallen off the back (which wasn't something he was allowed to do in the first place – play or fall!), but he had gotten one of his snow boots caught underneath the tailgate which, when he fell, twisted his leg and caused him to now dangle upside down with his head in the snow! Thankfully, his leg wasn't broken (and neither was his head), though both could've been had his angels not been close by. "Ah HA" I thought! "Didn't get me with THAT one!" With a deep sigh I muttered under my breath, "but the day is still young yet!" Oh, woman of great faith!

I barely had those words out of my mouth when I heard yet another familiar scream, this time from my youngest daughter who had also mastered the fine art of sobbing hysterically! As I peered out the front window I saw her face down in a snow bank with her boots and socks OFF! "Now why would she take those off?" I thought. "Is this really happening?" "Haven't I had enough for one week already?" Her feet were red and freezing, and she was covered with snow. "Why aren't any of the other kids helping her?" In the words of a famous cucumber I began to sing, "Oh WHERE is my husband . . . ?"

Friday looked very promising in spite of the fact that I had a zillion errands to run and the funeral to co-officiate in the evening. All was well in paradise when all of a sudden this ball of emotion welled up inside and I began to cry. Seeing ME cry, my kids also began to cry. No – they began to wail. Certainly we were acting like something horrible had just happened when in reality it was just the stress and tension of the week's events coming to a head. Pulling myself together I apologized to my children . . . they patted me on the back . . . we all hugged . . . and then we headed to the kitchen to bake Valentine cupcakes.

The evening service was fine. The family was blessed by the attendance and outpouring of love. And now I could relax and join in the family fun of "pizza, popcorn, soda, ice cream, cupcakes, and video party" the babysitter had joyfully started in my absence. Sincerely intending to sleep in the family room in the sleeping bag the kids "saved just for me," but not being able to, I headed for the comfort of my own bed at 2:30 a.m. Bliss at last.

The continuation of the night's party began promptly at 7:15 a.m. It's amazing to me that kids who get a full night's sleep and find it hard to get up for school can easily rise for FUN (and more goodies and videos) on a mere six hours of sleep! All six were well-behaved and enjoying their "before breakfast snacks" of Valentine candy, cookies, and popcorn when my oldest came down the stairs announcing that her bedroom door was locked and she couldn't get in. Having faced this situation more than once in the past, I felt equipped to handle the situation. I marched up the stairs with a screwdriver in hand. Ahhh. The sweet click of success. This wasn't going to be a bad **Saturday** after all.

I just knew **Sunday** was going to be a James 1:17 day – good and perfect – a real gift from my Heavenly Father Who never gives me more than I can handle. I wasn't deterred in my faith when I arose to the "fluff and flutter" of six (thankfully unused) diapers all torn, dismantled, and shredded in every possible direction in my laundry room. Our dog seemingly got a little restless in the night and needed an activity to keep her amused. To keep my astonishment in check, I promptly put her and her belongings in the garage for a cold, winter's nap while I cleaned up the mess and prepared to get the family ready for church. Beating the clock with five minutes to spare and no further calamities to ruin the feat, we headed to church for a wonderful service. I was more than ready to meet my Maker! Yes, indeed it WAS a glorious day!

Monday's freezing rain brought school closings all over the southern part of the county which meant our kids would be home for the day. Appreciating their delight at the prospect, and the fact that there were no broken bones during their intense indoor play, I chalked up another day to God's goodness. "One more day and Eric will be home . . . If only I can hold this pose!"

Having stayed up two hours longer than normal before going to bed, I wasn't ready to get up **Tuesday** when the alarm clock went off at 5:30 a.m. I had received two more frantic emails Monday night from a girl out west who used to be in our youth group some years ago. She was seeking my advice in regard to her marriage. Why she needed to ask someone now three-thousand miles from her and whom she hadn't seen in over eleven years was beyond me, but I responded to her with what wisdom and insight I possessed for knowing only one side of the story, while also encouraging her to talk to her pastor who, if he's like most pastors, had no clue she was having problems! (Why is it they are always the last to know anything?). Checking in on her in the morning, I was delighted to find that she and her husband had already scheduled an appointment with him for counseling. With a contented sigh and song in my heart I began to go about my early morning routine. Ah, yes, this IS the day the Lord has made! And it's the day Eric comes home!!! I certainly chose to rejoice and be glad in it, regardless of the catastrophe, calamity, trial, email, phone call, disaster, or situation! Happy days were here again!

Our trip to Buffalo to retrieve our happy traveler proved to be nothing like the week I had just experienced. Everything went fine! No flat tires. No throwing up in the back seat. Amazing. We loaded up our favorite guy with all of his belongings and headed for home.

I've come to appreciate my fourteen loads of laundry per week . . . twenty-one meals to prepare for and cook, . . . children to chase and taxi around, . . . endless phone calls to make and return, . . . errands to run, . . . lunches to pack, . . . questions to answer, . . . housework to do, ... meetings to make, . . . and friendship to extend, all of which, I must say, I also did in addition to the other recorded events I just mentioned. It was a long and hectic week, a time of stretching and testing, a time for me to realize that without God I would be in a loony bin. True, I failed as my faith weakened with some of the tests, my patience dwindled, and my spirit failed. But all in all, God was with me and saw me through. To that I can attest! And He will be with you too when you find yourself having "one of those days, or weeks!"

Dear Lord, the sweetness of Your presence reminds me that I have the victory in Christ. Thank You, Lord. In Jesus' name, Amen.

Listen Here, Doc!

~ A Reflection on Persistence ~

"Our God is the God of salvation; and to God the Lord belong escapes from death" (Psalm 68:20).

PEOPLE WITH SPECIAL NEEDS OFTEN times have quirky personalities that are sometimes hard to deal with. Our daughter is one of those people. As time went on and she grew a little older, she became harder and harder to deal with. She was as demanding as she was stubborn, and it seemed she was determined to stay that way. I, on the other hand, decided we needed something to change!

We headed to the doctor after I had had enough, to see what could be done from a medical standpoint. Surely nothing else was working. The doctor filled my ear with all of his wisdom and knowledge regarding this type of situation, suggesting that I take her to a counselor. That wasn't something I planned to do as the last group of counselors she talked to offered no help whatsoever. The more he spoke, the more irritated I became. He wasn't hearing me! So I told him again what the problems were and why I was in his office.

Erin had gotten the idea that she was in charge. And being such, she felt she could make her own decisions even though they went against our will. This is a typical teenager mentality, I know. But it went much deeper than that. She seemed depressed, very sad, and very much out of control. She was especially difficult at school and exceptionally difficult at home. No one could get along with her. She was irritable and anxious. I knew she didn't feel good about herself. We tried everything we could think of to shake her from this dark place. Finally, in desperation I sought the help of her pediatrician. Surely he would have some answers.

I talked to the doctor about medication that could possibly help stabilize her moods and behavior. It may have been the twitch of my lip or the crazed look in my eye but the doctor, after dancing around the topic for quite a while, finally agreed to prescribe some "mood changing drugs" for our daughter. It was a good thing. I had purposed before I got there that he was prescribing them for her or me, and I didn't care which!

The medication worked to help calm her down and get her through the tough spell she was having. Over time she got back to her same old self, which meant she didn't have to take the pills any longer. For quite a while she was off them altogether. But in recent months they have once again helped with her coping skills as different aspects in her life have changed. Medication isn't the answer for every person, I know that. But for us it was God's provision.

Never once did I discount the work of the Holy Spirit and what He was already doing to help in the situation. Eric and I had prayed and we believed He heard our cries. He pointed us in the direction of our doctor.

I know there are stigmas attached to taking anti-depressants. There are people with opinions on both sides of the matter. I never have understood that, really. My opinion is, if we need them, it's okay to take them. It may not be forever, but even if it is, our lives will be so much better when we're on more of an even keel.

Erin, even now at age twenty-nine, is still difficult to deal with at times. We don't see her every day so our experiences with her outbursts are few and far between. And really, she doesn't have them very often anymore, just every once in a while when her hormones rage out of control.

God made our complicated minds and wonderful bodies to function a certain way. Sometimes they get off-track, or go a little haywire. It's our responsibility to care for them the best way we know how, keeping them healthy and strong.

Medication is not a bad "ten letter word." Medication was created by man's intellect at God's inspiration so that when our bodies or minds get a little off, it can help to get us back on track.

Whether we take medicine or not, it's important to keep ourselves in good, working order. That means regular check-ups, a good diet, and exercise. It's as important to our overall health as spiritual nutrition. So today, let us be mindful of where we are. If we're up to date with our physicals and we're doing everything right, well, hallelujah! If we haven't been to the doctor in a while, why not make an appointment? The serious effects of most diseases can be averted by early detection. And if we're healthy and feeling good, our families will take notice and want to be around us all the more.

Take care of yourself ladies! You are a needed and valuable asset to all who love you!

Dear Lord, the sweetness of Your presence overshadows my very existence. Thank You for the wisdom You have given to mankind, and the health and healing that You have given to me. I stand on Your Word for all that I need. In Jesus' name, Amen.

The Surprise

~ A Reflection on Fear ~

"...perfect love casts out fear..." (1 John 4:18)

S ARAH HAD BEEN HOUNDING US for several years to get her ears pierced. All of her friends were getting them done; but because we didn't believe she was responsible enough to care for them yet, we kept putting it off. She wasn't particularly happy with our continual procrastination, but I think she understood just the same. When we saw a maturity level that demonstrated a higher level of responsibility, we'd let her know.

Her ninth birthday was quickly approaching; and since she had been showing more responsibility with her chores, her dad and I agreed it was now okay for her to get her ears pierced. We decided to surprise her at the end of a special mother-daughter birthday shopping trip to the mall. It wasn't very often she got me all to herself so her excitement grew as the day approached. So did mine.

The day before we were to go, we got the news that yet another little dumpling was going to join our family, Deborah. We needed to pick her up on the very same day I had planned with Sarah, so how would we manage to be in two places at once?

We came up with a solution to the problem. In order to streamline things, Eric and I made the drive to Buffalo without the kids so we could be home in time for Sarah and me to still go. A well-meaning friend of ours stopped by to see the new baby before we left and accidentally spilled the beans about the real reason for our trip to the city. (That's okay. We forgave her!). Sarah was excited and blessed at the news, but she also had time to think about it all the way to the city. As we drove to the city, I couldn't help but notice that she had been wringing her hands the whole way – in fact, they were clammy! She was obviously nervous as she anticipated the big event. Every time I asked her if she was ready to do it now, she would stall and ask to go into yet another store first. "What the heck is going on here?" I thought. Had she changed her mind? No, she hadn't. She just didn't like pain and she was afraid.

Finally, the moment of truth came. We couldn't wait any longer. She either had to get her ears done now, or we had to go home. We entered the store, picked out some cute birthstone stud earrings, and she hopped up in the stool. The nice lady with the ear piercing gun (they use a GUN?) explained what would happen and how quick it would be. But by this time Sarah was totally overcome with fear. Her big brown eyes that were now filled with huge crocodile tears stared right through me while I tried to remain calm. What was I doing to my daughter? Maybe she wasn't ready for this after all. Should we just forget the whole thing and try it another day?

The lady pulled the trigger and the earring went through Sarah's lobe. Sarah dropped off the stool and onto the floor on her knees. (She was always so dramatic!). Her head hit the floor and she didn't move for a second. What? Had she just fainted? I believe she worked herself up into such a dither *anticipating* the pain of the piercing, that when it actually happened she did black out for that split second! Oh my! And we still had another ear to do!

After some needed time and space to breathe, and much coaxing from the lady with the gun and me, Sarah decided she'd get the next ear done too. Not surprisingly, it wasn't as bad as the first. She came through it like a champ and I was impressed. But I was also pretty sweaty.

Fear can paralyze us if we let it. Fear of the unknown, fear of failure, fear of our enemy or enemies. It doesn't matter what or who it's from, fear is not of God. He tells us not to fear many times throughout Scripture. Why? Because He's always with us and He's big enough to handle any situation, person, or ear piercing gun that threatens us.

Fear, doubt, worry – none of them are good for us. They rob us of the true joy that God has for us and the surprises along the way. Like Sarah getting her ears pierced, we can faint in times of trouble, or we can invite the Lord's presence so we are not afraid at all. It's our choice.

Sarah's surprise was spoiled by a friend who didn't mean to. I was surprised by her dramatic reaction. But God is never surprised by anything we face or do. We can trust Him to see us through.

Dear Lord, the sweetness of Your presence reminds me that I have no reason to fear a thing! And for that, I thank You! In Jesus' name, Amen.

Where Did That Come From?

~ A Reflection on Focus ~

"The way of the lazy man is like a hedge of thorns, but the way of the upright is like a highway" (Proverbs 15:19).

THROUGH MOST OF MY MARRIED life I've been afforded the opportunity to be a stay-at-home mom and not work outside the home. True, there have been times when I've wanted to work, so I have. But the times when I've needed to work to help make ends meet I can probably count on one hand.

It was some years ago I decided to seek outside employment. Prices on most everything were going up, up, up and I knew it was a struggle for Eric to keep the bottom line in the black, so I volunteered to get a job. I had taken the Civil Service test a long time before; and since I was an honorably-discharged Air Force veteran, I knew I had an edge when it came to a "government job."

One of the neighboring post offices was looking for a relief mail carrier so I applied for the job and got it. I had been a permanent carrier in California when we lived there, but not for very long. By the time that position was offered we had moved about fifty miles away and it was too hard for me to get to the job, do it, get home, and still have a life with my family, so I quit. A relief carrier for a nearby post office was another story. I would be a fill-in when the regular carrier needed time off. Eric was good with it, so I was too.

Even though I had training in California for casing and delivering the mail and handling "accountables," I still had to have more training for this relief position. I was sent to the main post office in Rochester, NY for this week-long training, an hour's drive each way. It was rough getting up and out of the house so early, especially during the winter, but I managed to meet my obligations well. A woman I knew whose kids went to school with mine had also gotten a relief position at another post office so we decided to carpool to the training facility which definitely made the drives much more enjoyable.

Snow was piled high and deep on the sides of the road, in parking lots and in driveways. The streets had a light layer covering them as well, with an equal amount of road salt lying on top of that. I really dislike driving in winter, but I've learned to take it slow and allow extra time to get places.

My friend and I made it safely to Rochester this one morning even though the drive was excruciating. It snowed the whole way there and was still coming down pretty hard by the time we pulled into the parking lot. Spaces to park were at a premium with snow piled everywhere, so it wasn't easy finding a spot. I drove around and around until I spied a space I thought I could get into in another aisle. All I had to do was drive down THIS aisle and go up THAT aisle! It didn't matter to me that there was a big bank of snow at the end of the aisle I needed to drive down. I figured I could get through it. My eye was on that space and I was determined to get to it. So I drove carefully down the aisle, made the slight bend, and BUMP! Up and over something I went, and it was more than a pile of snow. It wasn't until I dropped off the other side that I realized it was a sidewalk! "Where did that come from?" I wondered.

I parked the car and we carefully walked into the building. It wasn't until I entered the classroom that I realized "other eyes" had witnessed me drive over the sidewalk – eyes of administrators and trainers who pointed out that mail carriers needed to stay OFF the sidewalks when they deliver mail! Real funny. Even though they tried to make light of the situation, I sensed a small but sincere displeasure in their voices which set me on edge. "Was I going to be fired before I even get started," I thought?

This story reminds me that God knows what's ahead in our path of life, and what obstacles (sidewalks) we're going to face along the way. He also knows what we must do to maneuver through, around, or over those obstacles. Our responsibility, then, is to keep our eyes focused on Him so we'll know our path. He is our GPS; and if we want to get where we're going safely, it's important the two of us are connected.

I didn't love that job as much as I have loved others, but the pay was decent and helped in a time of need. I can tell you, though, that I've never driven on another sidewalk – unintentionally or otherwise!

Dear Lord, the sweetness of Your presence helps me to focus on the path in front of me. Thank You for guiding me the whole way. In Jesus' name, Amen.

Genes, or Passion?

~ A Reflection on Gifting ~

"I will praise You, for I am fearfully and wonderfully made; marvelous are Your works, and that my soul knows very well" (Psalm 139:14).

I HAVE ALWAYS ENJOYED SPORTS, BUT not to the degree of my son. He lives and breathes for sports – specifically soccer, basketball, and track. He's not been as fired up for baseball (the one sport I adore!), but the truth is – he's good at everything he does! If guys were like girls he'd be "the guy you'd love to hate" because of his abilities. But guys take it in stride and "high five" each other when one of them does something fantastic like make the winning basket from half court, score a goal on a tough opponent, or beat the lead guy's time in a race. They're strange animals, though it's a good thing. Can you imagine just girls on the earth playing sports? I can't. We can be so catty and jealous and backbiting. It's so much easier for us to "weep with those who weep" than "rejoice with those who rejoice" (Romans 12:15). Why is that?

Josiah is the proverbial tall, dark and handsome guy. The fact that he has sports ability squirting out his eyes is a plus. Yes, he knows he's good, (remember – he became King at age eight). But he's definitely been given a gift to match his looks. This is a problem for some of his siblings who are constantly reminded that they are "Josiah's brother or sister," and "Oooh! Isn't it great?" "Uh, NO!" they say.

I know that someday Josiah will do great things with the gifts he's been given. It may be a college scholarship, or his involvement in youth ministry, or perhaps even professional sports somewhere down the line. I also know that it is our job to keep him grounded so that his head doesn't swell and he think too much of himself. Runaway pride does come before a fall. He needs to keep the important things in perspective.

God has given all of us abilities to do things that others can't. Some of us might wish we were like so-and-so, or had different talents than what we have. May I remind us both that it's God Who gave us the gifts He thought we should have. If we were meant to have different gifts we'd have them! So it's important that we use them appropriately and with the right attitude.

Josiah's future holds many promising opportunities. But so does ours. He's not any more special in God's eyes than the rest of us. Let us never forget that we have a mission on this earth. We were born because God had a plan. May we always seek to know His heart so that we may serve others in His Name.

Dear Lord, I love the sweetness of Your presence as I pursue the future You have purposed for my life. Thank You, Lord. In Jesus' name, Amen.

Tip-Toeing in Toe Socks

~ A Reflection on Grace ~

*"And be kind to one another, tender-hearted, forgiving one another,
even as God in Christ forgave you" (Ephesians 4:32).*

OUR HOUSE WAS BUILT IN the late 1890's so, needless to say, it has been a work in process to bring it up to acceptable standards. By the time we get done with the next project – the downstairs bathroom – we will have renovated every single room in the house. But you know what that means. It will then be time to start over with fresh paint in each room! Oh, the joys of home maintenance.

The dining room and kitchen floors needed facelifts long before they got them. Even though I appreciated the uniqueness of the original wooden floors, I wanted them covered with new flooring. The cracks between the planks were large enough to lodge cereal and other falling objects from kids' hands, not to mention loads of dirt; and it was just too much of an effort to keep them clean. Until the time came that we could put down new hardwood, we painted them every couple of years – "quite" a project! The paint took days to dry, and with a lot of bouncing kids living in the house, it was not a particularly fun period of time for any of us.

The weather in upstate New York can be anything from wet and humid, to cold and snappy, or just beginning to warm up and be pleasant. You just never know what you're going to get. It was May, and it was cold and rainy. The kids couldn't go outside to play, so I had to keep them corralled in the house and entertained while Dad, once again, repainted the floors. I'm sure you can imagine what work went into preparing the floors so they could be painted, not the least of which was moving all of the furniture.

Finally they were done and on the third day of drying. It was taking a bit longer than usual due to the humidity, but we were managing just fine. Hannah was upstairs playing dress up, and then Barbie's, when she decided she needed to be downstairs. She, like the others, had been instructed to stay off the floors and to use the planks that Daddy had rigged up. Up until this time, all of them had been pretty good about following our directions, so why she decided, all of a sudden, to bypass the planks and hop off the second stair and onto the still-tacky floor, I'll never know! The toe socks she was wearing stuck to the floor with each step, leaving little fuzzy remnants in her footprints. She didn't give it a second thought, however. She just kept on trucking.

My screams in disbelief, when I noticed, could have easily woken the dead. They weren't screams at her, but at the shock of the situation. My goodness! What was she thinking? That's just it – she wasn't thinking. She was a little girl just being a kid. They do that sometimes. But why, oh why, did it have to be on my still tacky floors that now had tiny footprints on them – from the stairs, through the dining room, and into the kitchen?

There wasn't much we could do about it now. The floors had to dry all the way before we could put another coat of paint on them. Until we could find the time to do that, the toe-sock footprints would be a constant reminder that our home is a work in process just like the people are who live here. They would also serve to remind us that our curly-haired, brown-eyed daughter needed new socks!

I have to confess that at first I wasn't very happy about the whole situation. But then I realized that we couldn't do anything about it so it wasn't worth losing sleep over. Hannah felt bad enough so I wasn't going to torture her by dwelling on it. We learned to take it in stride, and chalked it up as another one of those crazy, unintentional things that happened. We have had many good laughs about it through the years. And now that we recently put down new hardwood floors, I don't have to worry about wet paint!

If we find ourselves in situations that send us reeling, let's remember to pause before responding. We can take a few deep breaths if we need to. But we should be gracious, kind, tender-hearted, and forgiving. Let love abound in our hearts and homes so that the people we love know they are valued over any silly floor.

Dear Lord, thank You for the gift of grace. The sweetness of Your presence reminds me to keep my priorities straight, and those are always the people I love. In Jesus' name, Amen.

Imelda

~ A Reflection on Missions ~

"(S)he who has a generous eye will be blessed, for (s)he gives of (her) his bread to the poor" (Proverbs 22:9).

THE LITTLE VOLKSWAGEN WITH WINGS landed at the tiny Lake Elsinore airport. "That plane can't be for you," I thought. But it was. Missionary Aviation Fellowship (MAF) was doing some work in a tiny village in Mexico, and Eric had been invited to go with them. Their mission: dig wells far enough away from the latrines so the people would stop getting sick. It was a hard and arduous job, but Eric loved every minute of it. It was this first missionary adventure that sparked our interest in full-time missionary service.

Since that time Eric's been around the world at least six times to places like Haiti, China, Morocco, Kenya, Rwanda, Burundi, Singapore, Hong Kong, Kazakhstan, India, and more. His leadership and preaching gifts have certainly "made room for him" (Proverbs 18:16). He's such an encourager! I've always been "the girl behind the man," sending him off with blessings and love while I manned the home front and oversaw the happenings at the church.

I did get to go to Saltillo, Mexico with a group from our church once, and I loved it! We took curriculum and supplies for a make-shift VBS (Vacation Bible School) and preached in the streets to passersby. I actually got to play the part of a "hooker" in the drama we presented, which brought lots of laughs considering I was the "visiting pastor!" I preached at the Sunday morning church service and found that using a translator wasn't as intimidating as I thought!

My heart was really aching for Africa. Eric had now been several times, as well as others in our church too. So when the opportunity came for ME to go, I jumped on it! I led a team of five women to Kenya and our job was to minister to the widows and orphans during our week-long stay. I was again asked to bring the Sunday morning Word to the people at the church. Two interpreters down!

When my husband was in Suna, Kenya a year or two before, he challenged the leadership to begin a widows program where the widows would take orphans into their care. In return for their service they would be given cows. The cows produced enough milk for the children as well as more for the widows to sell. It seemed like a win/win situation and very doable so the Kenyan leadership decided they would do it!

Our team visited several of these widows' homes. I was beyond ecstatic to find the women flourishing in more ways than one. They felt their lives had purpose and meaning by caring for children not born to them (there's that adoption thing again!), and they now had means to make money to keep their homes going. It was so awesome to see what the Lord had done. I loved bringing home the good report!

We stayed in the church's mission house for the week and the pastor's wife had been our "tour guide." Lovely, lovely lady – truly! In our travels during that trip we happened upon a house that the pastor's wife knew of. As she entered the house she saw a little girl named Imelda lying on the dirt floor. Her mother had left the family a few years earlier and Imelda had become the house servant, caring for her father, siblings, and the women her father "entertained." She had been stricken with malaria and typhoid and was now crippled in her legs. Dehydration and dysentery only compounded her problems. Still, she was required to cook and clean so she pulled herself along the dirt floor day after day trying to accomplish the required tasks. By the time we found her she could barely move.

Our team lost it emotionally! We just couldn't believe the state of this beautiful little girl! Our hearts were broken in pieces so it didn't take us but two seconds to decide what to do. We asked Faith, our Kenyan pastor's wife, if we could take Imelda to the doctor for some necessary medical attention. She told the father that we were taking her (She didn't ask; she just did it!) and out the door we went. Imelda's big eyes filled with tears as we rode along the bumpy road to the clinic. We knew she was in pain. We were in pain for her too. I held her in my arms the whole way there. She didn't take her eyes off of me nor me her.

The doctor did archaic blood tests and started her on medication right away. Imelda was a very sick little girl and had to be "admitted" to the hospital for several days. The hospital was a brick building with holes for windows, yet no glass was in them. Flies were everywhere inside and on everything, even the food. It was really disheartening. How could "our little girl" get well in a place like this? She looked so small in that worn bed. I wanted to bring her home with me; in fact, I called home and asked Eric if I could!

Faith had several orphans in her care already but she agreed to make room for Imelda if we could pay her expenses. The five of us pooled our resources and bought the medicine she would need in the coming weeks, clothing to wear, even a year's tuition at the school she could now attend. We even paid for her physical therapy for the year so she could learn to walk again. Our "offering" for the care of this little child would never compare to the gratitude we had in our hearts. God had been so good to allow us the privilege of rescuing one of His own.

Now, I wish the story ended well but I'm sad to say it didn't. After Imelda had been with Faith and the other children for about two years, she ran away. She was healed from the diseases that ravaged her body; she no longer needed crutches with which to walk; she seemed to be happy in school; but one day she just left. No explanation. No good-bye. Just gone. It wasn't until weeks later that Faith learned she had gone back to her father's house.

I don't believe Imelda was a lost cause. Surely she would have died had we not "happened along." I do believe however, that while she went back to what was comfortable and familiar, she knows that she was given a second chance at life.

Someday we'll meet again in Heaven. And when we do, I hope she remembers this white face that loved her from the moment I laid my eyes on her! Until then, may she always know that she is "accepted in the Beloved," His daughter, and no one's slave.

Thinking about Imelda right now makes me smile, yet tears stream down my face as I write. They're happy tears though, for I was part of God's miracle in this little girl's life. There's no greater blessing on earth.

Dear Lord, I am Your handmaiden and desire to go where You lead. The sweetness of Your presence envelopes me as I share my life with those in need. In Jesus' name, Amen.

An Escapee

~ A Reflection on Knowing Where You Belong ~

"I love those who love Me; and those who seek Me diligently will find Me"
(Proverbs 8:17).

I COULDN'T HAVE BEEN MORE THRILLED when Nick started school. Finally, his energy would be channeled constructively, hopefully capturing his interest in learning. His teachers, on the other hand, weren't as excited to have him because they'd heard the stories from his siblings who went before him. But none of that mattered – it was their job; and they'd just have to learn to deal with it (and him) as I did.

We bought the usual supplies for the first day of kindergarten: a new backpack, crayons, markers, and paper for drawing. He looked so cute in his little pants and shirt. I wondered if he'd keep his shoes on the whole day but figured I'd find out when the day was done.

He was about three weeks into his first school year when I got a frantic call from the school. I needed to come home right away; Nick was missing! You can imagine the myriad of emotions after a call like that. But I wasted no time in getting home to find out what the heck had happened and how he managed to escape.

I couldn't quite fathom it considering there were teachers, teachers' aides, and other adults throughout the whole building. Didn't anybody notice? I began to think they were all inept and needed to be fired, a justifiable response to the situation I thought.

I pulled around the corner just in time to see my five year old son, with backpack on, running as fast as he could up our long driveway towards home. Hot on his heels about fifty feet behind him was his teacher, who was going as fast as she could in high heels. And about fifty feet behind her was the principal, who had practically sprinted out of his office once he learned of Nick's disappearance. I was watching a cartoon take place right in front of me! I couldn't believe my eyes! Nick . . . then his teacher . . . then the principal, all running to beat the band. I couldn't even begin to understand what I was seeing.

Nick ran to the back of the house and lodged himself between the back door and screen. Neither of them could find him when they looked back there. They wondered if he had gone into the woods. I'm sure they didn't want to think about the possibilities or their futures in education were he not found safe.

Finally finding his hiding place, I made him come out and face his teacher and principal. They were out of breath with looks of horror on their faces; but since Nick was okay, I assured them that everything was going to be fine. That's when they told me exactly what had happened.

Nick had been having some pretty good days in kindergarten. He seemed to be enjoying school and entered into each activity with energy, not surprisingly, I have to admit. He was one big bundle! Right after lunch he told his teacher that he was done with school for the day and wanted to go home. In fact, he *was* going home. Being her perky little self she patted him on the head and told him that school wasn't finished yet and he'd have to wait a couple more hours. When she wasn't looking, he slipped out of the room, grabbed his backpack, and walked right out the front doors of the school! He had already begun his trek home when they realized he was gone. That, needless to say, set off the alarms throughout the building that signaled a child was missing. I'm sure they thought their heads were going to roll.

Nick apologized (at my insistence) and his teacher and principal left. I talked to him about the importance of staying in school until it was time to go home when Mommy was there, and the dangers of a little boy walking around by himself, even if we do live behind the school. He seemed to understand. What melted my heart was his saying, "I just wanted to be home, Mommy." I so got that.

I asked him why he had hid in the back and he said, "Because I didn't want the police to get me!" "The police? What police?" He wasn't afraid of the teacher; she was nice. He was afraid of the police (he meant the principal) and what he would do if he got him. He was nice too, but obviously not too happy at the time. And to a little five year old escapee, all he knew to do was run . . . and then hide.

Nick has always been a home-body and, in fact, tells me all the time that he's never moving out! He likes to be home with his family where his world is safe and secure and he finds rest. His heart is towards home. And I hope it always will be!

Home is a place where most of us love to be, isn't it? It's where the people we love hang out, where we can be ourselves, and where we can be at rest. One day we'll go to our Heavenly Home but until that time we have the surreal privilege of watching unbelievable scenes like the one I just described, just because a little boy knew where his heart belonged.

Dear Lord, thank You for the place we call home and the people who live there. The sweetness of Your presence is the fragrance that binds us together. In Jesus' name, Amen.

Made In His Image

~ A Reflection on Being Satisfied ~

"Finally brethren, whatever things are true, whatever things are noble, whatever things are just, whatever things are pure, whatever things are lovely whatever things are of good report, if there is any virtue and if there is anything praiseworthy – meditate on these things"(Philippians 4:8).

GIRLS ARE NOTORIOUS FOR NOT liking what they have and who they are. If they're an only child, they wish they had siblings. If they are tall, they'd rather be short. If their skin is light, they'd rather have more color. If their hair is curly, they wish it were straight. I could go on and on with the list of complaints, and I know you could too. You've heard and seen it all as well, or may have even been a complainer like I was! For some reason we like to grumble. I don't know why exactly, though I do believe it stems from basic dissatisfaction and lack of a healthy self-image. Maybe it gives us something *else* to talk about! Heaven only knows our lips never stop moving!

Deborah is our one child who wishes she were more like her friends with long, straight hair (blonde if possible), fair skin, and taller. I understand her desire to fit in, but remind her that God may want her to stand out for a reason.

It is true that Deborah's features portray her black heritage more noticeably than the traits of her siblings. She lives in a white neighborhood, with no people of color living within a few miles of our home. Her school has only a few black kids in it, mostly her brothers and sisters, plus a couple of kids who just moved to the area. Even though we try to help her appreciate her uniqueness, we know her heart longs to look like everybody else. It's a desire her dad and I can't fulfill even if we had the notion to!

As adults we can sometimes fall into the same trap, can't we? We compare ourselves to the people around us and decide we're defective or deficient because we don't have a house as nice, or a car as new. Or maybe we don't have a slim and trim body, or the curves we once had. Maybe our husbands don't make the kind of money we'd prefer, enabling us to buy the things we would enjoy having.

Our lack of strong self-confidence – not believing we have value and worth when we're created in His image (Genesis 1:27), negates the truth of God's Word. Yes, we're all different. We come in different shapes and sizes and colors. That's a good thing! How boring would it be if we were all alike?

It is perfectly acceptable to want to improve our lives, providing more money at the end of the month for those extra little things we'd like to have. But it's a sin to want it at all costs or at the expense of our first priority which is to love God. His Word clearly says, "Seek first the Kingdom of God and His righteousness, and all these things will be added to you" (Matthew 6:33).

Because of Deborah's obvious black heritage, the kids who just moved to town who have even darker skin than she has feel more of a connection with, and a sense of belonging to, their new community. They relate to Deborah in a way they can't with the other girls who are carbon copies of one another. Maybe God planned it that way all along. He knew they'd need a friend who was more like them, and He had our daughter waiting in the wings. I'd say that's a pretty good reason, and definitely one of many, to appreciate who she is and what she has to offer.

The battle with self-image, or self-esteem, or self-worth, whichever you prefer to call it, begins in the heart and moves to the mind where it is either won or lost. Let's win the war before it even gets started by appreciating the way God made us, the many wonderful blessings He has given us in our family and friends, and the love that holds us all together.

Dear Lord, thank You for making me just the way I am! I have everything I need because I have You. I love the sweetness of Your presence. In Jesus' name, Amen.

Joy For The Journey

~ A Reflection on Enjoying Life ~

"So I commended enjoyment, because a man has nothing better under the sun than to eat, drink, and be merry; for this will remain with him in his labor all the days of his life which God gives him under the sun" (Ecclesiastes 8:15).

OUR CONGREGATION SURELY THOUGHT ERIC was having a mid-life crisis when he showed up to church one Sunday riding a new Harley-Davidson motorcycle. He had ordered it several months earlier, and drove the people at the dealership crazy as the time drew nearer for him to get it. It was behavior I'd never before seen him exhibit. He was acting like a little kid at Christmas! I doubt he could've helped control the excitement had he tried.

The fact that some people didn't think a pastor should have a motorcycle, much less a HARLEY, didn't deter him from riding it. He was going to be turning fifty and was having the time of his life. The church was healthy, our relationship was strong, and the kids were all doing well in their respective places in life. Let's see, Erin was twenty-three, Sarah seventeen; Josiah eleven;

Hannah ten; Nick nine, and Deborah eight – perfect timing to decide that the open roads were for him!

He got regular rude comments from ignorant people who thought he made too much money if he could afford a new Harley. (They should have seen our budget!). But he got just as many thumbs up from others we knew, both in and outside of our congregation, who were happy for him enjoying his life. Those have become his closest riding friends to this day.

I couldn't understand why he needed to start changing things on the bike as soon as he got it. First it was loud pipes. Then it was chrome, and lots of it. He'd exchange stock parts for the ones he preferred until the bike became what it is today – sleek, fast, and loud! I love it too, but not as much as he does!

I grew up riding dirt bikes so I was familiar with how the two-wheeled machines worked. Never in my wildest dreams would I have thought I'd be a passenger on a street bike much less own one myself! But I caved to his pleadings and eventually hopped on the back – and loved it. There I was content to ride until the following year. I decided I didn't like seeing the world as a passenger. I wanted to be sitting in my own saddle! I wanted my own bike!

I knew that our budget didn't allow for another purchase. After some discussion we decided that I could get a Harley IF I got a job to pay for it. No problem! Within a couple of weeks I got a job at a furniture store as part of their design and sales team. I loved that job. I got to shop with other peoples' money! It surely satisfied my shopping itch, if only somewhat.

I had done what was necessary for me to have a bike; so now, all I had to do was find the one I wanted. I was nervous and excited at the same time. Eric took me to our new favorite place – the dealership, and I came away with a brand new 2005 Sportster 883-Low in Chopper Blue Pearl. It was awesome! I smiled all the way home!

It was soon afterwards that I knew I needed a class on safe street riding. So Eric and I enrolled in a training that spanned three days at one of the colleges in Rochester, NY. It was an excellent class. I would recommend it to anyone who is considering riding a motorcycle on the street, even if they've been riding for years. Old dogs can always learn a few new tricks too, as Eric did.

I loved my Sportster and rode it whenever possible. I, too, changed stock parts for custom chrome ones – and put loud pipes on. It was a terrific little bike (if you can ever call a Harley "little"), but it didn't seem to have the "get up and go" that I wanted on the highways. So after a year, while still working at the furniture store, I traded it in on a 2006 Dyna Low Rider in Glacier White Pearl.

I changed a lot of things on that bike too. I had learned with my Sportster why Eric wasn't happy with his bike as it was. When you get a Harley, you want to make it "yours," with your personality in add-ons. The one thing that carried over from the Sportster to the Low Rider was the Bar and Shield logo. I don't like skulls and that sort of thing, but I really liked the logo, so I kept that.

About two years after I had the Low Rider, I saw and fell in love with a new bike at the dealership. It was in Red Hot Sunglo metal flake paint and was absolutely gorgeous! It was bigger than either of my previous bikes, but once I sat on it I KNEW I had to have it! So I did the unthinkable, I traded in my Low-Rider for this Softail Deluxe, beautiful in all its ways! It's actually the bike I should've gotten when I first started shopping for a motorcycle. But it was big and heavy and I wasn't sure I could handle it. I was intimidated by the thing, (with good reason), but she and I have a good relationship today. I take care of her and do my part in keeping us both safe, and she does me proud by handling like a dream! My goodness, how I love that bike! And I know it's one I'll have for a good long while, if not the rest of my life. It's tricked out just the way I like it, with the logo, lots more chrome, (my new favorite color!), loud pipes, fringe . . . it's just amazing! My husband even bought me "blingy" side plate covers – with rhinestones filling the Bar and Shield logo on a backdrop of shiny chrome, that even further makes her more my bike. She and I have a good thing going.

The people who thought Eric was having a mid-life crisis didn't know WHAT to think when I showed up with mine the first time, or the second, or the third! As their heads shook in disbelief, their smiles conveyed their messages that they were glad I was enjoying my life, even if they couldn't comprehend my methods. Eric and I have never looked back.

There have been times when we have thought about selling them due to financial crunches but as of this writing we haven't done that. God always seem to come through at the eleventh hour so it has worked out for us to keep them. We're glad because it's our special "something" that we do together as a couple. The wind in our faces, the bugs in our teeth, the world as we roar by – it's our personal bliss in the midst of life.

Age is a state of mind. If we think we're old, then we are! But if we refuse to grow old, even though the years are clicking away, we'll have much less regret when our life comes to an end. Life is hard enough, so why not enjoy the journey as much as we can? We should be doing things that are fun and energizing, things that make us go, "Wow! I did that!"

I think mid-life crises happen when people realize their lives are half over and they haven't accomplished any of the things they had hoped they would. Don't let that be your story. It definitely won't be mine! Next on my list – a zip-line adventure! You betcha baby! Strap me in and let me go! Are you coming with me?

Dear Lord, thank You for the gift of life. The sweetness of Your presence encourages me to make the most of it. In Jesus' name, Amen.

You've Got To Be You

~ A Reflection on Distinction ~

"For we are His workmanship, created in Christ Jesus for good works, which God prepared beforehand that we should walk in them" (Ephesians 2:10).

Y OU CAN IMAGINE OUR DELIGHT when Erin came home from school one day and announced that she'd been asked to the prom! To be truthful, we didn't even know her school held proms. We were glad to hear they did, of course, and even gladder at Erin's news; but now we had some preparations to take care of immediately. The prom was only a few weeks away!

She was giddy and red-faced with excitement as she pondered the night that Charlie would take her dancing. She even told me she thought Charlie might kiss her. When I asked what she thought about that possibility she very matter-of-factly stated, "I'll kiss him right back!" Eee-gads. A prom dress and shoes were the least of my concerns. Was I ready for this? Was she?

Erin had known Charlie for years since they had been long time classmates. We had suspected that Erin liked him as more than just a friend; but in all honesty, we thought it was just a passing phase. And we certainly didn't know that he liked her back! But now here they were preparing to go to their first prom together – the first, as time would tell, of several such events.

Erin didn't want a big, poofy dress like I wanted her to get. She didn't even want cute shoes. In fact, the idea of having to shop for an acceptable outfit was anathema to her as she detested shopping! She's gotten a little better about it now that she's gotten older, but back then it was an ordeal just to get her in the car to go.

Finally, after shopping for hours and hours, we found the perfect dress! And what do you know; we found some perfectly acceptable shoes to match – shoes that she would actually wear! My friend, the beautician, came over to do her hair; together we did her make-up; and when she left the house that night, she looked absolutely beautiful! She felt like a princess too.

We lived a good distance from the school where the prom was being held. Charlie lived a good distance the other way. To make it easier on his parents we volunteered to drive Erin to the school to meet her date. As planned, they met us at the door. It was really nice to finally meet them after our many phone conversations that led up to this night.

Charlie was long and lean and Erin was short and stout. They were darling together and it was obvious they had true affection for each other!

He looked quite dapper in his three-piece suit . . . and sneakers! Eric and I quietly giggled at this fine young, handsome boy – obviously done up for his girl, who, we were told, refused to wear anything on his feet but his favorite comfortable shoes! "No need to explain," we told his parents. "We completely understand." Boy, did we ever! Erin had a strong will too and we knew that once she made up her mind that was it! Apparently Charlie was the same way.

Erin's eyes danced as she looked at her date. She sheepishly blushed as they exchanged their corsage and boutonniere. We managed to snap a few pictures but before we knew it, they disappeared through the doorway into the cafeteria that, at least for the night, had been transformed into another world. A huge disco ball, loud music, plus decorations galore set the stage for a great evening of magical fun. The feast of food that was laid out for them was an extra treat that enhanced the event.

Dance . . . oh, how they danced! Not only did Erin tell us just how much as we drove her home afterwards, we saw it for ourselves too! No, unfortunately we hadn't been asked to be chaperones, but we did manage to eyeball the prom-goers without too much notice. We became peeping Toms! Love was as much in the air on the outside of those window panes as it was inside that room. Our hearts were indeed full.

This date was a first for Erin and Charlie. Like many other things in both of their lives, it was another milestone in the maturational process called growing up. My grandmother and mother went to the prom, and so did I. It was my hope that my daughter would have the opportunity to experience a prom night of her own with all of its magic and wonder. And thankfully she did three different times with the same boy!

If we're like Erin, preparing for milestones may be a bit harder for us than for others even though they're necessary. In order to feel like a princess she had to shop for the dress, and then shoes. In order for us to walk in obedience, there may be some things we have to do that we've never done before or don't like doing. That's okay. God's grace will be with us as we step out in faith.

I like Charlie's attitude though. He knew he needed to dress up for his night out with our daughter, and he did! But he also knew his limitations and refused to wear anything on his feet but his old sneakers. I admire him for standing his ground.

What are my limitations? What are yours? We are the only ones who can answer that question for ourselves. But if we strive to do and be our very best in everything, no one should ever have reason to be disappointed. And that's the way it is!

Dear Lord, thank You for my uniqueness. The sweetness of Your presence lets me live and move and have my being. In Jesus' name, Amen.

Losers!

~ A Reflection on Prejudice ~

"As the mountains surround Jerusalem, so the Lord surrounds His people from this time forth and forever" (Psalm 125:2).

I REMEMBER SO CLEARLY THE FIRST time I encountered a bigot. I was about twenty-three. She was a much older woman whom I didn't know very well, but who regularly expressed her opinion whether it was asked for or not. She was caustic and brash, and appeared to be very lonely even though she was married with a couple of kids.

We happened to be at a group event together at a lake one summer afternoon. Everyone was having a good time when the subject of black people came up. One of the other ladies mentioned she had just begun a friendship with a black woman, and how pleasant the woman was. She wasn't focusing on the color of her new friend's skin but rather on the joy of her new friendship. It was only for point of reference that she mentioned it in the first place.

This pitiful woman, without any invitation, decided she would throw her two cents worth in to the conversation. She shared her intense dislike of black people and the experiences she had had with them, which weren't many. The kicker was when she told us how she could "smell them," as if they had a definitive odor due to their skin color. My jaw hit the floor as I sat there in disbelief, as did everyone else. I was disgusted and indignant at her crude remarks and decided at that moment I didn't like her at all.

That was the first time I ever encountered someone with such strong prejudice. I had always heard about bigots, but I had never met one until that day. And it left a lasting impression on me. Every time I remember that experience I get all riled up inside again, like how I feel right now. My heart is beating faster and I am unsettled in my spirit. The audacity of such a person! I wish I had said something to correct her, but I was pretty quiet back in those days and didn't possess the boldness I do now. And since she has long since departed this world, I won't have a chance this side of heaven to express my opinion of her opinions!

Fast forward approximately twenty-three years to 2001 when Sarah was thirteen years old. She was usually a happy little girl who had lots of friends. She was involved in sports and clubs and had a pretty active and amazing life for one so young.

One day after school Sarah and I were chatting about our day. Something seemed to be bothering her so I pressed the issue until she told me what was going on. She began telling me about some of the remarks her classmates had been saying to and about her. They made jokes about her black heritage and referred to her with disrespectful and derogatory names, even the "n" word. Apparently it had been going on for some time. As she spoke her head dropped and her gaze fell to her lap where her folded hands were now fidgeting. She said they were just kidding and trying to be funny, but I didn't find one thing comical about what I was hearing. And neither did she! Those comments cut deep, even though she didn't believe the slightest truth of those words!

All of the feelings from that first experience with the lady bigot flooded my awareness as anger rose from my heart to my mouth! How could they be so cruel to say such hurtful things? I lost all sense of Christian dignity at the moment as I railed about these clueless losers and tried to comfort my daughter!

I got right on the phone to the principal and told him exactly what I thought about what had happened. He agreed that they were out of line and that racial slurs to any degree would not be tolerated at the school! He would handle it immediately, and the guilty ones would be rebuked and held accountable. I was glad that he took that stand and defended my daughter. I only wish I could say that was the end of their remarks and she never had to deal with such ugliness again, but that wasn't the case. They were quiet for a while because they knew they were in the principal's crosshairs, but it didn't stop them once his focus shifted.

Sarah eventually learned how to handle the offenders on her own. And the more she stood up for herself, the quieter they got. It's true that the only language a bully understands is being bullied right back. It shuts them up, good and fast. Sarah didn't retaliate with the same animosity as they dished out, but she did tell them where to go and what they could do once they got there . . . in the name of Jesus of course! And that was perfectly acceptable to me.

Kids will be kids, I know that. They'll say and do stupid things that they'll later regret. I know that too. These kids who spouted those words hadn't lived long enough on the earth to decide for themselves that they didn't like a particular race. I believe they were mimicking what they heard at home.

How can we bolster our kids to defend themselves when assaults like this come? The attacks may or may not be racially-based; they could be because a child wears glasses, or is clumsy, or overweight, or maybe because she's not so good in sports. No one is out of range when a bully decides to strike.

I pray for my kids daily. I know that we live in a predominantly white area where people of color are few and far between. I encourage them to speak up and tell adults when they are the target of someone's bad jokes, even when the bully insists he was "just teasing." I remind them who they are in Christ, who their parents are, and Who their God is! I quote scriptures that reinforce their beauty and identity, putting a shield about them in the name of the Lord!

We live in a wicked and fallen world and Christians are not exempt from being targets. In fact, as we get older it can be the very reason we're targeted. Until such time as our kids can do this for themselves, we have to remind them that they aren't dumping grounds so they do not have to accept anyone else's garbage!

Let's surround our kids with so much love and fill their hearts with so much truth that they'll be able to stand in the days of adversity (Proverbs 24:10). Let's give them tools that will help them recognize the enemy when he comes. Let's also remind them who wins in the end and who has the last word. It's NOT the bully!

Dear Lord, the sweetness of Your presence reminds me who I am in Christ. Thank You for putting a hedge of protection around me and for keeping me safe. I love You. In Jesus' name, Amen.

Clearance Puppy

~ A Reflection on Surprises ~

"God sets the solitary in families" (Psalm 68:6).

THE COMFORTER ENSEMBLE ON OUR bed had been looking tired for some time. It was faded in spots and well-worn in others. It was time for a new one.

The girls and I and one of Hannah's friends headed off for the mall in search of a new comforter set. Happily we shopped from store to store in search of "the one" that would beckon to me. While there were lots of pretty sets out there, none particularly stood out over the rest. I had a specific idea in mind of what I wanted and none seemed to fit within the budget that was allotted.

I knew I should have told the girls, "No". I knew I should have deliberately gone the other way. But I caved to "kid pressure" and we did the unthinkable . . . we stopped by the pet store on our way out of the mall "just to see what they had." And weren't those puppies out front just the cutest you ever saw? Of course they were!

Naturally, they had things we could care less about – rats and snakes and other creepy things that I wouldn't give a first look to, much less a second. But in the back of the store where we heard oodles of little voices pleading with their moms and dads were the puppies my kids wanted to check out. We're a pet family for sure. My adamancy that we were "only looking" was rock solid. I knew that once we stepped to the back of the store their hearts would be touched and their pleas would start. But I was determined that they wouldn't wear me down, no matter how hard they tried!

We petted and held many of the furry little things that barked and yapped and licked our faces. All of them were darling for sure. And yes, it would be fun to watch a little four-legged baby play with Amos, our St. Bernard. But no, it wasn't an option, period!

It was then that we spied the "Clearance Puppy" in a cage all by himself. He watched as all the other puppies got held and loved. We felt bad that he was left alone and no one seemed interested in him. So we asked to hold him and, as expected, we fell in love with him immediately. Yes, even me. But why was he priced so much lower than the others? He was just as cute as the rest, maybe a little less energetic (which was good) but still he would be a great addition to any family . . . maybe even our family! I could sense my resolve fading.

The straw that broke the proverbial camel's back was when we started taking pictures of the dog and sending them to Dad for his opinion. I had never in all my married years spent this much money at one time without consultation from my husband. He had – and more, but I hadn't. I just didn't feel comfortable doing it.

As we waited for replies from home, Dad sat wondering if I'd lost my mind as certainly this was not like me! What made matters worse on our end was the fact that this puppy's brother was there with his new owner – they just happened to stop in, and she held nothing back as she spoke to us about how happy they were that they got him!

Alright already! I'll do it, but only if Dad agrees. He did of course but with this one question, "Would he make a good comforter?" Ha! We'll talk about that later!

I signed the papers, bought a few "necessary" things for a new puppy and out the door we went with our new little bundle. I was still in shock at what I had done when I pulled into the driveway an hour later.

Since I did the purchasing, Dad got to name him. Harley Oliver Scott became the newest member of our family.

The lady was right. Cavalier King Charles Spaniel and Poodle mixes (aka Cavapoos) are wonderful dogs. He's not the "smartest tool in the shed," but he's faithful and friendly and loves each and every one of us. He loves to snuggle on the couch and nestle beneath the bed covers just as much as he loves to go bye-bye in the car. (He really does think he's a person!).

No, I haven't gotten a new comforter yet. The old one still adorns our equally old bed that should be replaced at some point too. But until we save enough money to make the purchases we'll enjoy and be thankful for what we have.

Oh! And for the record, there's nothing wrong with Harley. The "bad hips" they thought he had turned out to be nothing. So we got a perfectly good puppy at a greatly reduced price.

This story really isn't about finding a good deal at a pet store. It's about seizing and embracing a blessing when it comes, even when it's not in the "package" you might have expected.

Yes, I went looking for the blessing of a new comforter set. What I found was something that looked just as cute on the bed but who does much more than just lie there. To answer Eric's question, Yes – he has become a "comforter" for he's lain by the kids' sides when they were sick, offered love and licks when they were sad, played with them when their friends weren't around, and snuggled with them when they were cold. I'd say he's the best kind of comforter that you can buy.

I pray that God fills your life with wonderful surprises too!

Dear Lord, thank You for wonderful surprises that come in small packages. The sweetness of Your presence allows me to embrace them, even when they're not quite what I was expecting. In Jesus' name, Amen.

Little Drummer Boy

~ A Reflection on Mentorship ~

"Therefore, be imitators of God as dear children, and walk in love, as Christ also has loved us and given Himself for us" (Ephesians 5:1-2a).

WHEN JOSIAH WAS AN ADOLESCENT, he asked if he could learn to play the trumpet. We told him, "Of course," and rented an instrument through the school band department. He played that thing pretty well, earning "first chair" in the trumpet section of his band for a brief period of time. After a few years, however, he lost interest in the trumpet and band altogether. We were disappointed because he really had an ear for it, and ability, but we weren't going to force him to play if he really didn't want to.

What we didn't know was that he had really wanted to learn to play the drums. When he approached the band teacher about learning them, he was told, "No," and that he "should learn to play the trumpet." That's why he asked us about the trumpet in the first place instead of the drums, and then after a couple of years, lost interest in it altogether. His heart wasn't in the trumpet.

He was almost thirteen when he began hounding us about taking drum lessons. He was about fourteen when we were finally able to find a qualified teacher. Amazingly, one was right in our midst the whole time. The drummer at our church had one more year of high school to complete before he'd be leaving for college, so he agreed to give Josiah lessons after church each Sunday, which was very convenient and doable for us! The first few months of lessons were monotonous for Josiah. While he wanted to get on the whole drum set and really thump away on them, Rob took one drum into a back room to teach Josiah the basics. Over and over, Sunday after Sunday, they'd go through the basics, again and again. Josiah never said he wanted to quit, but I knew he wanted more from his lessons. Still, he was faithful to practice and go through it each time Rob gave direction, never complaining, never asking to do anything more, just being obedient to his teacher. He had submitted himself to Rob's tutelage and knew he had to do it his way.

One Sunday a few months into the lessons, quite to Josiah's surprise, Rob didn't take him in the back room, but to the big drum set. Josiah had learned the menial, routine reiterations to the degree they were now "in him," and Rob knew he was now ready to step it up and move on to the next level. Josiah understands now that Rob was building the foundation for his drum playing with those tedious repetitions, and appreciates the fact that Rob made him go through them. He realizes he couldn't jump to steps B or C without first learning step A.

Josiah learned how to play the drums well through the whole process – yes, but he learned much more than that. He learned that any new skill, craft, or trade is worth learning the right way. If you want to be good at it, you've got to take the time for the monotonous rituals – building the foundation, before you can advance. It's kind of like the story in the Bible about the man who built his house upon a rock in Matthew 7:24-25. He built it for the long haul to withstand the storms of life. In music, if you don't put forth the effort to build from the ground up, you'll either not master the instrument, or you'll lose interest and quit playing altogether.

Josiah continues to play the drums on one of our church worship teams. He's been faithful to practice at home and attends worship practices each week. He's doing very well; and he's being stretched with each new song he has to learn. I beg to differ with that band teacher who told him he shouldn't learn to play.

The story doesn't stop there though. Like Josiah, when he pursued Rob in order to learn how to play the drums, there's been a young boy in our church who has now been pursuing Josiah for lessons. And what has Josiah been doing with him? Taking him in the back room of course – going through the basics, week after week, Sunday after Sunday. When the time is right, Josiah will move him to the big drum set and teach him a few more new things.

We are so proud of our son who has not only been enriched in his own life, but who is now sowing into someone else's. He's giving back, and he's happy to be doing it. Of course there's a little stipend to compensate for time spent with this young boy, but that's not the sole reason he's doing it. It's nice and he appreciates it, but he also remembers when he had a dream too.

Let's make that our aim as well. Each of us is good at something, whether it's our musical talent, organizational skills, parenting a toddler, or something else. It could be anything. Someone we know, or will come to know, could benefit greatly by our willingness to share what wisdom we've learned and what tasks we've conquered. Mentorship doesn't have to be a long, drawn-out process, though it can be. Sometimes it's as simple as answering a question.

Dear Lord, thank You for equipping me for life. The sweetness of Your presence encourages me to sow into others' lives, and allow them to sow into mine, so all of us are blessed. We give You all the glory. In Jesus' name, Amen.

Sarah Bernhardt, or Not

~ A Reflection on Truth and Lies ~

"You shall no longer be termed Forsaken, nor shall your land any more be termed Desolate; but you shall be called Hephzibah, and your land Beulah; for the Lord delights in you" (Isaiah 62:4).

MY SISTER, KAREN, WAS THE drama queen of the family when we were growing up. Boy, could she pour it on at the blink of an eye. If she was trying to get her own way, she'd beg, plead and carry on like her request was her last and only dying wish – often times with real tears! When she was happy she'd be giddy and playful, always trying to draw others in to her act. While most of us were fairly predictable with our even temperaments, she had the ability to tear you to shreds with her words one minute, and love you with affection the next. She was the flavor of the family – like salt and pepper. She was also the one that gave my parents their "second-most" gray hairs. I came in first in that department! Tragically, Karen died when she was just thirty-six years old from breast cancer, leaving behind a husband and two daughters. Our family lost so much when we lost her. All of us miss her a lot.

When Karen would act up, my mom would refer to her as "Sarah Bernhardt." All I knew about Sarah Bernhardt was that she was an actress who lived many years ago. It wasn't until recently that I found out anything more about her. To be truthful, she was a bizarre person! She was born in 1844 and died in 1923. She was a bit of wild child who had a flair for the outrageous. At age fifteen she bought a rosewood coffin which she sometimes slept in. It is reported that, by the time she died, it was lined with letters from her stated one-thousand lovers. Can you imagine? Me neither. She was French, and the first great stage actress to appear in the medium of cinema films. She preferred playing characters that died at drama's end too. I can very easily picture the fainting couch in my mind – with her on it, as the curtains close and the audience cheers for more. She had a lion and six chameleons for household pets. I don't know why normal family pets wouldn't do, like a cat and dog, and maybe a goldfish, but if she wanted to be known for her fondness of wild animals, she certainly was! I wonder if she took any of them for walks – you know, to do "their duty." One of her peculiar tastes was her collection of chairs, which I, personally, find a bit odd just like everything else I have learned about her. I know many people who have collections of one thing or another, but she's the first that I know of to collect chairs. Just where did she put them all? She was only twenty when she gave birth to her only child in 1864. (One-thousand lovers and only one child?) Her son's father was Belgian Prince Henri de Ligne. She did marry a Greek diplomat, Aristide Damala, eighteen years after her son was born, but they were only married until the time of his death in 1898. I have to wonder what made him so special that she'd marry him. She was a widow for twenty-five years after her husband's death. Truly, she lived a unique life.

As Hannah entered toddlerhood, she too had an affinity for the dramatic. She could throw two-year old tantrums with the best of them. She could turn on the charm too. As she has gotten older, she knows just what nerve of mine needs to be played on to get what she wants. Sometimes it's hard resisting those big brown eyes and the darling girl behind them. She has always been able to make me laugh at her outrageous acts which are pretty frequent nowadays. Sometimes she'll grab me in the kitchen while I'm trying to make dinner and tango with me across the kitchen floor – cheek to cheek, hand in hand. At times she'll sing to me to soften me, and then drop her specific request in the middle of her performance. Yes, she's quite the actress too. It's no wonder I used to refer to her as Sarah Bernhardt just like my mom did to my sister.

It wasn't long after I found out about the real Sarah Bernhardt's life and reputation that my husband and I decided we needed to come up with another nickname for her. Sarah Bernhardt may have been a great stage actress, but she was a really weird person with traits that I don't want my daughter identified with. I'm still trying to come up with an actress's name that fits Hannah's personality and wholesomeness, but so far I've not come up with one.

I would assume that many of us have pet names, or nicknames, for at least one or two loved ones in our lives. How wonderful! I believe they are (or should be) names of affection and endorsement, perhaps names that sum up the person's personality or habits. Perhaps they are names that suggest accomplishment, goals desired, or places the person has travelled. As long as they are encouraging, they should be acceptable. Never would we want to refer to someone by a name that belittles them, causes shame or discouragement, or suggests failure. But you don't need me to tell you that.

It's not uncommon to give ourselves nicknames too, yet most of the time those names are not necessarily positive. For instance, I have never called myself, "Beautiful One," even though I resemble my Father in Heaven and that's one of His names. For many years I wore the name, "Rejected," because I was the only one without a baby when everyone in my life was having one. Even those who weren't trying to get pregnant got pregnant! That name affected everything I did and said – the way I carried myself and the way I spoke. I didn't present myself as having it together, but rather as dejected and defeated. The enemy spoke that name into my heart and I accepted, believed it, and embraced it. It was a lie. The truth is – I am accepted in the Beloved (Ephesians 1:6), blessed, and a blessing (Genesis 12:2). God delights in me (Isaiah 62:4)! I am not rejected! And neither are you!

Once I got ahold of God's Word, I was able to disassociate myself from the lie the enemy perpetrated by embracing the Truth of God's Word. Whenever I hear the name, Sarah Bernhardt, I think about my sister immediately. It was her pet name for so many years I can't help myself, even though Karen was nothing like Sarah except for her ability to entertain. It's easier to separate

Hannah from Sarah because I'm more knowledgeable now about Sarah's life, Hannah is still young, and we have stopped calling her by that name.

While you wait for the fulfillment of God's promises, believe His Truth. "Thus says the LORD, who makes a way in the sea and a path through the mighty waters, "Do not remember the former things, nor consider the things of old. Behold, I will do a new thing, now it shall spring forth; shall you not know it? I will even make a road in the wilderness and rivers in the desert" (Isaiah 43:16, 18-19).

God loves you, and He is up to something. "Blessed" is His nickname for you.

Dear Lord, the sweetness of Your presence helps me discern between Truth and lies. Thank You for Your Word which reminds me who I am, and more importantly, Who You are! In Jesus name, Amen.

We are FAMILY

~ A Reflection on Love ~

"For this reason I bow my knees to the Father of our Lord Jesus Christ, from whom the whole family in heaven and earth is named" (Ephesians 3:15).

I DON'T KNOW WHAT IT IS about old people – I just love them. Shortly after we got saved in 1985, we became friends with an elderly man who attended our church. Fred was in failing health and alone, so we spent as much time with him as possible until he passed away, which wasn't long after we met him. He entertained us with his stories of days gone by, and sincerely appreciated our attention to his life, especially since there was no one else to look after him.

Twenty-some years later, in another place and time, we became friends with yet another elderly man from church. Lloyd was approaching seventy when we met him – not old by today's standards, except that his mind was faltering and his body was thin and frail. Even so, he still lived in the same house in which he was born and raised. His parents and brothers had long since died; but he seemed to be getting along just fine, at least until he took one too many spills where he couldn't get up without help.

A friend of the family, who regularly stopped to check on Lloyd, happened by one afternoon to find him shivering on the bathroom floor. He had fallen again. We were in the midst of another northeast winter and it was really cold – even in the house! That prompted the family friend to start the paperwork so Lloyd could move into a skilled nursing facility where he would receive the care and oversight he needed. Lloyd didn't want to move, of course. He liked the independence of his own home. But he needed to go. His well-being was at stake.

Not long before he moved into that facility, about eighty-five of our church members planned to go on a white-water rafting trip down the Genesee River in Letchworth State Park. Lloyd REALLY wanted to go! We weren't too sure if he'd be able to handle it; but we agreed to let him participate if the organization we were rafting with was amenable. They were!

It was a fabulous trip! We started the day with quick instructions from our experienced leaders, put on our life vests, and set out for the river. Lloyd was driven down to the water's edge while the rest of us walked from the administration building, but he had just as much enthusiasm as the rest of us as we anticipated the day ahead. He had spunk, that guy, and chatted with the driver all the way to where the rest of us waited. We loved it that he was having such a good time already – and we hadn't even gotten started yet.

Lloyd could barely get into his raft so we knew he wouldn't be able to handle and use a paddle, much less use it while sitting on the raft's edge. He finally stumbled over the side and landed on the raft's bottom where he promptly stayed the entire day – butt down, and grinning face up. He quickly adopted a "peel me a grape attitude" as the three trained instructors, two in the front and one in the back, paddled his raft from the start of the trip to its very end. You could hear Lloyd laughing and having a good time the entire day, sometimes yelling, "Whee!" like a little boy. It was a great time, made even better because Lloyd got to experience it with us.

I'm so glad Lloyd got to participate in adventurous activities even though his body was breaking down. His sheer will allowed him to accomplish things he would have otherwise never gotten to do. He loved life; and he loved living it with the people who cared about him.

From the day that Lloyd moved to the nursing home, his body went rapidly downhill. Dementia and marks of disease finally ran their courses, and Lloyd went to be with Jesus. His passing left a huge hole in our hearts. True, it took us extra time to go anywhere or do anything when he was with us because he walked, ate, and got to the points of his stories so slowly, but we loved him. And we knew he had loved us in return. We had become family.

To me, "family" isn't just those who are born or marry into a family tree. Family extends beyond those borders to those who are connected in the heart. In some cases, the sense of connection can be stronger than between blood relatives. I know I feel a particular family bond with those whom I worship with every week, and those on whom I can always count – my friends. I am grateful for each and every one who has enriched my life just by them being in it.

Lloyd may not have been a relative in the literal sense, but he was family just the same. And because he was family, we made time for him – including him in family activities and spending time with him, even when it would have been easier in the long run not to.

Who is your "family?" Who are you connected to at the heart? It may be those in your family tree, but it might also include a few elderly men or women who are lonely and alone. Whoever it is, make sure you make memorable moments together that will be relived for years to come. They'll appreciate the time you invest in recognizing the significance of their lives; and you'll be blessed in return – in much greater measure. And that, dear sister, is what family is all about!

Dear Lord, I love it that You have surrounded me with people to love. The sweetness of Your presence helps me to appreciate each of them for the wonderful blessings they are, and to make the most of our times together. I love You. In Jesus' name, Amen.

Who Needs a Picnic Table Anyway?

~ A Reflection on Pace Maintenance and Priorities ~

"I will instruct you and teach you in the way you should go; I will guide you with My eye" (Psalm 32:8).

ERIC AND I HAVE BEEN motorcycle enthusiasts for a long time – years in fact. Our kids had wanted to learn to ride motorcycles for quite a while too, so we saved enough money to buy a couple of dirt bikes, a Honda 70 and a Honda 50, – perfect sizes for our young children at the time.

The kids sat patiently and listened intently to Dad as he explained everything he knew about motorcycles – how they worked and what each part's function was, how to use them, what not to do when riding, and what to do if something went wrong. He also explained the reasons for wearing safety equipment – helmets and long pants, shoes that went above the ankle, and coats. The kids were eager to get on the bikes so one by one, after the lecture was over, they each took a turn around the yard. They all did great! I can't say I was too surprised. After all, look who their models are!

As their confidence grew, their speed increased, giving us reason to keep an even closer eye on them. The motorcycles became the kids' favorite pastimes. But since they weren't allowed on the bikes unless Dad or I were home and able to watch them, they didn't get to ride them as often as they would have liked. Still, they maintained good attitudes about it.

One day the kids had the bikes out while Eric was outside doing something in the yard. A friend was over visiting with Eric, and I was just coming home from the store. When I left all was well. Peace and harmony abounded in our yard where all of the activity was. When I returned my picture-perfect day was disintegrating right before my eyes!

As I drove up our driveway I could hear Eric yelling continuously at Nick, who was on the Honda 50, to "Lay OFF the throttle" as he chased after him! I pulled in just in time to see Nick slam into our hand-made Hemlock picnic table which sat in the front yard under one of our biggest trees. Nick didn't lay off the throttle. He rammed that picnic table with such force, that it fell over in one big heap from the continuous pressure against it. Eric, out of breath, caught up to Nick about the same time the picnic table collapsed, incredulous as to what had just happened!

"Why didn't you stop?" asked Dad. "I didn't know how to!" replied Nick. At that moment Eric and I realized that Nick needed more intensive training before getting on the bike again! Eric's heart eventually calmed, but the reality of what could have happened haunted him for days.

Our friend picked up the remnants of our once-standing, big, heavy picnic table. He made a nice pile of the pieces so if Eric got the chance at some future point, he could try to put it together again. We weren't sure how it would look afterwards, but it was worth a try. I'm happy to report that the picnic table stands in its place to this day. It has a few dings, dents, and gouges that remind us of its earlier misfortune, but Eric did a fine job putting it back together again.

I can identify with both Nick and the table in this story. Like Nick, sometimes I get going so fast through life that I forget how to slow down, or that I even need to. The demands of my busy life keep me going from thing to thing; and if I'm not careful, I can end up exhausted and frustrated.

Like the table, sometimes I get mowed down and kicked off my footing by the crazy things that happen in the course of a day. It's when I don't see them coming that I'm most susceptible.

So today's lesson is two-fold. One, maintain your speed. Don't go so fast that you wear yourself out and end up regretting your existence. Don't go so slowly that you never get anything accomplished. There will be days when you'll need to speed it up or slow it down from your normal pace, but those days should be the exception and not the rule. Enjoy the journey. If there is no joy and only chaos, take a deeper look and see what can be changed to improve your life.

Two, honor your priorities. Take time for the important things first. It's when I get taken down that I remember I haven't prayed, or stood on God's Word, or praised His holy name! The enemy of our souls wants to knock us down and keep us there, but he'll not have an easy time of it if we're securely grounded.

Nick still likes to ride motorcycles as much as the other kids. We let him, though we insist he keep his speed under control and that he stay away from the yard furniture. It's a copacetic arrangement that keeps us both happy.

Dear Lord, thank You that You show me good balance for my life that brings both joy and productivity. The sweetness of Your presence gives me joy for the journey. In Jesus' name, Amen.

Angels on Duty

~ A Reflection on God's Protection ~

"For He shall give His angels charge over you, to keep you in all your ways"
(Psalm 91:11).

BEING A LARGE FAMILY OUR vehicles are constantly in motion, running kids to and from sports activities, doctor appointments, friends' houses, school, and just about everywhere imaginable. We put hundreds of miles on them each month. We also sink lots of money into repairs when needed to keep them operational. Being down a car means life stops for this family.

Deborah has always liked going in the car just for the sake of going. Most of the time we don't mind, but sometimes it's just plain inconvenient. When I want to slip out of the house and make a quick run to the store, I'll invariably hear her little voice yell, "Wait for me! I want to go too!" Dinner will be on the table and I just need some milk real quick. "Do you HAVE to go, Deb?" I'll ask. I already know the answer before the question is even asked. "YES!" Truthfully, this drives me crazy when I'm pressed for time. It's so much easier when I can hop in the car, drive to the store, buy the milk, get back in the car, and drive back home. I don't have to wait for her to get her shoes and seatbelt on, and tell her, "No," when she asks for other things in the store we're not there to buy. Customarily I let her go, even though it takes longer, unless there's a pretty good reason why she can't.

Like her brothers and sisters before her, Deborah learned to ski when she was quite young. It came as natural to her as riding a bike. She was good at it too, and we were impressed, me especially, who still hasn't quite mastered it gracefully. As each night or weekend came for her dad to serve on the Ski Patrol, we'd repeatedly hear her chime in, "I'm going too," and off she'd go to gather her things! She got her ride AND was able to ski with Dad for several hours – a double bonus!

Eric is a pretty good skier. When he is patrolling, he makes several runs down each hill before taking a break. And Deb, not wanting to leave his side, skis right behind him hour after hour while they remain on the hill. I'm sure it has been this activity, time after time, that has perfected her skills. She'd be a good candidate for the ski team at her school, that's for sure.

It was the last day of the ski season. Spring had finally sprung and the climbing temperatures were melting the snow slowly, making it like mashed potatoes – lumpy, bumpy and sticky. Deb and her dad had been skiing all afternoon and were preparing for their last run before they headed for home. It had been a good day!

They headed over to Last Will, the black diamond slope that only expert skiers dare to ski, and Deb decided she didn't want to follow Dad this time – she wanted to go first! She had skied this hill with him several times before so Eric didn't think a thing about it. "Sure," he said, "go ahead." Over the top of the head wall she went. Dad scooted over to the edge just in time to see his daughter doing flying cartwheels in the air. With an abrupt stop she landed in a heap, her feet completely out of her boots. She isn't a crier like her sister, but the pain she was experiencing brought lots of tears. Eric knew she had done it this time, but to what extent he wasn't sure. Another patroller helped Eric get her down off the hill, and Eric called me at home. I needed to take her to the hospital for further examination.

I left instructions for the other kids whom I had to leave at home. I didn't dilly-dally getting to the ski resort where Deb was. As the patrollers loaded her up in the back of my car, Deb recounted the whole story in living detail.

The long and the short of it is this – she was doing fine but going too fast. The snow grabbed her skis as she tried to make a turn over one of the bumps and she was abruptly yanked out of her boots and over the front of her skis. And now her leg hurt mid-way up her calf.

Well, this is one car ride Deb wished she could've sat out. She was in pain and very anxious about going to the hospital. With each mile I reassured her that everything was going to be okay; she just needed to relax. We made it there in record time and the nursing staff met us at the car.

"Is it broken?" I asked. After x-rays it was determined that Deb had a green stick fracture at the very place where the top of her ski boot rested on her leg. A moving target had met an immovable force. The two didn't work too well together.

Deb came home with a bright blue cast that spanned the length of her leg from her toes clear to the top of her thigh. She also sported a pair of shiny crutches that helped her get around after a few days' rest on the couch.

I thank God that her condition wasn't worse because it certainly could have been. Broken bones heal over time, but a life lost is just that – lost. And this is one situation that very easily could have turned out quite differently. Skiing is dangerous, and we know it. That's why I'm so glad our angels never stop to rest even when we do.

Deb had three different casts over the course of her healing. The crutches lasted only a few weeks before she learned how to walk with her new red walking cast. Her favorite was the final air cast that allowed for full bathing. I understand that completely.

I'm sure that you, like me, have wondered how you escaped a car accident when you thought you were headed right for one, or didn't break your ankle when you missed the bottom step on the stairs, or slipped in the shower on that soap! How about when your child stepped in front of a car and it didn't hit him, or the attacking dog all of a sudden decided to go another way?

God's Word tells us that He has assigned His angels to us for our protection. Aren't you glad He has? Where would we be if it were not so? I can think of several times when I should have died from foolish last-minute decisions while driving, or stupid things that only cost me a twisted ankle or arm. Let's remember that God's heart is for us, and part of that is keeping us safe.

Dear Lord, I love the sweetness of Your presence, everywhere I go, and in everything I do. Thank You for always being with me. In Jesus' name, Amen.

Christmas Socks

~ A Reflection on Holiday Spirit ~

"The light shines in the darkness, and the darkness did not comprehend it"
(John 1:5).

I LOVE CHRISTMAS, AS MOST OF you probably do too. I love everything about the holiday season – twinkling lights, music-filled air, gift exchanging, family get-togethers, Christmas programs at church, and socks – Christmas socks to be exact. My growing collection of the silly things suggests just how much. I have red ones, green ones, black ones, white ones, and blue ones, some with stripes, polka dots or a combination of the two. Some have snowballs or snowmen, mittens, candy canes, Santa Clauses, or reindeer. Some have little sayings like, "Ho Ho Ho," "'Tis the Season," or "Merry Christmas." Each year as stores put out their Christmas things, I'm one of the first in line to peruse their sock stock, to see what the new styles are, and which ones I must buy for myself and friends. I actually have a hard time choosing because I like them all. Christmas socks make me happy – they add to my holiday mood, making me feel festive. So, from the Friday after Thanksgiving to a week or so into the New Year, they are the only things I wear on my feet besides shoes.

Christmas is a time to rejoice, be happy, and celebrate the Lord's birth. It's a time to reconnect with old friends, and make new ones. It's a time for feasting (definitely not fasting!) and a time to decorate our world. That's why we put up trees in our living rooms, lights on our houses, and garlands on our staircases and mantles. It's also the reason we wear colorful holiday sweaters and throw neighborhood parties.

I realize that the commercialism of the holiday tries to detract from the true meaning of Christmas. To a certain degree it has affected all of us. But if we keep the Reason for the Season as our focus, then it won't matter how loudly merchants' ads cry to us to buy their wares. We will be better able to keep things in perspective, and our gift-buying within our means.

I also realize that the Christmas season can be a really stressful time for some who already feel overwhelmed. Instead of it being a magical and wonderful time, it can be a period that adds to the growing pressures of raising a family on a very limited income, requiring we shop and wrap when we'd rather take a nap, or attend usually-enjoyable get-togethers when we'd prefer to stay home. Our kids' eyes dance as they read us their Christmas lists. Parents, no matter how much they'd like to get these things for their children, are required to pick and choose, often times settling for less. The demands on our time and pocket books can rise to unimaginable heights as Christmas Day approaches. Did you know that there are more suicides and suicide attempts during the holiday season than any other? I was shocked to learn this.

As Christians, our mission in life is to be salt and light to a dark and hurting world. We should shine brightly in the darkness. The joy in our hearts should be reflected to everyone we know and encounter. And that joy should be infectious, sprinkling out everywhere we go. Our demeanor – with smiles, affirmation, encouragement, and blessing, should mirror the hope we hold dear in our hearts. While some grumble and complain, our mission should be to smile, be cheery, and demonstrate holiday spirit.

In comparison to the symbols of true Christmas celebration – angels proclaiming Good News, shepherds tending their flocks, wise men following a star, and a baby born in a lowly manger, festive socks don't even rank with the truth of those other things. Yet, somehow they add a childlike joy to the whole holiday experience.

Whatever form it takes, spread a little holiday cheer wherever you go. Wish strangers on the street a "Merry Christmas," bake your favorite cookies with your kids, turn up the music and sing along when the radio plays Christmas carols, and buy at least two pairs of Christmas socks – one for you to keep, and one to give away. In the grander scheme of things, they mean absolutely nothing. But if they make you happy, they'll certainly make someone else happy too.

Dear Lord, thank You for coming as a baby and living in our hearts forever. The sweetness of Your presence reminds me of the real reason we celebrate. In Jesus' name, Amen.

Graduating With Honors

~ A Reflection on Accomplishment ~

The Lord will perfect that which concerns me; Your mercy, O Lord, endures forever; do not forsake the work of Your hands" (Psalm 138:8).

I DON'T KNOW ABOUT YOU, BUT I enjoy going to high school graduations. I like to watch the kids I knew as babies, now grown and moving into the next phase of their lives, walk across that platform and receive the evidence of a job well done – their diplomas. The smiles on their faces portray the inner feelings of accomplishment and satisfaction. The spring in their steps suggests an "I Did It" attitude! In the audience are the families who prayed for and raised those kids, who also possess that same sense of accomplishment. It's a great day for everyone involved.

The opportunity to be recognized for having completed this important segment of their lives is just as important, if not more so, for kids with special needs. They have had to work especially hard to master even the most basic of skills, let alone achieve academic competency.

When we moved to New York we enrolled Erin in an extraordinary school that served only kids with special needs. She had a tailor-made program that helped fine tune the areas she was good at, as well as strengthen the areas that needed work. It was a wonderful environment for her as she was surrounded by her peers – other kids like her, and teachers and faculty who absolutely loved their jobs! The feelings of love and appreciation for each student permeated the classrooms and hallways of that school, and we were very blessed that Erin had been afforded the opportunity to be a student there for many years. She grew so much during her tenure. The attention to life skills helped to prepare her for life as an adult – holding down a job, interacting with the world, and living "on her own."

Individual Education Programs in the United States provide for school attendance through age twenty-one if desired, giving the student an extra three years of educational opportunity. We opted for this extension because we believed it would be beneficial to Erin's overall development. So it was, on a warm sunny day in June 2004, at age twenty-one, that Erin graduated from high school. She had that same spring in her step and smile on her face as every other graduate we had ever encountered.

We prepared for graduation day as we would for any of our kids. We shopped for a suitable outfit and shoes as well as an appropriate gift to commemorate the day! We brought flowers, and shouted cheers of pride as her name was called and she made her way across the stage to the principal of the school who held her reward.

What touched me is that each student also graduated "with honors," not honors for best achievement, but honors that spotlighted a quality the student was known for – Best Smile, Best Friend, Best Helper, Hardest Worker, Fastest Runner, Best Ball Thrower, Best Laugh, and so on. The kids practically ran back up to the platform to receive their honorable mentions while the audience clapped and cheered even louder than before. And they basked in the glory of the moment as they stood center stage in front of a filled auditorium.

It was the best graduation ceremony of any I'd ever attended, and not just because it was Erin's. The teachers and faculty had determined, as probably they'd done all the many years prior, to make it a day of remembrance, a day of celebration, and a day of personal appreciation for the extra effort these precious ones had exerted in order to make it to this day. This mama's heart was as full as it could be with gratitude for the many years of experience Erin had received at this wonderful school, and the privilege I had of being a part of this most delightful day.

Graduating from high school is a maturational experience that is marked with pride and achievement. It also signals a new facet of life that will be marked with more challenges. It's important that we stay focused as we reach for our dreams.

If adopting children is a goal that you sincerely want to obtain, then stay in the process. Don't give up because you have to attend classes, or write papers, or have a home study, or pay money. Set your mind on the prize – the end result, the fulfillment of your efforts. Give yourself an "IEP" if you need one, with plans and strategies that will help you get there. Jesus is in the audience waiting for your name to be called. And He has some "honors" He wants to bestow on you as well. I can only imagine what they might be.

Dear Lord, I love the sweetness of Your presence as I accomplish every task and reach my goals. In Jesus' name, Amen.

Who Cares?

~ A Reflection on Appreciation ~

"... recognize those who labor among you ..."(1 Thessalonians 5:12)

SARAH BECAME INTERESTED IN SPORTS about the time she entered kindergarten. Throughout elementary school she earned quite a few awards for her long jump, mile run and ball throw. As she progressed through middle school she participated in modified sports, specifically soccer and track, though she did have a brief interest in basketball too. In high school, she played the position of sweeper on her soccer teams and participated in the 4x1 relay, long jump, and triple jump in track.

We were glad that Sarah got involved in sports. We knew she had natural talents and abilities that would be a good foundation on which her coaches could build to make her an incredible athlete. Apparently, they saw potential in her too. With each passing year and more practices, games, and meets than I care to count, she became a force to be reckoned with as they helped her hone her skills. This solidified her reputation as a strong athlete. In eighth grade, even though she was still in middle school, she was the only girl awarded with a high school varsity letter. Sadly, we didn't know about this honor until after the fact. We never received a letter from the school regarding the award or the sports banquet at which it would be given, and Sarah never bothered to tell us when she found out. Apparently, at the time, she didn't realize how much of a big deal it was, so she didn't pay close attention to the athletic director as he spoke to her about it. As a consequence, she missed the glory of the whole experience, and so did we! She was handed her "K" during gym class the day after the banquet, and that was that! How very disappointing for us all!

Sarah never participated in sports for the recognition, though that came with each track meet or game she played. She was a formidable opponent who did her job well. Our little brown-eyed, curly-haired antagonist made her coaches and family very proud, and the opposing team very wary as they came up against her.

We didn't encourage her to compete for the recognition it brought. We believe that if you're going to do something though, do it with all of your heart and to the best of your ability, "as unto the Lord." A by-product of hard work and diligence is recognition, not necessarily for how well you actually did, but for how hard you tried. People do take notice, even though they don't express it as often as they should.

I feel good when someone acknowledges my efforts, whether I am completely successful in reaching my goal or not. The fact that I tried is what is important. The fact that someone else noticed my effort and appreciated it is like chocolate frosting on a chocolate cake.

My goal for today's story is to encourage us to be more vocal in our appreciation of others as they serve us. In our families, churches, and community we have many servants who give of their free time because they want to make a difference. I think of my older kids who have watched the younger ones so that I didn't have to cancel a much-needed hair appointment when my other arrangements fell through at the last minute. I also think of our Sunday school teachers and nursery workers who teach, care for, and interact with our kids so that we can be attentive in the morning service and enjoy the time with the other adults in attendance. How about our school board members? They give countless, tiresome hours in an effort to be problem-solvers and not problem-makers as they attempt to make good decisions in regard to our children's educations and learning environments.

Do we ever take time to tell them, "Thank you?" We may not always agree with their decisions, but they should be commended for their efforts.

I want us to be mindful today of those who serve us, making our lives better, more manageable, or easier in one way or another. Let's remember to tell them we appreciate them. We can write them a note, call them on the phone, or stop them in the market when we see them. And we shouldn't just do it once and forget about it. Periodically we should remind them. Our appreciation may very well be the words of encouragement they need to keep doing what they do, their "letter," if you will, of service, accomplishment, and importance to us. In our church we have yearly acknowledgements for our workers and servants as a small token of appreciation for all of their hard work. These times of recognition go a long way. However, the personal touch and impartation by those whom they serve goes a lot further.

I am reminded of Aaron (Moses' brother), and Hur (Moses's friend), who upheld Moses's arms when he was weary (Exodus 17:10-12). When Moses's arms were raised, his army prevailed against the Amalekites. When his arms were lowered, the enemy prevailed. The encouragement from his friends made all the difference in the world.

All of us could use a little extra juice – encouragement and appreciation, for our batteries. (And since we can, we know others can too.). So let's purpose today to acknowledge those people in our lives who bless us by their service. However we do it, let's honor them by recognizing their efforts. God's Word says we should, so let's get started!

Dear Lord, thank You for helping me to be mindful of those who labor in my midst. The sweetness of Your presence fills their lives as they serve, and mine as I receive their blessing. In Jesus' name, Amen.

Chips Anonymous

~ A Reflection on Confession ~

"Confess your trespasses to one another, and pray for one another, that you may be healed" (James 5:16).

I THINK I SHOULD START A 12-step program for people like me. No, it's not drugs or alcohol to which I'm addicted – it's potato chips! You may laugh but I'm serious! I've tried so many times before to stay away from them, but it's the one thing that's knocked me off my diet wagon more times than I care to count. Even this afternoon, right before I sat down to write this piece, I had myself a few big hands full. I don't know what it is about those savory little devils – I just love them!

I do know people who have struggled with bigger things. Alcohol has damaged many relationships I've known, as has drug use. I've seen the ugly grip each has had on its victims. It's really very sad.

For those who have no addictions, or pet comfort foods, or habits they wish they could unload, I applaud you! For the rest of us though, it's a battle each and every day. I've gotten to where I don't buy the kind I love the most because I KNOW I won't stay out of them.

Sometimes I can go for days with a strong resolve to steer clear of the pantry where they're kept. But then the urge to eat that salt and crispy yumminess overwhelms me till I cave in to the longing. Sometimes it takes no effort at all to stay away. Other times it only takes a glance and I'm done for.

Potato chips may be my downfall. What's yours? Is there something in your life that you'd like to once and for all be done with? Just as I know Jesus is my Helper, He's also yours. When He gives deliverance, we need to walk in discipline . . . which is something I wish I had more of!

This is kind of a crazy confession, I know. Heaven only knows there are other, more "impressive" things I could talk about in my life. But this is the one thing that gets me over and over, and it's worth my being transparent about it even if you laugh. If for no other reason, it will give you something to pray about if you are inclined to pray for me.

Let us remember that we're all fighting a hard battle every day. Your friend's personal struggle may not be the same as yours, but it's a battle just the same. Anything we can do to lighten another's load and bring encouragement will always be appreciated.

Dear Lord, the sweetness of Your presence helps me to pray for my friends and family who face battles every day. Thank You for being their very present help in time of trouble, and for being mine too. I love You. In Jesus' name, Amen.

Daniel Boone Wannabes

~ A Reflection on Heeding Dad's Instruction ~

"Now therefore, listen to me, my children; pay attention to the words of my mouth" (Proverbs 7:24).

I CAN HEAR THE LYRICS PLAYING in my head every time I think of Eric and his muzzle loader or bow perched in a tree in our woods, "Daniel Boone was a man . . ." You probably don't remember that song because you weren't born yet. This tune was the theme song to the television show where the adventures of Mr. Boone were shared. He was a hunter and trapper and regular nice guy, but the thing I remembered the most about him were the dead animals on his head and the fact that he hunted everything he ate! Neither of those qualities appeals to me, but they make my husband feel all warm and fuzzy inside! He was born one hundred years too late, I tell him. In fact, he's happiest when he's strapped in a tree-stand in the frigid winter *alone*! And he's taught his sons to be the exact same way.

It all started years ago when he was a boy. He and his brother would pick off squirrels and other unsuspecting animals on their overnights alone in the woods by their house. They were quite young at the time which makes me wonder how their mother let them shoot guns unsupervised. Wasn't she afraid of one of them putting the other's eye out? If you know them like I know them, I wouldn't put it past them. It would have been a very real possibility.

Their days of "plunkin' vermin" together lasted through high school until they each went their separate ways. It wasn't until they were much older and living in the same area that they took it to another level.

Eric calls them "rendezvouses;" I call them ridiculous. A bunch of normal (I use the term loosely) men *and women* get together and act like they did in the old days. They all wear hides on their bodies for clothes, dead animals on their heads for hats, and bones for jewelry. They each carry a tomahawk and musket and compete in different games that Eric has won a few times. No coolers. No sleeping bags. Just animal jerky and an Indian blanket. Weird if you ask me. I'd make Eric take his clothes off in the garage when he got home from one of his three or four day binges with the wild folk because he smelled as bad as he looked.

While our boys have only experienced rendezvouses by the stories their dad tells, they have practiced firsthand the thrill of the hunt. Dad is a meticulous and detailed instructor of how to sight in bows, handle the shotgun, or gut the animal when it's down. The boys thrive on this exercise and try to get in the woods as much as possible when Dad can take them. Actually, the girls enjoy this too, come to think of it. They certainly do not take after me in this regard.

Josiah has been particularly successful in his hunting efforts because he paid attention to his father's instructions. More than that, he put them into practice. His first year bow hunting he got a big doe, and his second year an eight-point buck. "Alfonzo," as Josiah likes to call him, is stuffed and hanging over our mantle.

Dads instruct their children all the time. Do the children always listen and obey? I wish I could say, "Yes," but we know better. The kids who do, however, are usually rewarded in one way or another while the kids who don't, aren't. Had Josiah not paid attention to his father, I doubt Alfonzo would be our family room's main attraction.

Jesus gave us His Word so we'd know how to live and have happy, successful lives. As Christians we know the way we're supposed to walk. As "children," we don't always do what we're told.

My challenge for us today is to get back to basics. If life doesn't seem to be going too well, back up and regroup. Read again what God expects, and then put those practices into action. If you do, things will turn around and you'll end up with a trophy life! It's never too late to start.

Dear Lord, thank You for Your Word that teaches me how I should live. The sweetness of Your presence compels me to examine my life on a regular basis so that I can grow to be more like You. In Jesus' name, Amen.

Constipation, Huh?

~ A Reflection on Thanksgiving ~

"Rejoice in the Lord always. Again I will say, rejoice" (Philippians 4:4)!

HANNAH HAD BEEN COMPLAINING OF a stomach ache for a while, and the cause didn't seem to want to release its grip on her insides. I finally took her to the doctor who said it was constipation. The follow-up x-rays confirmed the diagnosis. Hannah needed to get more exercise and drink more water. That was easy enough!

Day after day she told us how badly her stomach hurt. We basically told her to suck it up and drink more fluids. It wasn't anything more than needing to go potty. The pain in her abdomen seemed to come and go with each passing day. One day she'd be fine; the next she was in agony. We thought she was a wimp.

Then one night a month later we were on our way home from a baseball game when she cried out in excruciating pain! We had several church people in the van with us so after dropping them and the family off, Hannah and I headed for the hospital. We knew that something was terribly wrong.

We were barely ten minutes into our thirty minute drive when Hannah said she wanted to go home. The Ibuprofen seemed to be working and she was tired; she just wanted to get some sleep. I pulled to the side of the road; we talked about it for a bit; and then we both decided that a good night's sleep would do her well. In the morning, however, we called the doctor. This just wasn't normal!

The doctor instructed us to go right to his house. It was a holiday weekend so his office was closed. Short of going to the emergency room, this was the best way for her to be seen. He's always been good about this sort of thing. I don't know if he has a life outside of his medical practice, but we like him as a doctor.

We weren't there five minutes when he instructed us to go to the hospital. He called ahead for tests. Hannah was still in pain and it was getting worse, but what was he looking for? Hadn't they decided it was constipation?

The hospital was only five minutes away. After an hour and half in the waiting room, she finally got a room where the staff drew her blood, started an IV, and took her for the tests that were ordered. Her temperature was taken every thirty minutes as well as her blood pressure and pulse. The hours clicked away until the doctor finally came in. He had wanted to wait until they had the test results back before seeing her further.

We were quite surprised when he came into the room and declared that the surgeon had already been called! The blood tests had shown an infection; but it was the CT scan that showed fluid in her abdomen and a possible ruptured appendix. The operating room team arrived and she was wheeled into surgery. It was amazing how calm she was. I was a wreck on the inside but knew she was in good hands. I had met the surgeon and the anesthesiologist and felt very comfortable with them being in charge of her life this side of Heaven. I prayed that God would guide their hands and give them wisdom as they cared for my daughter.

Eric was holding down the proverbial fort at home while I was at the hospital. As much as he wanted to be at the hospital with me, the other kids' comings and goings required that one of us stay so they weren't left to themselves. I kept in constant contact with him by text and phone with each new development.

My friend, Roxanne, rushed to the hospital. She stopped by McDonald's and brought dinner for the two of us. This was very much appreciated as I was so hungry, having been at the hospital all day. What a joy she was to my heart! I have the best friends on the face of the earth.

An hour and a half later the surgeon came out to tell me the news. They couldn't find Hannah's appendix when they opened her up, but rather they found an abscess the size of a small peach where the appendix should have been, and it had ruptured filling her abdomen with poison. He said her appendix, he suspects, ruptured a month before. (Constipation, huh?) I couldn't believe my ears. She could have died from this! Why wasn't this caught before?

Hannah did well throughout the whole procedure. The surgeon drained her abdomen of the poison and cleaned the "ooze" from her insides. He left the wound open for more draining, and attached a grenade-looking thing to the end of another drain tube that poked out her abdomen on one end, and laid right on the spot where the abscess had been on the other. It pumped out a lot more icky stuff. Poor thing. Eric and I felt terrible that we had been telling her repeatedly to drink more water, take a walk, and get a bit of exercise, instead of letting her lie on the couch watching food shows. She had been in some serious pain. Why, she wasn't a wimp after all! Come to find out, she had a very high pain tolerance and a great immune system. Never once did she get a fever with all of that infection raging inside her body until the day the abscess burst. She was a bonafide miracle!

Our hearts are full of gratitude to God. He spared her life when it certainly could have gone the other way. Our attitude is one of celebration *with thanksgiving* for what He did for our daughter. He is good, all the time, and we know it!

God is still in the business of doing miracles. I'm pretty sure you can recall times when a situation could have gone either way and you were pleasantly surprised with a good report or a favorable outcome. Maybe you didn't lose your job when your company downsized, or an unexpected check came in the mail enabling you to pay your rent on time. Maybe your husband didn't get the diagnosis you were expecting, and instead got a clean bill of health.

God's hand is on our lives all the time. Nothing escapes His gaze. Let's express our gratitude daily and thank Him for always being with us – through the big trials like a medical emergency, to the smaller ones like finding an up-close parking spot when it's pouring, and of course everything in between. He likes it when we notice and appreciate what He has done.

Dear Lord, I thank You for Your miraculous ways in my life. The sweetness of Your presence shows me just how much You love me. In Jesus' name, Amen.

I Want Quiet!

~ A Reflection on Rest ~

"To everything there is a season, a time for every purpose under heaven"
(Ecclesiastes 3:1).

W E HAD JUST COME THROUGH a particularly busy season in our lives, and I was tired. I just wanted to veg. I didn't want the kids going anywhere because it meant I would have to drive them. I didn't want their friends coming over because it meant I would have to be responsible for more people. I wanted quiet for about a week and I intended to have it.

The kids weren't thrilled with the imposed sentence on their lives. Neither did they beg me for very long for a stay of execution. I was immovable. I needed some down time from the hustle and bustle of active kids' lives, demands at the church, and life in general. And the way I saw it, they needed it too. They had become edgy and irritable and barked at the each other instead of talking in a reasonable voice. I'm sure they got that from me because that's how I felt too. I just wasn't myself.

The break from our normal routine was good, or shall I say, g . . . o . . . o . . . d! It was just what the doctor ordered for a family that needed to once again find enjoyment in one another.

I don't know about you, but when those opportunities come, I seize them! They're few and far between anymore, but they do seem to come right when I'm about ready to implode from all the pressure of running to and from. Add to a normal family life the responsibility and care of a couple hundred more people and you REALLY learn to appreciate those Calgon days, or as this was, a Calgon week!

Life isn't fun when it becomes a drudgery just to get up in the morning, or when interest is lost in the things that usually give us enjoyment. Let's not get to that point. Let's opt for Sabbaths of rest, even when our kids balk. Coming through on the other side they'll agree that it was as good for them as it was you.

God rested on the seventh day. It's more than okay for us to do the same. Let go of those To Do Lists and just be. It's good for what ails you!

Dear Lord, thank You that You have provided rest for me when I'm weary. The sweetness of Your presence helps me appreciate it all the more. In Jesus' name, Amen.

It Was an Accident!

~ A Reflection on Mercy ~

"Let us therefore come boldly before the throne of grace, that we may obtain mercy and find grace to help in time of need" (Hebrews 4:16).

YOU MAY HAVE ALREADY GUESSED that Nick has been a handful since day one. We never know what a day will bring when it comes to our not-so-little-anymore son, who now towers over me by almost a foot! We can't for the life of us grasp how he comes up with the stuff he does! What prompts his impulses? Isn't there any common sense occupying his cranial cavity? One thing's for sure – we're tired. But that's not a good enough reason to quit, though we'd like to sometimes.

Nick has always loved balls – all sizes, all types, all colors, all balls! He's got scads of them in his room. His prize possession, however, is his box of golf balls – all 200+ of them! Regularly he'll bring down the box, empty it out, line them up, and make each of us count them so he knows just how many there are. He can count them himself but he gets lost with his numbers after a while, so we count them for him even though we'd rather be doing something else. I mean, how many times do we NEED to count them anyway?

He finds these golf balls everywhere – on the school lawn, in the field by our house, under bushes in our yard. No matter where he goes, he always manages to come home with at least a few more. It's uncanny how this works for him.

Nick also has a couple sets of golf clubs with which to whack those golf balls across our yard. And man, he sends them sailing! He's got quite a good drive. We've told him time and time again that he is NOT to hit those balls towards the house – ever! Why? Because we said so, that's why! And because we know what can happen if one of those babies meets up with a window!

Of course he has to be reminded on a regular basis. Of course he doesn't like it when we "nag" him. But the reason we've been so relentless in our words is because we were hoping to avoid the thing that actually did happen!

It was a sunny afternoon and Nick was playing outside with his golf balls and clubs. He was smacking them this way, and then that way, and I was keeping a good eye on what was going on. About the time I turned my back for a moment, I heard the crack of a window, the shattering of glass, and the thud of a ball landing inches from my china closet on the dining room table! I was horrified!

Nick came running into the house hollering, "I'm sorry!" "It was an accident!" I didn't care at the moment . . . I wanted to choke him! I was so mad that I could barely speak, and that's a state I don't usually find myself in. (I'm never at a loss for words, or so my husband tells me!). He knew he had done it this time in a big way. He knew he was in trouble. And he knew that I knew that he knew that he wasn't supposed to hit towards the house – ever.

He really deserved a good finger-wagging "I told you blah, blah blah" session, but what I tried to express was my compassion for him. I kept my voice low, kept my finger in my pocket, and just loved on him. He felt bad. I felt bad. Besides, yelling at him wouldn't help the situation at all. He would only get defensive and my blood pressure would go up. And that was a lose/lose situation I didn't want to get into.

Both of us learned a lesson on mercy that afternoon. Grace is unmerited favor of God – getting something you don't deserve – like eternal life. Justice is getting what you do deserve – like a speeding ticket when you're driving over the speed limit. And mercy is not getting what you do deserve. Jesus dying on the cross for our sins is the humblest form of mercy we will ever know.

Nick needed several things that day – money to buy a new window, a broom to clean up the mess, grounding, whatever. But what he got was a good dose of Mommy's compassion and mercy, if for no other reason than I love him. The fact that he was demonstrably shaken and repentant for what he had done told me he loves me too.

I wish I could say that I always handled things this well. I, like my son, am a work in progress who makes more mistakes than I care to admit. I've learned to say, "I'm sorry," too.

I think today is a good day to remember those who have spurred us on as they've imparted wisdom into our hearts. From our parents and grandparents to our friends, pastors and other Christian leaders, it's easy to acknowledge that we wouldn't be where we are today were it not for them. And for that I am eternally grateful.

Dear Lord, thank You for the influence of godly men and women whom you have put in my life. The sweetness of Your presence envelopes them as it does me. In Jesus' name, Amen.

Prayers That Avail Much

~ A Reflection on Divine Appointments ~

"Preach the word! Be ready in season and out of season. Convince, rebuke, exhort, with all long-suffering and teaching" (2 Timothy 4:2).

ONE AFTERNOON DEBORAH AND I were sitting in the Emergency Room at the hospital with Nick who had a very obvious dislocated thumb. He had been playing soccer with his brother and friends, and as usual, Nick was the goalie. They had been playing for an hour or so when one of them kicked the ball so hard that, when Nick tried to get it, it banged his thumb right out of joint. It looked as bad as it no doubt felt. It was crooked and distorted and needed immediate attention. Deborah hopped in the car with me and we headed off over the mountain to the hospital.

There were tons of people in the waiting room that day. Our doctor had told us before that you never want to go to the ER on a weekend, holiday or night because of the long wait. Even though it was a weekday the waiting room was jam packed. Old people. Young people. Little kids crying. Older ones writhing in pain waiting to be seen. Nick had been given an ice pack to help with swelling while we waited. Thankfully his injury had calmed his normally active behavior to the point where he actually sat still!

There was a young lady in her late teens or early twenties who sat rocking back and forth with tears streaming down her face. Deborah kept whispering to me that she hoped the girl would be okay. She even asked if I knew what was wrong with her. "No," I told her, "but as soon as she's seen they'll help her."

We sat there a while longer. The girl kept on rocking. And it was quite unsettling for Deborah who by this time asked if she could talk to her. I'm glad she asked first. It proved she was aware of stranger danger.

I told her, "Of course!" Deborah introduced herself which put the girl at ease and took her mind off her problems. She even quit rocking for a bit. Deborah began asking her name, where she lived, and why she was at the hospital. They had a nice little conversation, overheard by all of the people in the waiting room. Moments later Deborah whispered again in my ear. "Can we pray for her?" I was humbled by her heart and wondered why I hadn't thought of it first! Deborah got out of her chair once again, grabbed my hand, asked the girl if it would be okay if we prayed for her, and then said, "Ok, Mommy. You pray!" It wasn't that she didn't know how to pray because she certainly did. She wasn't embarrassed or afraid because she had already demonstrated that she could start a conversation with a total stranger. For some reason she wanted me to pray, so I did, and loud enough so everyone in the room could hear. They all stopped their own conversations out of respect which I thought was really something!

Amy's name was called. Finally they would get to the bottom of her agony and she would be freed from the pain. Deborah and I both smiled with relief. I was so touched by my daughter's heart of compassion.

Nick's name was finally called and we were put in a room off the main corridor. We were still waiting to be seen by the doctor when Amy was released to go home. Before she left she stopped by our room to thank Deborah for her kindness and prayers because "they helped." They exchanged addresses and telephone numbers and Amy was gone. Deborah's heart danced as she watched Amy leave the hospital. I know because her eyes told a story as they danced. God and I couldn't have been more proud

Deborah knew the importance and value of prayer. She also believed in God's healing power. And she wasn't afraid to share the good news with Amy, a total stranger in need of a touch from God. I believe Amy was drawn a little closer to the Kingdom because of Deborah's boldness.

How often do we miss opportunities like this? Do we get embarrassed or afraid and remain silent when someone can benefit from prayer? Or are we bold enough to step outside of our comfort zones and lay hands on the sick and needy? I know I've missed opportunities for one reason or another. And I felt horrible afterwards! Like my daughter, it is my desire to be used of God to share Jesus Christ, the Hope of glory, and His salvation for their need – and not miss one more opportunity! I know it is your desire as well.

So let's be mindful as we go through our days. Let's keep our hearts and eyes open, watching for those to whom we might minister. We get the easy part. All we have to do is pray. The rest is up to Him. And we know He's got that in the bag!

Dear Lord, You are marvelous in all of Your ways! Use me this day to bring glory to Your name. I love the sweetness of Your presence. In Jesus' name, Amen.

Calm Down, Mrs. Scott!

~ A Reflection on Boldness ~

"Open your mouth, judge righteously, and plead the cause of the poor and needy" (Proverbs 31:9).

I'M A STICKLER ABOUT CERTAIN things. You treat others like you want to be treated. You clean up your own messes. And you don't wear your pajamas out of the house! I abhor seeing grown, hairy men at Wal-Mart in Sponge Bob pajama bottoms, looking like they just crawled out from under the covers! I can almost understand why kids wear them. They're comfortable. And, they want to be like everybody else. But, grown men? Give me a break! Where's your pride, men? Before going into public you may want to take a quick peek in the mirror to see what the world sees as we look at you. I mean, if first impressions mean anything, you may want to at least consider a decent pair of pants, and maybe a hairbrush!

My kids know where I stand on the issue so they don't bother asking anymore if they can wear their pajamas in public, even for Spirit Week at school. The rules are the rules, period. Pajamas are for home wear and sleeping. Jeans are appropriate school attire.

Usually Spirit Week consists of days like Crazy Hair Day, Favorite Sports Team Day, School Colors Day, Backwards Day, and Hat Day. All of these are pretty harmless events when you come right down to it. Since they don't cross any sacred line of etiquette – old-fashioned or not, we support our kids by helping them figure out what they're going to wear each day, and by fixing their hair all weird and crazy.

A few years back the administration at our school thought it was a good idea to incorporate Pajama Day into the Spirit Week line-up. I thought they were crazy for even considering it! In my opinion, it was totally inappropriate and unacceptable to even suggest it. But I held my tongue and didn't rock the boat as I'd been known to do in the past – and since. My kids tried to wear me down so I would allow them to wear their pajamas, but I held firm to my rules and would not budge. ("Talk to the hand because the ears aren't listening!"). The closest they got to bed clothes that school day was sweat pants! Am I sorry? Did I feel bad? Nope. As long as they live in my house they will not be wearing their sleeping clothes to school, to the bank, the store, the park, their friend's house, the ball game, . . . nowhere but at home! There are some hills worth dying on, and this is one of them.

Pajama Day has become a regular event during Spirit Week; and every year since the outfits have become more and more outrageous. I'm not talking about my kids who continue to wear sweat pants, but about the other kids! Who would've known that teenage girls would be wearing pieces of lingerie to school, and that every teenage boy would have bugging eyes all day? (Can you see me raising my hand? I did! I did!). Kids will push the envelope. They will try to get away with as much as they can. And sometimes administrators won't have the guts to reverse a decision even if it's a bad one from years ago. I don't like it but there's really nothing I can do about it now. It is one of those sacred cows that, unfortunately, is here to stay.

As if Pajama Day wasn't bad enough, last year our educated administrators thought it was a good idea to incorporate yet another special day into the Spirit Week line-up – Cross Dressing Day! Yes, you read that right. They expected the boys to dress like girls and the girls to dress like boys! I totally lost it with that one. I couldn't imagine what they were thinking! I fussed and fumed until I decided I HAD to go to the school and address the issue. Without a shower or make-up, I made myself as presentable as possible and headed towards the superintendent's office. I wasn't fooling around with secretaries and principals. I was going straight to the top as the accountability rested with her, whether or not she was directly responsible! Even if she didn't personally decide to host Cross Dressing Day, one of her administrators did and she didn't stop it when she got the memo.

"Is Mrs. So-and-So expecting you?" the nice secretary asked. "No," I replied. "Well, it might be a while," she said. "That's okay. I'll wait, thank you!" While I waited I rehearsed in my mind everything I wanted to say to this lady, with whom I was not impressed. I had had a run-in with her a few years earlier over a situation between her son and my daughter. The language he used in emails to her was offensive, including four-letter words, and she needed to know. Her response to our complaint was that we didn't understand kids these days. It was "the way they talk." And, "didn't we know that those words don't mean the same thing as they did back then?" What was she smoking? Was she kidding me? It was at that moment that she lost all respect in our eyes. And now here I was, ready to bring a matter to her attention yet again! I wasn't sure just what she'd do with what I had to say, but I was darn certain she was going to hear me out!

After waiting nearly a half hour, I was called into her office. We sat at a small, round table just a little over an arm's reach from one another. Good thing too. There were times during our conversation that I wanted to choke her!

I guess I was pretty animated in expressing my angst at their stupid idea. As she tried to shift the blame, I held her on task. Being in a position of leadership myself, I know how it works. If someone on your team does something crazy, you take the responsibility for it. And if she didn't take care of the situation by cancelling Cross Dressing Day, I was going to the school board.

"Calm down, Mrs. Scott!" she said. It's true, I was practically foaming at the mouth as I spoke and she resisted. I think what finally opened her eyes was my suggestion that they were promoting homosexuality and lewd behavior. Were they purposely doing this? Did they want kids to explore their sexuality? I was incredulous and angry and expected better from them. Eventually she agreed that Cross Dressing Day would be cancelled. I also demanded that a letter of apology be sent home to the parents regarding the whole situation. That very afternoon a letter was sent home – but not from her office. She had one of her guidance counselors write it.

Evil prospers when good men (and women) do nothing. Just like Pajama Day wasn't a good idea when it was proposed and has progressed to what it is today, I knew that Cross Dressing Day was even more harmful and would also progress. It was a really, really bad idea. What would have happened had I not challenged them? Would another parent have had the boldness to confront the issue? Did anybody else care? What do we do when we're faced with issues like this? Do we speak up, regardless of what anybody else thinks? Or, do we keep our opinions to ourselves, wishing and hoping someone else will do something?

I believe God wants us to have a voice, to make a difference, and to safe guard our families. Evil is out there lurking, trying to find an open door by which to enter our lives. We must be on guard at all times, and expose it as it comes, even when it appears to be something harmless, like pajamas, or costumes. We need to consider the consequences of our decisions. Are we failing as a society? I believe we are. Look how far we've fallen from righteousness. Homosexual marriage and acceptance of such as normal behavior came about because people in the Truth did not speak up with one voice to be heard!

This reminds me of another situation I faced with a relative. This man, whom I love dearly, has been living with his girlfriend for years. They decided they were coming for a visit and would be staying about a week. Great! We welcomed the idea. Before they bought plane tickets I wanted them to know up front that they would not be occupying the same room, let alone the same bed, while they were in our home. I wanted all of the cards on the table so there were no surprises. When I shared this fact and the reasons thereof, he got angry and decided they would not be coming after all. I was quite sad and disappointed, but I could not compromise my faith. What kind of a message would that have sent to my kids, especially after all of my teaching, preaching and harping on the sin and perils of pre-marital sex? They know it happens. But for me to import and condone it under our own roof would be double-speak to them and cause them to question other things that I've also taught them. As a result of my insistence to not allow it, my relationship with this relative hasn't been quite as chummy as it had been. My stand for righteousness cost me a great deal, but I have no regrets.

Today, let's be bold to speak up when lines are being challenged or crossed. Let's not wait for someone else to do it; it's our responsibility as children of the King. If we don't, we will have no one to blame but ourselves for the way things are. We all have voices; let's use them to the glory of His name!

"Dear Lord, thank You that You have given me wisdom to discern between right and wrong. The sweetness of Your presence gives me boldness to speak up when righteousness is threatened. I love You, Lord. In Jesus' name, Amen.

March 1, 2005

~ A Reflection on Change ~

"And my God shall supply all your need according to His riches in glory by Christ Jesus" (Philippians 4:19).

THE DAY HAD FINALLY ARRIVED! Erin was moving to her own place! And we couldn't have been more thrilled had we tried. Erin, on the other hand, wasn't quite as excited. In fact, she refused to get out of the car when we got there!

Let's back up a little bit. We weren't *pushing* our daughter out of the nest like birds do to their young. We had been preparing for this day for a long, long time. And it was finally here. And we were smiling big!

One thing you'll have to know about Erin is she doesn't like change. Any change. It takes her a while to warm up to new ideas; and after she's mulled them over in her mind for days, weeks, months, or even years as in this case, she may or may not go along with your program. She's stubborn when it comes to things she doesn't want to do. And it's difficult to move her. She's a big girl so if the notion doesn't suit her, she plops down on the ground and won't be budged. We knew this going into it.

We'd been assigned a Service Coordinator with Heritage Christian Services from the moment our application was accepted. We didn't know exactly how to maneuver through the expanding world of possibilities for people with disabilities, so we welcomed the experience and insight Julia had to offer. We especially liked the fact that the organization was Christian-based. We came to find out soon after beginning our relationship with Heritage that not all of the workers themselves are Christians. But at least the organization had a foundation of Christian values. That was important to us.

Like our own lives, there are maturational milestones for people with disabilities as they move along the age continuum. Kids without those special needs usually graduate from high school, go to college, move out, or get married – eventually. They move along. They keep going. We felt it should be no different for Erin.

One of the things we thought important for her was to be settled into her "own home" long before we ever left this earth for our heavenly homes. Should she still be with us when she was up in years and that time came for her father and me, she would have double the anxiety and turmoil of not only losing her parents but her home as well! We didn't want that for her, or us, to be honest. We wanted her to be settled and enjoying her adult life first.

It took a long time to get through the whole application process for her to be eligible to live in a group home. And we were told there were hundreds, if not thousands, of people on the waiting list to be placed. Of course our hopes were a bit dashed at the prospect of her moving anytime soon, but somehow we knew that God would work it all out in His time. We were okay with that.

Julia went to work seeing what she could do to help Erin find a home. And then miracle of all miracles, as if one is grander than the other, she found one that had an opening. This was a couple of years after we had applied, but even so, we thought that was pretty good timing considering the alternatives. We met with her to find out all the details – how many ladies in the house, (no coed situations, please!), how far away it was, how many people on staff, what about her job at the farm, etc. We felt confident that, after Julia explained the situation and answered all of our questions, we should at least visit it and continue the process of moving forward. We could pull out anytime along the way so why not keep going?

As it turned out, things were meant to be. We completed everything necessary for Erin to be able to move to her new home and we planned for the big day which was still months away. She had pretty much decided she wasn't moving so we talked it up as much as we could to spark her interest and approval, but she wouldn't move. When moving day came she barked and sputtered and dragged her feet at every turn! She wouldn't pack – I had to do it; she wouldn't get in the car – we practically had to hog-tie her; and once we arrived at the destination, she wouldn't get out of the car! It had been an exhausting day before we pulled into her driveway. Eric and I decided to leave her in the car as we went inside with her things. She WAS moving in! And we knew that eventually she would come inside herself but it had to be HER idea.

The interesting thing about this story is that once Erin decided she liked her new house and housemates, she never wanted to come back home – even for a visit! She went from not wanting to move or get out of the car to now not wanting to come home – ever! I'm sure it's because she thought we'd never want to let her go back. Little did she know that couldn't have been further from the truth!

But see, it's that *change* thing. Once she settles in she's fine. Change has never come easy for her. She's a pretty predictable girl in terms of lifestyle and patterns of behavior.

This is as much a story on change and how Erin does or doesn't face it, as it is God's provision for her. It is true that she doesn't handle change easily, yet she still has to embrace it. It is also true that God provided a home for her to call her own when it didn't look too promising as we waited and prayed.

All of our cares and concerns, our dreams and desires, our needs and our wants, can be safely placed with our Savior. He does provide for us. He does help us through difficult times. And He will never stop surprising us with answers to our prayers when we continue to seek His face.

So that's my word to you today. Keep praying. Stand on His Word. If the adoption process seems to be taking forever, hold fast. If God can part the Red Sea He can certainly part the red tape that stands between you and the fulfillment of your dreams.

I'm happy to report that we now enjoy a normal relationship where Erin loves to come home for regular visits. And she likes it when we visit her too! It took a long time to get to this point, but we made it. And with God's help, you will too. Where He guides, He absolutely provides. You can take that to the bank!

Dear Lord, thank You that I can trust You for my every need. The sweetness of Your presence helps me as I wait. I know I won't be disappointed. In Jesus' name, Amen.

Sarah's Flying Lesson

~ A Reflection on Rebellion ~

"As for me and my house, we WILL serve the Lord" (Joshua 24:15).

THE TITLE OF THIS STORY suggests I'm going to be talking about airplanes. Actually, I'm not, though it is about flying – specifically the time Sarah sent her car sailing through the air trying to get home before we found out where she had been. Her full-blown rebellion had caught up with her and she now had to face the music.

Sarah got her learner's permit when she turned fifteen. We frequently let her get behind the wheel of our car so she'd get the practice she needed to pass her driver's test when the time came.

Once she turned sixteen she pleaded with us to take her to the local Department of Motor Vehicles. In due course we did, but that also meant that she needed to get a job because she would have to pay for her insurance as well as gasoline. We believe that, along with the privilege of driving an automobile comes the responsibility of paying the costs. Even if we had the funds to pay, we wouldn't have given them to her. Hard work goes hand-in-hand with getting things we desire. This teaches a good work ethic and leaves no room for an entitlement attitude.

Sarah got a job at the local Arrow Mart in the deli section. She made pizzas, sandwiches, and ice cream cones for hours on end. She was a hard worker and was commended fairly regularly by her boss and customers. Everyone liked Sarah!

Eric and I decided to get a new car which meant we had the other one available for her to drive. Her school schedule and after school activities, as well as her job, became increasingly more demanding so we offered her the opportunity to buy the other car from us. It was a little Eagle with a sunroof and kicking stereo system! The body was perfect and the interior immaculate, at least until she got her hands on it. That's one thing she's never been known for – keeping a clean room or a clean car! But I still believe she will . . . someday!

Because she had a job we let her make payments on the car. How well I remember the day of her maiden voyage. We stood on the sidewalk waving as she drove away for the first time *alone*. Although she thought it was ridiculous, I captured that proud moment with my camera. But since she was able to get herself around, we didn't have to be shuttling her around everywhere she needed to go. It was an arrangement that made my life easier.

Sarah became interested in a boy I'll call Mitch. Mitch was a loser (with a capital L!) and definitely a boy I wouldn't have picked for my daughter had he been the last boy on earth! My husband and I didn't like him at all, but Sarah found him to be charming. I think he was the first boy who ever really liked her so of course she was infatuated with him. We could see right through him, however, so we kept a pretty good eye on him as he wooed our daughter.

The more experience we had with him, the more reasons we had for not trusting him and not letting Sarah hang around with him too often. We tried our very best to explain the whys and wherefores, but she was unreasonable. We began telling her, "No" more often than, "Yes" when she asked to go somewhere with him, even if it was with a group of friends. She became angry at us because we were so hard-hearted. She felt we singled him out (we did) and that we were punishing her. No, we were trying to protect her. It was our job. And we would do it again in a hot second!

To get around us and do what she wanted, Sarah started fudging the truth about her whereabouts and with whom she was with. We followed up on our hunches and found that she had been sneaking around with Mitch, not doing anything naughty but just hanging out together at his house when his mother was not at home – a definite no-no! Our trust was being eroded with each lie which made home-life pretty unpredictable.

One night she was supposed to get off work at 10:00 p.m. We lived a mile from the Arrow Mart so surely she should be home by 10:15 p.m. at the latest. We waited for her to drive up the driveway but no Sarah. No phone call. No nothing. We set out to find her but couldn't, so we had to sit and wait.

Around midnight we got a hysterical call from her telling us she had crashed her car. She had gotten off work early, around 8:00 p.m., and had gone to Mitch's house in a neighboring town. Realizing the time and the fact that she was going to be late, she hopped in her car and sped off towards home, not making the corner turn at the end of the street.

The village road crew had been making some improvements to the street onto which she was attempting to turn. The surface was built up with new asphalt about three inches thick. Sarah, racing down the road from Mitch's house, hit that raised asphalt while trying to make the turn at her high speed which launched her car into the air, across the road, and into the ditch on the other side. She was okay, she promised, but she was visibly shaken from the experience and the knowledge that her dad and I were going to kill her even when the accident hadn't.

Mitch lived out in the country with no neighbors nearby. She walked a pretty good way to a friend's house and called home. She didn't have a cell phone at the time so this was the best she could do. Dad threw on his clothes and went to her rescue. We'd get the car the next day we figured. When we got there, we found it was beyond repair. The frame had been bent so badly it couldn't be fixed. She was without a car again and I became her taxi driver once again, though I was pretty choosy about the places I'd take her after this event! But those problems were minimal compared to the underlying problems with our daughter.

Many years have passed since that night that ripped our hearts out. She was in all-out rebellion and did what she wanted no matter what we said. She paid dearly for that choice in many ways, not the least of which was making the rest of the car payments for the car she could no longer drive.

In recent years she has confessed a lot of the things she did as a kid with apologies, and again, we extended our forgiveness. Some of the things I have been shocked to learn; others I already knew. I find it interesting that she now wants to keep us in the light. I think that comes with maturity.

Why do we resort to rebellion? Does the thing we want to do have that much of a pull on us that we can't resist its temptations? I think it's that insidious battle that rages between spirit and flesh. We know the right thing, yet we do the wrong thing, either not believing we'll get caught or choosing to live with the consequences when we do. And teenagers aren't the only ones who fall victim to it. Adults do too. We always tell our kids, "We may not always know at the time that you're doing something wrong, but we will find out eventually. And when we do, you WILL suffer the consequences! Don't do the crime if you can't do the time."

Sarah took a flying lesson that night that probably caused her life to flash in front of her eyes. She knew she had messed up good. She also knew we were going to be mad as heck, and she was right.

The important thing for me to know in this story is that Sarah really was sorry. It wasn't just that she had gotten caught. It was that she had allowed herself to cross a line she hadn't intended on crossing. She was repentant; we forgave her; and she lived with the ultimate consequences that included having to pay for the car, but also rebuilding the trust that was destroyed by her behavior.

Mitch didn't stick around very long afterwards, I'm happy to report. When he realized he couldn't get his agenda over on her, and that her dad had full intentions to do him bodily harm if he didn't back off, his sights were set on another girl.

Eric and I have many gray hairs today. Most have come from being in the ministry but a good many others are the result of Sarah's teen years. She gave us a run for our money, for sure! Thank the Lord she's now in her twenties with a little more common sense now, and attempting to go in the right direction. She doesn't live at home anymore so there are some things I have no need to know. But I do know the One who sees everything. And I believe He will continue to soften her heart more and more each day until she's completely and fully surrendered to His will. He has some amazing things for her to see and do once she is. As I wait, I will pray in faith believing that it will be as He has purposed. And it will be good, yes, very good.

> *Dear Lord, thank You that Your desire is for our whole family to be saved and walking in the Light. The sweetness of Your presence encourages me to keep praying in faith until I see it in the natural. In Jesus' name, Amen.*

Those Darn Chickens!

~ A Reflection on Tolerance ~

"And let us not grow weary while doing good, for in due season we shall reap if we do not lose heart" (Galatians 6:9).

WE LIVE IN SMALL TOWN, USA. This is not even considered a village – it's a hamlet. Living in a hamlet allows you to have farm animals on your property if you so desire, and living on several acres, we do. The kids have hounded me for years about getting horses, a cow, or a pig! But I know what would happen. Even though they insist they'd be the ones feeding, watering, walking, brushing, and taking care of the things, I know I'd end up being the one to do it. And so I've held my mantra strong and true every time it's brought up, "NO! Read my lips! NO! Not a chance! Forget it! "I have enough (pardon the expression) crap to deal with. I don't need YOU importing more for me!" But they did wear me down enough to get chickens.

We had chickens ten or eleven years ago; and they were a fun novelty at first. The four younger kids were just babies so really, it was Erin and Sarah's job to gather the eggs, change their water, and make sure their grain pail was filled. Often times we'd send Sarah in the pen to grab one of them by the feathers just to prove that a ten-year old could outwit them. I took some evil pleasure in seeing her succeed!

Those chickens met their demise when a predator got into the pen. We never did quite figure out how. It was just one of those things that happen sometimes. And frankly, once they were all gone, I didn't mind that we were chicken-less. In fact, if I never had another chicken in my whole life it would be okay with me. I was not a farm girl at heart and never intended to be such.

Last summer the notion to try it again became the talk of the family. For months we weighed it out. Should we, or shouldn't we? Deborah wanted to make a little extra spending money and the eggs would help her do that, so we decided to get some. But she had to take care of them, that was the deal. No chicken care, no egg money. And so far she's done pretty well with it.

The family outing to the farm store was uneventful. We picked out thirty baby chicks and headed for home. I hadn't realized they'd need to stay together in a big blue tub in the DINING ROOM with a light on them because it was still too cold outside for them to be out. I wasn't entirely thrilled with that idea but I did go along with it. After a couple of weeks Eric put them in the pen he had made in the garage. Good! They were starting to smell and I did NOT like that, though I did kind of enjoy their little chirps!

They grew and the garage started to smell. It was time for them to be put in their new house – a nice coop with nesting boxes and perches, and a big pen in which to roam. Of course they didn't start laying eggs right away; they had to grow some more before that happened. But they seemed to be doing pretty well when summer vacation rolled around and we made our plans for the lake. A neighbor girl agreed to care for them while we were gone even though she hated birds!

We came home to ten less chickens than when we left. We thought for sure that Brooke had forgotten to close the pen gate because we hadn't had any problems before we went out of town. But it wasn't long afterwards that we found another dead chicken, then another, then others, that we realized we had another unwanted guest in the chicken house!

Deb had been good about closing the door to the coop at dusk and opening it in the morning, so it was hard to decipher exactly how a murderer was getting in the coop at night. As Eric spied the situation he realized that "something" was climbing on the Sumac tree outside of the pen area, jumping off its branches onto the top of the coop, swinging under the overhangs that allowed for ventilation, climbing inside, terrorizing the ladies and boys inside, and then partaking of its chosen victim. Nothing like being in a locked room with a murderer! We felt awful that that had happened so Eric nailed the eaves closed. To date we have had no further problems. And, we have decided it was a raccoon that was probably doing the killing.

Because of the nightly havoc in the chicken coop, six of the ten remaining chickens have decided to have sleepovers in one of the apple trees instead of sleeping in the coop. I can't say that I blame them really. But it's really bad behavior on their parts. They come running in the morning because it's breakfast time and their food is in the coop. Once they've eaten, back over the fence they go so they now free range the whole yard all day long. That really gets me! I want them to stay in their pen where they belong!

I've tried countless times to rally them together and get them back in. Even when I'm successful, as soon as I walk away, they fly right back over the fence. This has been going on for months. They even got the remaining "faithful four" – the chickens who had never flown over before, to follow them! Darn chickens! Who do they think they are? This is MY yard! Obviously chicken poop doesn't bother them as much as it does me.

I've given up trying to make them do as I want. I've learned to tolerate their behavior. I know that one day, as they venture further and further from the house, they'll get their just rewards. They'll end up a raccoon's or fox's lunch which will, sadly, totally put the kibosh on Deb's business!

Tolerating chickens' behavior is a bit different than tolerating our kids' behavior when it's bad. The Bible says that "foolishness is bound up in the heart of a child" (Proverbs 22:15). That means that they're going to try every crazy thing before they learn. I know because mine have. It's sometimes hard to deal with but you'll survive when it's your turn too.

My prayer is that each of my kids is equipped for the job God has given them in life. May my training, (teaching, nagging, rallying, harping, reminding, pleading, demanding, and bargaining), lead to their desire to follow God's will. As they stay within the confines of His Word, they will be safe from evil as it lurks beyond the fence. May they have ears to hear Wisdom when She calls.

Dear Lord, thank You that You love me even when I'm being unreasonable. The sweetness of Your presence challenges me to go along with Your program and not my own. In Jesus' name, Amen.

Breathe

~ A Reflection on Readiness ~

"Rejoice always, pray without ceasing, in everything give thanks; for this is the will of God in Christ Jesus for you" (1 Thessalonians 5:16-18).

IT WAS A NORMAL AFTERNOON with activity happening all around me. The laundry was systematically getting done, the dishwasher was running, the television was on, and whoever wasn't watching it was doing something else in another part of the house or outside. The dog was even busy following me from room to room as I puttered around, cleaning and tidying up.

Josiah seemed to be quieter than usual though. I had noticed it for a couple of days but every time I asked him what was wrong, he'd say, "Nothing." "Ok," I thought. I knew he'd talk to me when he was ready. And then out of the blue, caught between the upstairs bathroom and my craft room, he approached me with this question, "Mom, why was I adopted?"

"Be still my beating heart." That question stopped my heart for a brief second, not because I didn't want to answer it, but because I never expected it from him.

Whenever the topic of adoption would come up he'd seem disinterested, even about his own story. He wasn't like the girls who wanted to know every detail! Josiah would never comment or ask questions, and often times he'd leave the room. I never thought much about it because my sister's son who is also adopted and around the same age is pretty much the same way. So I thought it was just a guy thing. They didn't have a need to know like the girls . . . nor did they necessarily care.

I felt my stomach drop to the bottom of my belly as I realized I was holding my breath. "Breathe," I thought to myself. "It's okay."

I've always wanted my kids to know their individual stories, and at the right moments in time, to know their birth families. I believe it's important for them to be able to put the pieces of their lives together so they feel complete and not lacking in any way. It was okay and perfectly natural that Josiah was asking the question. And right now it was my job to give him the answers he was looking for.

We stood in the hallway as I shared what I knew. But what made an impact and satisfied his curiosity were the letters I got out for him to read. They were letters from his birth mom expressing her love for him and the reason she placed him in adoption. More letters were from his birth grandmother who also expressed her love and the great admiration she had for her daughter for making such a hard decision.

Josiah knelt by the side of his bed as he read each and every one. Periodically I would go in and ask how he was doing. Each time his reply was, "Good." After he was done with the dozen or so letters, he bundled them back up and gave them to me for safe keeping. His curiosity had been satisfied, or shall I say, his friends' curiosity was satisfied! What I came to find out later was not that he had a burning desire to know his adoption story; it was his friends that were asking questions he couldn't answer. Either way, I felt good that my son was a little better educated in the things that concerned him. He knows he wasn't "given up" as most like to say. His birth mom made a hard decision out of deep love for her son so she "placed him" in adoption so he would have the things he needed while growing up, not the least of which were a mother AND a father.

It's true what the Bible says. We do need to be ready "in season and out of season." But that's not just in instances of sharing our faith. It's also when, in the midst of doing piles of laundry and cleaning the house, a question comes from one of your kids that stops you in your tracks. At that moment that child's question becomes the most important thing on your To Do List. Be ready. Have any information readily available. And when the question is sufficiently answered and the conversation is over, then go on about your day. Whether you accomplish the rest of your intended goals or not doesn't matter. The most important event of the day was handled. And God's grace was there overshadowing each word spoken, each touch or embrace, each hug and kiss. And for that I am perpetually amazed and grateful.

Dear Lord, thank You that You give me words to speak when I need them. Thank You, too, for my children's hearts that are so tender before You. The sweetness of Your presence gives us all grace for the moments we share. In Jesus' name, Amen.

Bringing Home the Bacon

~ A Reflection on Success ~

*"This Book of the Law shall not depart from your mouth, but you shall
meditate in it day and night, that you may observe to do according to all
that is written in it. For then you will make your way prosperous,
and then you will have good success" (Joshua 1:8).*

SHORTLY AFTER WE GOT SAVED our pastor challenged us about tithing
our income which, to be honest, didn't set too well with my husband.
He owned a construction business at the time and made a good
living for us. Eric was mad at our pastor for suggesting it, but he took the
challenge anyway, purposing to prove that it wouldn't do anything except
give us less to live on. He was surprised to find that our pastor was right.
Our obedience to God's Word brought God's favor on our lives. Not only
were our finances blessed, we were blessed in other areas too – relationally,
spiritually, emotionally, in health, at work – you name it, we were blessed!
God really does reward those who are faithful to His Word. We had learned
an important lesson and never regretted it or looked back. That's not to say
we have never had any problems in any of those areas since that time. The

choices we make today do affect our tomorrows. But even in our mistakes God has been there for us. If there's one thing we have learned, it's that God takes care of His own. He has always met our needs. Sometimes we don't understand how or why, He just does.

You can be sure that we wanted each of our children to learn the discipline of tithing as well. From the time they were old enough to babysit or mow lawns, or whatever job they chose, we've instructed them in the tithe – why they must do it with a *happy* heart, what favor it brings from the throne room of God, and how their lives will be blessed in every area when they obey.

Hannah is the one who really got it. She never questioned or argued about it; she just did it. Even when she received birthday or Christmas money, she sometimes tithed it. As a result of her heart to put Him first, God has blessed her in amazing ways.

Her first job was, and still is, an after-school babysitting job. At first she only made twenty-five dollars a week because she only worked an hour a day. The job has progressed into more hours now, which Hannah appreciates, but she's looking forward to the day when she is able to work at a different job and make even more money. Even so, the money she has amassed to this point has grown to a sizeable sum as she's been faithful to the Lord and us, her parents.

In addition to the tithe, we have required that our kids also save forty percent of what they make. They tithe their ten percent, save forty percent, and live on – spend – the other fifty percent. Our belief is that by teaching them to save and not spend it all, they will learn good budgeting habits that will carry them into adulthood. And if they save enough now, they will have more buying power later when it comes time for them to buy cars of their own. Again, Hannah has been faithful to put that money aside with no argument, and sometimes even more than the forty percent, which means she will be getting a car sooner rather than later. Her bank account grows weekly as she is faithful to do what is required of her. The remaining fifty percent has been more than ample for her to enjoy. Out of that, she often times gives offerings to specific outreaches the church is doing – like Thanksgiving-To-Go where we prepare and home deliver a couple hundred complete Thanksgiving meals to elderly, shut-ins, and families in need. She has given to missionaries as they have spoken at church. She can be frivolous with sodas, gum, and candy like most kids, but for the most part she is selective and deliberate in the parceling of her funds. It doesn't matter how much she gives, she always has more than enough for herself. It's God's multiplication system. It's how He does things. He says in Luke 6:38, "Give, and it will be given to you; good measure, pressed down, shaken together, and running over will be put into your bosom. For with the same measure that you use, it will be measured back to you." It boils down to our hearts, and to what extent we choose to cooperate with God. Hannah's plans are succeeding because she has purposed to do things God's way. As a result, she is a blessed young lady, and in more ways than just financially.

Today's encouragement is Joshua 1:8. Meditate on God's Word day and night. Observe to do according to all that is written in it. In so doing, we will be making our way prosperous and successful. We've got to do our part first – like the old man with the wood stove. The man says to the stove, "Give me some heat." The stove replies, "Give me some wood." As we honor God by doing what is expected of us, putting in our wood, so to speak, the heat – the blessings, will follow. All that He has is ours if we follow His commands. Like Eric did, as we step out in faith and obey His Word, we will be happily surprised at how He works in our lives from that point forward. Like Mikey on an old TV commercial, "Try it! You'll like it!"

Dear Lord, thank You for outlining Your plan for our success in Your Word. The sweetness of Your presence encourages me to walk in Your ways and fulfill Your commands every day of my life. I appreciate that You loved me so much that You showed me the way. In Jesus' name, Amen.

My Riding Buddy

~ A Reflection on Friendship ~

"A (wo)man who has friends must (her)self be friendly" (Proverbs 18:24a).

A T THE TIME I GOT my Harley there weren't many women riders that I knew. In fact, I can't think of one who had her own bike. There were several who rode on the backs with their husbands, but not one who enjoyed a saddle of her own. And that was okay. I didn't mind being the anomaly when a group of us would set out for the back hills of western New York. I enjoyed the freedom of the open road and being with our friends. Still, I longed for a female friend with whom I could ride when Eric was available to man the home front, so it became an object of my personal prayer time.

Eric spoke at our "parent" church one Sunday morning; and during his message he mentioned that he and I both ride motorcycles. After the service a woman and her husband, about our age, came up to tell us that they both ride. Not only did he have a bike, she did too. I had a little Hallelujah Chorus time inside my heart as they spoke! Not only was she a Christian, she rode a motorcycle too! I had hoped that she was God's answer to my prayer and that she would become my riding buddy. We lived fairly close to one another and could easily hook up with some forethought.

Linda is a sign language interpreter so she literally talks with her hands – on purpose. Her job takes her far and near as different assignments are given by the organization with which she's partnered. Her husband, Phil, works on heavy equipment at a company not far from their home. Their kids are grown and gone so they have a lot of flexible hours at their disposal.

From the moment I met Linda I liked her. She's opinionated and direct, but I like the fact that I know just where she stands on everything we talk about. She loves the Lord with her whole heart and uses her motorcycle as a tool to minister to the down and outers she meets along the way. The fact that she's a woman riding a bike is a great conversation starter. When curious onlookers comment on her bike, she comments back, and before you know it, they're in full blown conversation. I can't tell you how many people she's had the opportunity to minister to as a result of her riding adventures. Some have remained her long-time friends.

What impresses me about Linda is that she likes to be with me as much as I like to be with her. I haven't had a real close friend outside the church in a long, long time. We can enjoy one another's company without the threat of someone in the church feeling like I'm showing partiality. That's something that leaders have to be very careful about.

Linda has had her bike a lot longer than I have had mine, and she knows the back hills like the back of her hand. When we ride, she usually leads as she knows where the roads will take us. She insists that her pipes are louder than mine so I let her think that I believe it too! She's a good egg – a little cracked – but so full of God inside that one can't help but like her!

We have had some amazing times together. I know we'll have many more of those times as the days ahead unfold and the upstate New York weather cooperates. I just love having a friend, one on whom I can count for prayer, counsel, and yes, good riding times. Husbands are wonderful; kids are great; but friends are just as important as they enrich our lives in ways that no other person can.

I have had other friends through the years too, some closer to me than others. Some I remain in contact with to this day, while others have long since moved along for one reason or another. Both ends of the spectrum are okay. Not all friends are with us for life. Some are sent by God to be with us for just a season. I believe Linda will be a friend for life, even though miles may one day part us as they talk about moving south and we talk about moving west.

I believe that it is important to express our gratitude for the people in our lives who mean the most. It's easy to tell our husbands and kids we love and appreciate them, but when was the last time we told our friend? Let's make it our aim today to "be friendly first" and convey our appreciation for all the friends in our lives. They're truly gifts from God.

Dear Lord, thank You for my special gifts called friends. The sweetness of Your presence encapsulates each of us as we share our lives together. In Jesus' name, Amen.

How Can I Miss You If You Won't Go Away?

~ A Reflection on Endurance ~

"For you have need of endurance, so that after you have done the will of God, you may receive the promise" (Hebrews 10:36).

THE NEW SCHOOL YEAR STARTED like every other – with excitement, anticipation, and a sigh of relief that we had made it through yet another busy summer. It took about two weeks for the enthusiasm to wear off however, once homework started coming. Being back to school also meant earlier bedtimes and morning get up times, neither of which suited the kids. But that was the way it was. If we were going to keep the ship sailing smoothly, we had to stick to the routine.

Nick was the most vocal about not liking his school schedule. He balked when it was time to go to bed. He balked when it was time to get up. He dragged his feet getting ready every morning because, quite frankly, he just didn't like school and didn't want to go. Well, he liked recess and lunch but that was about it. The rest of the day, forget it! He would have been quite content just to stay at home.

His teachers weren't ready for his attitude or angst at having to go to school. Certainly he was an oddity because most kids his age liked it. They used every trick in the book to try to capture his attention and actually get him to learn something, but for the most part, it was to no avail. Nick couldn't have cared less about them or their agendas. He just wanted to play outside, period.

As time went on, he became a bit more amenable to their ploys to engage him, which resulted in him actually learning a few things. But to say that it was an effort and uphill battle from day one is an understatement.

Because of Nick's special needs we have always kept a home-to-school communication journal going back and forth each day. The notes in the new year's journal were at first just a few lines about how hard he was trying and what new things the teacher was trying. There was an obvious positive attitude in the things she had to say, but we knew, as time went on, he would test her endurance as he resisted her tactics. In no time at all, her frustration rose and the simple notes became full paragraphs, and then entire pages which suggested nothing she tried was working. Before long we were getting regular phone calls because the teacher, who really should have retired years before, couldn't take it anymore. She was at her wit's end as to what to do with our son. Really? The year was barely half over!

The straw that broke the camel's back was when she began meeting us in the school lobby every day after school as we arrived to pick up our kids. She wanted to make sure she informed us about all of the things he did *wrong* throughout the day. Forget the journal. Forget the phone calls! She wanted eye contact with us! The day-after-day monotony became so disheartening that neither of us wanted to do the afternoon pick-ups. Feeling overwhelmed, we finally resorted to meeting Nick outside the school on the front lawn just so we could avoid her! It didn't take long for her to catch on though. Within days she began escorting him out to meet us, just to make sure she'd catch us. "Come on, lady! How can we miss you if you won't go away?" As you can imagine, our patience with this tenured educator had worn very thin by this point in time.

One day right before the end of the school year she met us outside with a startled look on her face and tears in her eyes. After everything else she had to say about his learned academics, or lack thereof, she told us how he had hurt her feelings by saying, "You're fat, and ugly, and I don't like you!" While we definitely don't condone hurting someone else's feelings, we did understand why he said those things. She was grossly overweight, ugly in his eyes, and, no, he didn't like her at all! She badgered, taunted, and scolded him every day. Even though we have always told him that, "If he doesn't have anything nice to say, then he shouldn't say anything at all," we couldn't fault him for his retaliation. He had reached his breaking point. We weren't far behind ourselves.

We made it through the rest of the school year with our skin still on and our sanity intact, but only barely. Every time we saw that lady coming, we'd want to run the other way. And that's not usually like us. Nick hated school even more because of her. When the school year ended and we no longer had to deal with her, we totally rejoiced! I suspect she sighed in relief as well because I don't think it was any more fun for her than it was for us. She was as glad to be rid of us as we were to be rid of her.

Is there someone in your life who drives you to the point of distraction like this teacher did to us and our son? Is there a situation that pushes you nearer and nearer the edge of your endurance or patience? If so, I'd like to encourage you today in a couple of areas. First of all, acknowledge you're at the breaking point. We run into trouble when we're not honest about where we are emotionally. Talk about it with your husband, or a trusted friend. Strategize new plans of dealing with it, or alleviating it altogether, if possible. Secondly, and most importantly, talk to the Lord about it. He will equip you with everything you need to handle the situation properly. Like He did for us, He will give you strength and grace to endure when you don't think you can go one step further.

Maybe your antagonist is, like mine was, a frumpy old school teacher. Maybe it's your mother-in-law – but I hope not! Maybe it's the discouragement of being passed over *again* for a baby. Maybe it's an impossible budget that never seems to work no matter what you try. Whatever or whoever it is, don't try to ignore it because it will not go away on its own. With God's help, you WILL be an overcomer.

May today be filled with blessing and honor, and new opportunities to praise His name for all He has done and seen you through!

Dear Lord, I am amazed by Your love and grace. The sweetness of Your presence helps me to bless others and honor You, even when the road is rough. In Jesus' name, Amen.

The Snackster

~ A Reflection on Self-Centeredness ~

"The heart is deceitful above all things, and desperately wicked; who can know it" (Jeremiah 17:9).

I COULDN'T FOR THE LIFE OF me figure out what was happening to all of our snacks in the pantry. Each week I would buy a box or two of at least eight snacks in each, allowing several after-school choices for the kids when they got home, but by week's end, there were more individual packets missing than should have been! Where were they going?

This went on for weeks until I began finding the lost packs of oatmeal cookies, granola bars, and gummies in places other than where they should have been. They weren't opened or eaten, but they were definitely stashed for later enjoyment – that was obvious. As usual, none of the kids knew anything about it so it was evident that "Not Me" had once again visited! I had an idea who the culprit was though, so I kept a close eye on her until I knew for sure. And just as I suspected, I was right.

Deborah seemed to be in the pantry more often than she should have been. She also seemed to disappear a lot more than usual, most of the time to her room but sometimes outside as well. One of our rules is that no food is allowed upstairs, so once I started finding empty wrappers in the upstairs bathroom and her bedroom, and outside by the blueberry bushes, I knew I had her. I wasn't trying to trap her, but I did want her to know I had proof of her wrongdoing.

Actually, I wish she had confessed in the first place. Lying is a big no-no at our house. But since she didn't, I had to confront her with my knowledge. She actually took it better than expected.

She told me that she feels that if she doesn't hide the snacks she likes, they won't be there later when she wants one because everybody else likes them too. Okay. I understood her childish reasoning. While her suspicions were very possible considering the number of people who live here, her actions were selfish and self-centered. I wanted her to understand that.

We had a pretty intense talk about self-centeredness, and lying, and how neither is acceptable behavior for a young girl purposing to follow Jesus. She apologized, of course, but I was more concerned with the root of the problem than the out workings of it. Was she feeling cheated in some way by being the youngest, or imagining that she wasn't being cared for properly? When was the last time she went without? Certainly there are plenty of snacks to go around. As we talked I realized it was none of those things, but rather just her flesh saying, "I want what I want when I want it." That's never good because that is not God's way. And she knew it. She knew it before she even did it, of that I am sure.

Today I want to examine my heart to see if there is "any wicked thing in me." Adults are not exempt from flesh demanding to be satisfied. Am I selfish? Am I self-centered? Do I consider others before myself? Am I cheating God? Am I fulfilling my destiny? Am I the best wife and mother I can possibly be? Do I offer my time freely? The questions we could ask ourselves are endless.

I think that if we take time to regularly examine our hearts and actions in light of God's Word and His Holy Spirit, we will be a lot less likely to fall into selfish habits where what I want becomes more important than what He expects. Let us decide to be open, honest, and transparent before our families and our God so that it can never be said of us that we only think about ourselves. We all have the same goal in mind – to have Him say, "Well done, good and faithful servant . . . enter into the joy of your Lord" (Matthew 25:23).

Dear Lord, I love the sweetness of Your presence which keeps my heart open to Your will and Your ways. Thank You for Your Word and Your Holy Spirit Who always speak to me about my heart attitudes. I love You, Lord. In Jesus' name, Amen.

Aunt Spanky

~ A Reflection on Keeping Short Accounts ~

"Be angry, and do not sin; do not let the sun go down on your wrath"
(Ephesians 4:26).

WE RECENTLY HAD THE PRIVILEGE of having one of our nephews stay with us for several days during the Christmas break from school. We don't get to see him or his family except once or twice a year because they live two-hundred and fifty miles away – a good five-hour drive depending on traffic conditions and how many potty stops we have to make along the way. Each of us has a busy life with our own family so it's not always easy to carve out time from our full schedules for mutually-desired get-togethers. We agree, however, that we need to prioritize more visits before the years pass us by. It's important for the cousins to spend time together as much as it is for their parents.

This year we were afforded the pleasurable opportunity to see our nephew and his mom on Thanksgiving when they came for our holiday celebrations, and again on Christmas Day when his parents delivered him to begin an almost week-long stay with us. He had never asked to stay with us before; and to be honest, I never considered asking him. I guess I never thought he had an interest; and with us having a house full already, I suppose it didn't occur to me to extend an invitation.

I have to confess that he wasn't always the charming, well-mannered, and pleasant young man that he is today. As a toddler he was definitely cute, but he was a bit of a brat who didn't listen very well to his parents. In his defense, he was just a kid like every other one who had "foolishness bound up in his heart" at that age (Proverbs 22:15a). I believe he needed more applications of the "rod of correction" to his backside (Proverbs 22:15b), but even though he didn't receive them, he turned out to be an amazing young man.

One summer when he was maybe two or three years old, his family came for a few days' visit. As we were hiking through our woods on a particularly sunny afternoon, he and our son, Nick, ran ahead out of sight after being reminded repeatedly not to. I ran after them; and after explaining in three-year old language why I was upset and had to discipline them, I swatted each of them on their rumps for disobeying. Apparently, that discharge of discipline offended my nephew, so much so that he decided he didn't like me from that day forward. I never knew this, of course. And I certainly didn't know that he referred to me as, "Aunt Spanky" from then on. I wonder why no one ever told me.

It wasn't until a few years ago at a family reunion that he finally decided I was an okay person. Apparently the damage I had caused to his ego and emotions was gone. Had I of known that I had been redeemed and forgiven, I would have rejoiced with him, but not knowing about the offense in the first place, I was clueless when he let it go.

As I was driving him to meet his mom after his recent visit, my dear nephew shared with me about the offense he had carried for so many years. He didn't make a big deal out of it – he smiled and kind of laughed as he told the story in colorful detail, but I knew it was still very real for him, and was an event that left a negative, lasting impression. How easy it is to relive those experiences that, even though they're forgiven, are not easily forgotten. How I wish this issue could have been resolved when he was a child. I wasn't sorry I had disciplined him – he needed it, just like my son did. But I certainly did not mean to hurt his feelings to the extent that he didn't like me. (The light just dawned! Maybe that's why he never wanted to stay with us in the past!). His issue wasn't with the fact that he was disciplined. It was with the fact that it came from me – his aunt. In his two or three-year old mind, only his parents had that right. He certainly was not aware of my stand on such matters. If a child in my care is deserving of a swat, by golly, he's going to get one! It will never be a wild, out of control flailing, but rather a zap that reminds him who is in charge. The same goes for my children in the care of someone else. If they need a little encouragement to keep them behaving correctly, give it to them! Discipline is both good and necessary, though it is never pleasant at the time.

All of us have the ability to offend others, and sometimes we do it without realizing it. The reality of my nephew's angst all those years hit me squarely between the eyes as I drove and he spoke, and I felt horrible about it. Why hadn't he ever told me? Was he afraid of me? Come to think of it, he never had much to say to me at family reunions or get-togethers when we had them. Sadly, I never realized he most likely had avoided me at those gatherings.

Let's keep short accounts. Let's tell the other person when they offend us. Allowing years to pass without speaking up serves only the devil's purposes to steal, kill, and destroy. What if my nephew never reconciled this event and carried the offense into adulthood? It would have robbed him of opportunities to be with his cousins through the years and from knowing the truth about his hopefully now favorite aunt – that I'm not an ogre. He knows now that I only had his best interests in mind. And yes, I did apologize for hurting his feelings.

I love my nephew. He's a great young man with an awesome future ahead. And I'm not too bad of an aunt when you come right down to it, even if I have earned the name, "Aunt Spanky." I can live with it if it is the truth – and I guess it is. Oh well. I've been called far worse.

Dear Lord, I am so thankful for Your Word that reminds me I need to keep short accounts and not hold offenses in my heart. The sweetness of Your presence helps me to do just that! Thank You. In Jesus' name, Amen.

I Have a Present For You!

~ A Reflection on Giving ~

"But as for you, brethren, do not grow weary in doing good"
(2 Thessalonians 3:13).

IT HAS BECOME FAIRLY COMMONPLACE for Erin to show up for weekend visits with heavily wrapped gifts for everyone, and I mean HEAVILY WRAPPED! There are so many layers of paper and tape that it's virtually impossible to unveil the gifts inside without totally destroying them! They aren't particularly great wrap jobs, but they are meticulous with obvious signs of effort to keep the gift inside covered . . . many times over.

The presents are usually things she's made like pages she's colored, or necklaces she's beaded, or a craft she's made somewhere. Sometimes they are store-bought items too; but for the most part, they are creations she has made that denote her affection for her family.

Erin takes great delight in making each present. She takes even greater delight in giving each one to its intended recipient. Erin waits with anticipation, watching every response and giggling with joy as the receiver unwraps the gift – layer upon layer. More often than not, she gets the response she was hoping for – a bright smile, a heartfelt thank you and a warm embrace that reminds her once again that she is loved.

Why does Erin take such delight in giving? I believe it's one of the spiritual gifts that God has given her. But Erin has special needs . . . how can she have a spiritual gift? That's an easy one. Just because her mind is somewhat limited, her spirit is very much alive and well and willing to do the work of the Lord. God implanted that gift into her when she was created, and the fulfillment of its purpose will not be hindered by her mental disabilities. In fact, it's a gift that God has given to each one of us.

Giving handmade gifts is not the only area in which Erin gives of herself. Each time she's home she grabs the vacuum and cleans the floors at least once, or scours the sink in the bathroom, or unloads the dishwasher! She takes the dog outside to go potty, and she helps with the laundry. When she doesn't have to, why does she do it? It is her gift of giving in operation again. Its sole purpose is to participate in the blessing and benefit of others.

As moms (and moms to be), we're all givers, aren't we? It's our second nature to welcome a new neighbor with cookies, or make a meal for a family whose mom just had a new baby, or babysit some friends' dog for a week so they can go on vacation. We throw birthday parties, and make special trips back to the school with the science project or gym clothes our child forgot. We phone people when they're not feeling well, and we take time in the grocery aisle to chat with people we haven't seen in a while. We take great pleasure in interacting and blessing others so they will feel loved and cared for, even when the demands of our own lives keep us plenty busy.

Our Heavenly Father is the biggest giver of anyone we know. It's true that the most wonderful gift He has given is His Son, Jesus Christ. But each new sunrise is a gift to us from God Himself too, reminding us that we have a future. Tucked inside the day on a beautiful, hand-painted landscape are His special creations – you and I, on which He has promised His attention and faithfulness through every joy and sorrow we'll face. His gift of love is filled with promise, possibility and opportunity. Like Erin, He takes great delight in watching our faces as we enjoy the gift we've been given with grateful appreciation.

Today I feel especially grateful for all the many blessings in my life. I think I will make a favorite dessert for my family to enjoy after tonight's supper. I'm also going to spend a little extra time with Him, the One Who has shown me the deepest love of all.

Dear Lord, thank You for my friends and family and the opportunities to bless others. I love the sweetness of Your presence with every meal I make and conversation I have. May my actions bring glory to Your name! In Jesus' name, Amen.

A Life Worth Living

~ A Reflection on Reputation ~

"Let your light so shine before men, that they may see your good works and glorify your Father in heaven" (Matthew 5:16).

OUR KIDS LEARNED AT A young age, as most do I suspect, that money allows them to buy things. Since we have never been ones to just hand it over at their every whim, we've instilled in them the fact that they need to work hard in order to earn it. The by-product will be satisfaction of a job well done, plus the reward of a paycheck that goes a long way towards getting the things they desire. We also teach them the principles of tithing and saving, as I have already mentioned.

Knowing this, as soon as Sarah was old enough to get a job, she did. We signed the necessary papers allowing her to work, and coached her for the upcoming interview. "Dress up, not down. Shake his or her hand. Be confident. Be polite. Think through your answers. Look the person in the eye. And smile." Because she followed our instruction, she got the first job she applied for. She was as thrilled as we were because that meant new possibilities on her horizon.

She worked at a delicatessen where she made submarine sandwiches, pizzas, wings, and ice cream cones, and that job meant the world to her. She worked hard. She treated the customers with respect. And she always made it a point to do the job to the best of her ability. Before long she had "regulars" – those who habitually stopped in to engage her, whose orders she knew before they even asked. She got good tips and rave reviews from her boss as she became proficient at each job, moving up from ice cream girl to the manager's right hand aide.

Sarah had that job until she went away to college. She had earned an excellent reputation for being a diligent and hard worker, so much so that the manager would often call our house asking when Sarah was going to be home for vacations because she had hours Sarah could work if she wanted. That fact speaks volumes.

Sarah has held a few jobs since that initial one. Each time she has been a faithful employee who does her work to the highest degree of her ability. It's what makes her valuable, and the reason her employers hate to see her leave when she finds she has to quit due to a conflict in her crazy schedule.

I believe that any job is worth doing well. Why do it at all if we're not going to do it right? I tell that to my younger kids all the time, especially at room-cleaning time. They argue about it of course, especially as they try to hide their dirty clothes under their beds or their clean, unfolded clothes in the backs of their closets. They'll eventually get it, I'm sure, but for now I'm just a broken record – one they wish they could turn off!

I've worked with both kinds of people – those with integrity who do their jobs to the very best of their abilities, and those who merely show up and go through the motions in order to collect a pay check. I'm sure you, like me, would rather work with those who always give it their best effort.

Our lives preach every day, and sometimes we use words. It matters what people hear us say, or see us do. What kind of mixed message is conveyed if we are known as church-going, faith-filled Christians, but slackers at the office? If we are going to let our lights shine, then we need to shine brightly in all areas, especially when those who aren't Christians are watching.

The scripture passage for today's reading is Matthew 5:16, one of my favorites. I am reminded every time I read it that people can be drawn to the Father by what they see in me. If they know me as good, hard worker, one who doesn't complain or backbite, and one who is a joy to be around regardless of personal circumstances, then I'll have a much better chance to share the Good News of Jesus Christ with them.

Let your light shine brightly for Jesus today. Let it speak volumes about your character, love for God, and relationship with Him. Let Him be the reason you do everything to the best of your ability. Not only are others watching – He is too. When we do our very best, He is well-pleased, the enemy is confounded, and our reputations of being Christians in deed as well as in word, remains intact. And sometimes our good effort pays off in the form of a raise at our jobs!

So, be blessed today as you purpose to "shine, Baby, shine!"

Dear Lord, thank You for filling me with Your light. The sweetness of Your presence allows me to shine for You – everywhere I go, and in everything I do. In Jesus' name, Amen.

Just Keep Swimming

~ A Reflection on Steadfastness ~

"Therefore, my beloved brethren, be steadfast, immovable, always abounding in the work of the Lord, knowing that your labor is not in vain in the Lord"
(1 Corinthians 15:58)

MY MORNING RITUAL ON SCHOOL days is to get up, make coffee, watch the news, pack lunches, and keep the kids moving in the right direction so everybody gets to school on time. After Eric loads them in the car and they head down the driveway, it's then that I clean up the breakfast dishes, tidy up the living room, make our bed, get my shower, and then go over my day's list of activities which usually entails work, picking up the kids from school, stopping at the store, making dinner, and more dishes, plus laundry and light housework, and whatever else I see that needs attention, like the dog. Did anybody bother to feed him? Probably not. And then I remember the cat and figure nobody fed him either. And what about the chickens? Did anybody get the eggs yesterday? My mind never sleeps, and that's probably why at times my body can't either – that, and the joys of menopause!

It would be very easy for me to feel overwhelmed because most every waking moment is subordinated to the needs of my family. Any "me" time I get is usually late at night or early in the morning when no one else is up. And this could be very discouraging if I let it be. I've learned instead how to seize the moments I have and make the most of them.

Even as I am writing now I'm in the middle of preparing dinner, finishing up the sixth of seven loads of laundry, helping my daughter with her homework, and preparing for the soccer game we're heading to once dinner is done. Talk about wearing lots of hats at the same time!

I chose this life, however, so I will not allow myself a pity party, even though one may be deserved every now and then. I don't like whiners and I refuse to be one myself, so I plod along, day after day, doing what I have to do, with a happy face *most* of the time!

It's those *other* times I want to talk about. What do we do when we feel over-extended, under-appreciated, and lost in the needs of those whom we love most? Do we get mad? Do we go on strike? Do we cry? What do we do?

I confess that I've done all of the above at one time or another, and on occasion some of them at the same time! But at no time was fruit produced in my life when I did. I usually end up having to legitimately apologize, which resulted in yet another guilt trip for not being the perfect wife and mother. Yep, I needed to get over myself!

What I found was this. At those times when I felt like I was losing it or going to explode because the demands on my time did not include enough hours in the day to get them done, I wasn't praying or reading the Word enough. The joy in the menial things was gone and drudgery set in.

Once I realized it I had to create an action plan. My "To Do" List had to be prioritized with, #1 – things that HAD to be done, #2 – things that were less important, and #3 – things of even lesser importance. As I focused on the #1s I had more time to pray and read my Bible. And the more I prayed and read my Bible, the more time I had for the less important tasks too. All I can say is it worked! I don't know why, but I've learned that it's God's way. You make time for Him and He makes sure you have time for everything else.

My favorite line out of the Finding Nemo movie is from the little blue fish, Dory. "Just keep swimming," she says, and always with a joyful heart!

And that's my encouragement to you today. Keep swimming. Keep moving. Keep a good attitude. Yes, we ladies ARE busy. Yes, there are a great many demands on our time. But if we don't forget the One Who gives us strength for each new day, then we won't find ourselves reacting to pressure and then having to apologize.

Dear Lord, thank You for Your grace which helps me through the demands of each day. The sweetness of Your presence helps me to keep my priorities in perspective, and not fuss when some things are left for another day. In Jesus' name, Amen.

The Invitation of a Lifetime

~ A Reflection on Opportunity ~

"A man's gift makes room for him, and brings him before great men"
(Proverbs 18:16).

I ACTUALLY DECIDED TO WRITE THIS story instead of another one I had been planning to write. Josiah has just received the invitation of a lifetime and I wanted to tell you about it. I'm so excited I can hardly stand it!

As you no doubt already know by reading thus far, Josiah is quite the athlete. He's good at every sport in which he participates, but his heart is in soccer. He eats and breathes soccer. He has had his picture in the local paper on more than one occasion. He has been named Athlete of the Week on a local level, and was chosen Athlete of the Month on a county level. He watches soccer games on TV that the rest of us can't stand to watch (because of the horns the fans continually blow, making an irritating noise). He has favorite soccer teams and favorite players that he likes to follow. He's in it heart and lungs, as they say, and would actually like to play on a college team after he graduates from high school.

This past Friday he was called into his coach's office. Josiah didn't have a clue why or what his coach wanted, but he went just the same. They've always had a good rapport. Josiah's mouth dropped open and hit the floor as he read the letter he had been given. The heading read, "Barcelona, Spain." The letter began, "Dear Section V All Star, Congratulations on being chosen to the Section V European Select Soccer Team. This selection recognizes you as one of the outstanding soccer players in Section V. You have already been honored by your league for your achievements, and for this program, we have attempted to select the best players to represent Section V in Europe." In other words, Josiah has been invited to go to Europe to "experience the thrill of representing the U.S.A. and New York State, both on and off the playing field." In addition to some cultural opportunities and other experiences, he will also "learn from the superior coaching of our staff coaches, participate in international matches, and experience other activities, events, and thrills that, up to this point, he has only dreamed about." I'd say that's one heck of an invitation! There were only three young men chosen from our school – two seniors and Josiah, a junior. The seniors will be "finishing their high school career playing with the area's finest players." Josiah will be experiencing an "opportunity where he'll be challenged by Europe's best and still have time to display his new-found talent next fall."

Kids like to dream about what they'll be when they grow up and where their talents will take them. Josiah could never have imagined this opportunity, even if he'd wanted to! It's a true honor to be chosen for such an experience, and one he's going to have to work hard to see become a reality.

He has to raise a minimum of $3500 for the trip, but that includes everything – airfare, ground transportation, breakfasts and dinners, matches and team fees, tour guide assistance, and a personalized Nike uniform. He'll have to come up with some spending money for souvenirs and lunches, but I'm sure he'll be able to do it as he's set his heart on it.

My point is this. We never know what dreams can become a reality until we pursue them. We don't know where our gifts will take us unless we use them. Josiah is almost seventeen years old and already God is opening doors for him. He gifted Josiah with sports abilities way beyond any other I know.

Who knows what other doors will open as a result of him taking advantage of the opportunities before him. My mind soars as I only imagine.

We don't have $3500 to give him, and neither would he expect us to if we did. He knows that the burden of raising this kind of money lies with him, so that means sending out support letters, fund-raising, working hard, and trusting in the Lord for the difference.

What are your dreams? To what heights do you desire to go? It can happen, and will, in the fullness of His time, if it is His will. Keep using those gifts.

Should I write a sequel to this book, I will be sure to include the "rest of the story" about Josiah's invitation so you'll know how it all worked out and what wonderful things he experienced, both on and off the playing field. In the meantime, would you pray with us as we look to the One Who opened this door in the first place? We would appreciate it.

Just so you know, I volunteered to be a chaperone on the trip but sadly, they don't need any more. If they did, however, I'd be first in line! Barcelona, Spain – I'd love to go there some day. Maybe when Josiah plays in the World Cup I'll go. Hey! You never know!

Dear Lord, thank You for all of the wonderful opportunities you place before me. The sweetness of Your presence helps me to trust You more as I walk through the doors You have opened. In Jesus' name, Amen.

The Little Red Hen

~ A Reflection on Passion ~

"Delight yourself also in the Lord, and he shall give you the desires of your heart" (Psalm 37:4-5).

SARAH WAS THE BAKER OF the family until Hannah came along and learned to read cookbooks. As she experimented with different ingredients and made a total mess of my kitchen, she found that the end results were as yummy as they were satisfying. The accolades from the family encouraged her to keep her apron on. As a result she's really stepped it up a notch or two by experimenting with fondant and other materials that makes a cake over the top awesome. Her friends always ask her to make their birthday cakes for casual school celebrations; and she's the one who was asked by a lady at church to make cupcakes for a baby shower she was hosting. We see great promise for this young lady with such passion for making sheer deliciousness out of ingredients I myself may never have thought to use together.

What makes her times in the kitchen so much more enjoyable for her than my times do for me? I believe it's passion for what she's doing. It's in her blood. She's happiest when she's creating and has always been that way. When she was little she'd make wonderful creations out of trash – toilet paper tubes, napkins, ribbons, paper, beads, whatever she could find. She'd sit for hours and put this on that, and then that on this. She amazed us with her finished projects.

I think that creative gift has carried over into something more satisfying than an animal made from a cardboard tube with yarn hair and beady eyes. She loves making each distinct creation and especially loves the kudos she gets as people take their first bites. Her goal at this juncture in life is to go to the Culinary Institute so she can perfect her gift. She sees herself someday being a pastry chef or owning a bakery. We see that for her as well, or maybe a home economics teacher as she also has a gift with children.

Being in high school still she has a lot to look forward to and plan for. In the meantime, she watches every TV food show known to mankind. When she was home recuperating from her appendectomy, those shows were on all day, every day. It got to be annoying for the rest of us but she loved them. And since then she's tried new things with what she's learned on those shows.

I love having Hannah in the house because she doesn't just enjoy baking, she thrives on it! When I'm pressed for time and need a quick dessert, she'll whip one up with hardly a second thought. It's what makes her good at what she does. Now if I can only get her to clean up afterwards, that will be true progress!

What's your passion? What fuels your motivation? Is it baking like Hannah? Is it full – blown cooking, or catering? Maybe it's sewing or crafting in some way. Maybe it's serving at church or teaching in a classroom. Whatever it is, don't let the joy of it fizzle out and die. Do something with it! Pursue that dream! Water it until it grows to become all that God intended for it to be.

When you're good at something you generally know it. Your friends and family generally know it too. So get moving. Your future awaits!

Dear Lord, thank You for the dreams and good gifts You have given me. The sweetness of Your presence pushes me onward so that I may attain all that You have purposed for my life. In Jesus' name, Amen.

Seven Stitches Later

~ A Reflection on Sin ~

"For the wages of sin is death, but the gift of God is eternal life in Christ Jesus our Lord" (Romans 6:23).

I'D BET IF I WERE to ask right now what the Golden Rule is, most of you would be able to recite it to me with hardly a thought. "Do unto others as you would have them do unto you." Right? We should always want to treat others as we would like to be treated. I don't see this as being so hard, but one young boy in our family found it difficult.

One year many Christmases ago we got our kids a dog as a family gift. Amos wasn't just any dog though – he was a St. Bernard. No, we didn't put him under the tree with all of the other presents. But we did put a stuffed animal under the tree which looked exactly like him, with a note tied around his neck telling the kids that he would be arriving from the Midwest in about four weeks. The kids couldn't have been more thrilled! Eric and I were a bit excited too as we anticipated his arrival. We had come across him online as we searched for possible pets, and chose him because he was the runt of one of the litters. He was so cute and small. Thinking back I'm not sure we were in our right minds to even consider such a hairy dog that wasn't going to stay small for very long, but at the time it seemed like a good idea. The kids took turns sleeping with the stuffed animal until the day came that we were to pick up the real dog from the airport. We had had a couple of false starts due to weather, but the third time was a charm and we got the green light.

We piled into the van and drove to the cargo receiving area of the Buffalo airport where our new puppy would be arriving, and waited. As each piece of cargo was unloaded from the plane, other crates with animals included, our excitement grew. Finally, we saw him!

As the attendant put Amos's crate on the table for us to inspect, all of us huddled around it with peering eyes and prodding fingers, causing Amos to cower in the back. He wasn't coming out for anything, even when we opened the door for him!

It took two full days for him to become the playful pup we were expecting. He was so traumatized by his journey across the United States; all he wanted to do was sleep. On day three, however, he came alive! He romped, played, and chased the kids just like we had imagined. Getting him in the middle of winter meant that one of us – Eric or I, had to walk him to do his business outside. He wasn't "Mr. Quick" at all! As much as we tried to prod him along, he determinably took his time. Meanwhile, it was our austere privilege to freeze until he decided to accomplish the objective.

Amos never grew to be a very big dog. I've seen some Saints that are massive and quite slobbery. Amos, being a different type of St. Bernard and a runt to boot, was smaller in size and didn't drool at all. He was a dry mouth, and for that I was quite appreciative.

The kids loved Amos. They used him for a pillow every time they lay on the floor to watch TV, as a conversation starter when they took him to school for show-and-tell, and as their playmate when their two-legged friends weren't around. He wasn't allowed upstairs because of his constant shedding, but he'd wait for them at the bottom of the stairs each morning to greet them as they got up. Aside from the hair everywhere, which I could have knit together and made sweaters, he was a great family pet. He had a good disposition and was well-behaved in the house, which is important if you have a big dog. Amos had the ability to clear the coffee table with one swish of his tail.

Even though Amos was a good sport, Nick wasn't. He wouldn't leave the dog alone. He poked, prodded, pulled, and yanked on Amos all the time, even when he was reminded to leave him alone. He certainly didn't treat the dog like he wanted to be treated. He would have had a fit if one of us did to him what he did to the dog.

Eric and I had just stepped out of the room. The kids were getting ready for school so activity was happening in just about every room. All of a sudden we heard a blood-curdling scream coming from the family room. It was Nick. By the time we got to him, blood was dripping through his fingers as he held onto the back of his head. Amos had run out of the room to get away from the scene, but probably too because he knew he had stepped over a sacred line. You don't bite your family!

Nick stuck his head one too many times in Amos's face, so Amos retaliated. Amos's reaction to Nick required that Nick go to the emergency room right away. Seven stitches later, he lamented the whole experience but the damage was already done. For a St. Bernard's bite, seven stitches wasn't bad. There certainly could have been more!

We tried to make it work, but shortly after the incident we decided we needed to find another home for Amos. A couple of the other kids wanted us to find another home for Nick instead. Even though our four-legged fur ball was absolutely perfect with the other kids, and all adults, he couldn't tolerate Nick. If we couldn't trust Nick to keep his hands to himself, then Amos had to go. We gave Amos to some friends who had a female St. Bernard, which made Amos a very happy dog! I guess you could say he was rewarded for bad behavior!

This reminds me so clearly how sin works in our lives. We entertain it a little when we know better; we play around with it when we should run the other way, believing we will always have it under control; and before we know it, it turns around and bites us – trapping us in its vices with the consequences it brings.

Think of your life as a big, delicious cookie with lots of chocolate chips. Think of sin as mud. How much mud would you be willing to put in your cookie and still eat it? Right! None! It's important that we be "sober and diligent; because our adversary the devil walks about like a roaring lion, seeking whom he may devour" (1 Peter 5:8). We don't want it to be us!

May we always stay true to our Lord – pursuing righteousness and, with determination, avoiding sin.

Dear Lord, the sweetness of Your presence exposes sin for what it is – death. Thank You for Your Word and salvation that grants me eternal life. May I never take it for granted. I love the way You love me. In Jesus' name, Amen.

Going For the Gold

~ A Reflection on Effort ~

"For with God nothing will be impossible" (Luke 1:37).

DEBORAH IS THE ONLY KID in our family who didn't like the feel of grass when she was a baby. If we tried to put her down in it, she'd draw up her legs and scurry to our necks. She hated the feel of the stuff and cried if we sat her down anyway. I'm not sure what made her not like it, she just didn't.

Her phobia was magically healed once she started walking. Then she wanted to be outside all the time – with or without us, in the grass, dirt, flowerbeds, and in our dog's food bowls. She loved to explore her surroundings and quickly found her new love – running. From then on my job was to keep up with her as she ran from place to place, and thing to thing. She was a happy baby who was very easy to parent. She had personality to match her running legs so it was a joy to be her mom. All of my other kids loved to run too – like most kids, so I didn't give it a second thought that she was anything special or extraordinary. When she hit elementary school age however, my opinion changed.

From kindergarten through fifth grade, she set school records one after another in most track running events. By her last year in elementary school, fifth grade, those records overshadowed even the boys' records, beating their times as well. She was the only girl to ever do so; and she still holds the records in several events today. It's been three years since she was in fifth grade; and no one has even come close. She was really good – and fast! We hoped she might be offered a college scholarship if she continued with a good track record through High school.

When Deborah broke her leg a couple years back, her confidence took a major hit. Her energy level dropped, and her drive to win practically left her completely. This isn't the same little girl who took great pleasure in undercutting everybody's time.

My husband and I ran into the new varsity track coach at the supermarket one day not long ago. He has known our family for years, having had each of our kids in his gym class at one time or another. He told us he is especially interested in having Deborah on his team this year because she has the goods to be a real winner. In fact, he said, "She's a champion. I want to take her to State competition." Now, you and I both know that some things need to change for that to happen. Three years ago I would have agreed that taking home a State medal was a very real possibility. Today, I'm not so sure – not because I don't believe she has what it takes, but because I don't believe *she* thinks she does anymore. Deborah needs to shake a few things off before she can go forward. Then, and only then, can the drive return to allow her to go the distance.

This makes me wonder about my own life. What cloak of lies have I put on that are stopping me from going forward and realizing my goals? For years I have struggled with my weight, which is kind of ironic since I was underweight when I joined the Air Force in 1976. I was skinny until ten years or so ago, when my metabolism slowed down and I started putting on close to fifty extra pounds. I'm not proud of it; I don't like admitting it; and I'm having a really hard time getting it off. I've tried different diets but none have been successful. I think my weight-loss success story is going to come about the old-fashioned way – by eating a lot less food and exercising a lot more.

What effort do you need to put forth in order to realize your dreams? How badly do you want a family, or a doctorate degree, or the business you've always dreamed of having? Do you, like me, have a book in your heart that you want to write "someday?" Perhaps your dream is to travel the world, or be a missionary, or perhaps a school teacher. What do you need to do to move closer to your goal? This book has been in process for close to ten years. It would not be published today had I not sat down and reflected back on my life, written each story, and pursued a publisher. I had to do it. No one was going to do it for me.

Let me encourage you today. Elbow grease is a good and necessary thing. We'll never go anywhere, or do anything, without it. Heck, our homes won't get cleaned unless we muster the energy to vacuum and dust. Pursuing our dreams is going to take a lot more effort than that! If we never try, then it's a sure thing that they will remain only dreams.

I believe that, as we continue to follow the Lord and His will for our lives, and work toward our goals, we'll make it. Like anyone you know who has ever accomplished anything, our dreams can become reality because "nothing is impossible with God." He said it in His Word and He doesn't lie. Believe it, then get going!

Dear Lord, thank You for the drive in my heart to pursue my dreams. The sweetness of Your presence helps me to believe they can – and will – happen if I put forth some effort. Help me to strategize the steps I need to take. In Jesus' name, Amen.

The Knock That Rocked
Our World

~ A Lesson on Acceptance ~

". . . seek those things which are above, where Christ is, sitting at the right hand of God. Set your mind on things above, not on things on the earth" (Colossians 3:1b-2).

AS I WRAP UP MY reflections on my life's journey thus far, I would like to tell you the story of another incredible life that came into ours when he was just ten years old. We were minding our own business, enjoying life in southern California when our attention was captured, not by a ringing phone, but by a knock on the door.

The mailman held a manila envelope in his hand that my husband needed to sign for. Since Eric wasn't home and I couldn't sign for it, he had to go to the post office after he got home from work. We had no idea what it could be or who it was from. Of course different scenarios played through our minds, but we couldn't have been further from the truth once the package was retrieved.

Eric was gone for what seemed like hours. When he finally got home from his "quick trip" to the post office, he was white as a ghost, (if ghosts are white), with the strangest look on his face. He didn't say a word to me; he just handed me the envelope.

Opening it, the contents fell out – letters, pictures, and even a birth certificate. Julie, Paul's mother, had decided it was time for Paul to know his dad so she had hired a private investigator to find him. Once that was accomplished, she set out to tell Eric the story of the boy she had given birth to just seven months before he and I were married and the reasons she never told him.

You can imagine the myriad of emotions I struggled with while perusing all of the information I held in my hand. And now I understood why Eric took so long at the post office. He had been trying to process it as well.

I was glad that my husband had been afforded the knowledge he had a son, and even glad that Paul wanted to meet him. I was not happy, though, that this precious boy was from another woman! The one thing I so desperately wanted to give my husband I couldn't give, and this other woman not only gave it to him but withheld his existence until ten years later! Boing! Boing! Boing! My emotions hit the roof and fell to the floor several times in succession as we both tried to get a handle on the news we had just received.

This was October of 1987. Thank goodness we were saved by this time. Considering the rockiness of our marriage prior to our coming to the Lord, I doubt we would have been able to survive this devastating news, if for no other reason than my own insecurities.

As Eric and I processed the situation as best as we knew how, immediately the Lord gave me a scripture, 1 Timothy 4:4, "For every creature of God is good, and nothing is to be refused if it is received with thanksgiving." Now obviously this passage specifically refers to foods that have been created by God which are to be received with thanksgiving by believers who know the Truth. But it spoke right to my heart that I had a choice to make. I could either receive this "creature" created by God as one of my own, *with thanksgiving*, or I could refuse him. The choice was mine to make and it was easy! If this boy was my husband's child, then he was mine as well, and I received him as such!

We were foster parents at the time with only one child in the home besides Erin who was five. Wanting to give a clear picture of the whole scenario so the kids could understand it better, we decided to fly both Paul and his mom, Julie, to California from Washington State so we could meet. Needless to say, we had a whole slew of things to discuss prior to their arrival.

We learned of Paul in mid-October. With Thanksgiving right around the corner, we thought it a good idea for them to come then. It gave them time to prepare for the meeting, and us too. Major earthquakes demand planned attention.

The first people we told were our pastor and his wife. They were most encouraging and supportive once they picked their jaws up off the floor.

Since we were youth leaders at our church, we had to talk to the kids in the group about our recent discovery. What a living, breathing, perfect example of the need for abstinence from sexual relations prior to marriage. We most assuredly were not ashamed about Paul's existence, but his life was evidence that babies are born as a result of sexual intercourse!

We also had to tell the whole church body so they would receive Paul and Julie with the same welcoming heart that we had extended to them. You could hear the little old ladies in the church gasp as Eric spoke that Sunday. But they were proud of us just the same for our Christ-like attitude and decision to honor them both.

It was a little harder telling our families; why, I'm not sure. But even they received the news with the best possible attitudes. It was all of our intentions to embrace these two people now in our lives "for better or for worse." Life throws curve balls sometimes and you either learn to swing the bat or strike out.

We greeted our new son and his mom at the airport with "Welcome!" signs, streamers and balloons. While I was happy on the outside, my insides were like Jello as I prepared to meet this "other woman." I knew I was going to embrace Paul with no problems or qualms whatsoever; he was a child! But I was very nervous to meet the woman who, together with MY husband, created a life.

"What if she's a curvaceous blond bombshell with long legs," the very thing I wasn't? "What if she's even prettier than Eric remembered her?" Even though Paul was conceived during a momentary lapse of judgment due to an alcohol stupor, a one-night stand shall we say, knowing my husband's tastes meant she was definitely something to look at. How thrilled I was when she got off the plane and she was anything but! A rounder woman with pretty red hair accompanied our son off the plane, and I couldn't have been more delighted! Inwardly I was rejoicing, sad to say, but it's the truth. And if you're honest, and it was you, you'd probably have to admit it too!

That visit was the beginning of an on again / off again relationship with Paul that has spanned the years since. Though we never intended to, we lost touch with Paul for several years when he went to Iraq with General Dynamics – the company he worked for at that time, and the subsequent several years. But through the miracle of modern technology – Facebook to be exact, we were reunited once again! He's married to a beautiful woman and they have two wonderful daughters! That makes us grandparents!!! They still live in Washington and we in New York so our visits aren't as frequent as we'd like, but we have vowed to stay connected through phone calls, emails, texts, Facebook Wall posts, and Skype!

Every day we face a number of choices that need to be made. Some most assuredly are easier to make than others. We can decide what to wear or eat, who to see or where to go with hardly a thought. Other decisions, like the one we faced in 1987, caused us to look deeply within the heart of God Who not only fashioned us in our mother's wombs, but Paul as well. He was a gift from God then and continues to be that same gift now. Our choice to receive him with thanksgiving brings glory to the Lord, and manifests the good work He's done in our lives.

We can't do anything about the years gone by that have been lost, but we can certainly do something about the future. And if God is in it, which He is, then we can rest assured that it's going to be a good future, filled with hope and promise!

I love You Lord.

Dear Lord, thank You for Your Son. The sweetness of Your presence gives me reason to celebrate and be thankful. In Jesus' name, Amen.

Epilogue

"The glory of young men is their strength and the splendor of old men
(and women) is their gray head" (Proverbs 20:29).

It has been a joy to write this book for you. As I have penned each page, I have relived every experience – laughing, crying, and thanking God for each of the final outcomes. All of us have life experiences that help to mold and shape us into the people we are today. My family has done that for me; and they are truly my pride and joy. Our lives together have not always been easy, but they've been good. And for that I am grateful.

I would like to express my love and admiration for each of our birth moms who made it possible for us to be a family. My prayer for them is that they would be rewarded for their selfless love and sacrifice, and one day be afforded the awesome opportunity of knowing the children they have held in their hearts all these years.

I know that life is just that – life. You get out of it what you put into it, but sometimes even more. Things may not always go the way we plan, but as long as we are determined to follow Him, no matter which way the road turns, it's sure to be okay.

Stay on the conveyor belt. Keep growing and moving along life's path. Take time to stop and smell the roses, the saying goes, and find the silver lining in each day. Make lemonade when you're dealt lemons. Be forgiving, and honest, and trustworthy. Be a good friend, and role model. Give love freely – and be a good recipient of love in return. You're worth everything God has poured into and given you. And when all else fails, learn to laugh and find humor whenever you can. Make sure you don't take yourself too seriously because, honestly, nobody else does!

My sister, may I say again that God is already in your future. Don't try to take the easy way out because it's easy, but rather plod along as He directs even though the journey seems long. It will be worth the destination if you do. Invite the sweetness of His presence – the sugar, if you will, into every day you are given breath, for He makes all the difference! And when you find that you have sprouted a few gray hairs of your own, rejoice, for then you will know that you too have lived an abundantly satisfying life.

Acknowledgements

I would like to acknowledge and personally thank Mrs. Carolyn Pollock for her countless hours and energy in editing this book. Her mastery of the English language and grammatical punctuation has helped me attain the level of excellence I had hoped.

Thank you, Carolyn, for all of your hard work these past months. Your labor of love has kept me on the straight and narrow path that has led to my dream becoming a reality. You are a faithful and true friend. I am grateful that God saw fit to put you in my life so many years ago.

I would also like to acknowledge Pastor Jack Hempfling of Living Waters Church in LeRoy, NY, himself a published author, ("Before You Go," Xulon Press). Jack, your encouragement spurred me on to keep going to the very end! Thank you for sowing into this project in a literal way, and for being another faithful friend whom I have been pleased to know for many years as well.

Noteworthy of acknowledgment as well are the following people for "eyeballing" my manuscript one last time before I submitted it: Ann Abbey, Maureen Dally, Linda Egge, Maria Reimer, Eric Scott, and Nancy Scott. An extra-special special thank you goes out to Peter and Ruth Lavin and Kim Leach, who each offered final editorial comments, as well as Connie Vellekoop, who herself is a published author, ("A Man After God's Own Heart – the Jack Schisler story", Bethany House International).

About The Author

"... clearly you are an epistle of Christ ..." (2 Corinthians 3:3a)

Deby Scott is wife to one, mother to seven, and grandmother to two. She ministers alongside her husband, Eric, at Celebrate! Family Church in Leicester, New York. She is a Licensed Minister with Elim Fellowship in Lima, New York. She works part-time at her church as an office administrator and special events coordinator ("Cruise Director"). She also oversees the small group ministry as the Vitality Department Director.

She has been a guest speaker at women's events and conferences, and desires to see women fulfilled in their desires to be moms. She has been sought out by countless couples for direction, encouragement, and wisdom as they set out on their adoption journeys.

Her hobbies include riding her Harley, teaching and making paper crafts, including cards of encouragement, and now writing about her family.

Her future goals include writing more books and possibly pursuing a nursing degree.

She and her family make their home in Dalton, New York.

CPSIA information can be obtained at www.ICGtesting.com
Printed in the USA
BVOW020820050612

291717BV00002B/4/P